THE ONE VOICE THAT MATTERS

What Worship Leaders Need To Hear From Their Shepherd

JEANELLE REIDER

The One Voice That Matters

By Jeanelle Reider

First Edition eBook: 2014
First Edition Paperback: 2014

ISBN (ePub): 978-1-938596-21-6
ISBN (Paperback): 978-1-938596-22-3

Cover photography and design by Stephanie Blaser

Published in the United States of America
NCC Publishing
Meridian, Idaho, 83642, USA
www.nccpublishing.com

All Scripture references in this book, unless otherwise noted, are taken from the New American Standard Bible (NASB), Copyright © 1960, 1962, 1963, 1968, 1971, 1972, 1973, 1975, 1977, 1995 by The Lockman Foundation. Used by Permission.

20140417

I was a child, thoughts of losing heaven driving fear deep. You took me to the Shepherd who follows hard after one lost sheep until He finds it.

I was a young adult, doubts slamming my once-bedrock faith. You brought me before the Shepherd, knowing He would speak to me in His good time.

I was your worship leader, complications of ministry blurring my vision. You worshiped the Shepherd alongside me, gamely attempting unfamiliar melodies and strange rhythms.

I'm an author now. And you? Most days words jumble and confusion clouds. But your hearty nods when I quote Scripture, and your countenance when I pray, and your "Beautiful!" when I sing—oh, you still hear your Shepherd.

This book is for you, Mom. For teaching me how to listen. Even now.

THE ONE VOICE THAT MATTERS

TABLE OF CONTENTS

INTRODUCTION

This is a book for worship leaders, whether you direct an entire worship ministry or are one of those who stand up front as your brothers and sisters join you in worship. It's a book about worship leaders listening to their Shepherd as they serve in the fields where He's called them.

I've been involved in worship ministry my entire adult life. I play the piano and guitar, and I'm trying to convince myself that I can also play the drums. I love to sing, though I much prefer to do so without a microphone in front of me. I was our church's worship director for nine years, and I continue to pour my heart and soul into our worship ministry.

I'm married to Greg, who also happens to be my pastor. He and I together have served our present church for 25 years. We love the local church and believe with all our hearts that it's meant to be a place of love, encouragement, service, and worship. But sometimes our church lets us down. Other times—and this grieves us far more—we let our church down. Because none of the Shepherd's sheep are perfect.

In my years as director of worship ministry, I often wrestled with the disconnect between how things should be in the church and how they really are. I frequently fretted over the tension between how I should be as a worship leader and how I really was.

Even as I prayed for the spiritual renewal of my congregation, I'd sense my own spirit running dry. Even while I chose God-exalting songs to strengthen the hearts of my fellow sheep, I'd see my own heart succumbing to weariness or self-doubt. Even as I lamented over my brothers' and sisters' lack of love, I'd find myself sitting in judgment of them.

If you're in worship ministry, you have struggles of your own. If you're preparing to serve in worship ministry, these struggles are sure to come (if they haven't already). In writing this book, my driving desire is to bolster your courage by reminding you that our Shepherd meets you in these hard places. He does speak, and His words are well worth hearing. In fact, they are indispensable.

As you read each page and do each devotional, my hope is that you will have an ongoing conversation with your Shepherd. I pray that, as you talk with Him, you will hear beautiful things from His heart to yours.

CHAPTER 1

OUR SHEPHERD SPEAKS

DAY 1: THE VOICE THAT MATTERS MOST

I had been here before; hadn't I? Signs overhead reflecting the familiar words: "Interstate 5." Slate-gray ocean stretching vast, endless and dark, to the west. The same view I'd seen out the car window time and time again traveling as a passenger to Dana Point to go sailing with my in-laws.

Yet, as the sun sank over the horizon and the shadows lengthened and the California traffic rushed by, nothing was the same. This time I was alone in the car. I was lost, and I was the only one who could do anything about it. The farther I drove the less familiar everything became, until it finally felt that I might as well have been in a foreign country. As light faded to darkness, I felt small and vulnerable, and at that point, I would have paid a good sum of money to have a friendly guide along with me saying, "I know the way. I'll show you."

In those days, GPS and cell phones were still the stuff of science fiction, and even the attendant at the gas station I eventually located had no idea how to direct me to my destination. By the time I finally stumbled onto the winding road that led to Dana Point and drove up to where my very concerned husband and his parents were waiting, I was exhausted and ready to be anywhere in the world but behind the wheel of that car.

Years later, I found myself lost again in vaguely familiar territory. For the first time in my life, I was directing a worship ministry, and I was gripped with fear. I had been part of my church family for fifteen years and integrally involved in the worship ministry all that time, surrounded by brothers and sisters with whom I felt safe. Yet, as the one now behind the wheel, somehow my world seemed more intimidating than before. Daunting. Strangely shadowed. Friends were waiting for me to find my way, even cheering me on, and yet I felt lost. Alone at the wheel, I desperately needed to hear my Shepherd's voice saying, "I know the way. I'll show you."

How did I come to be in this fragile, magnificent place? What movements of God's Spirit, what trajectory of events, and what passions of my heart coalesced, so that in the most impractical and unlikely of moments, I was bequeathed this unspeakable privilege, this impossible calling? To lead God's people in worship—how is it that any fallible human gets to do this?

I imagine I am not alone in asking this question; perhaps you have asked it too. It's an important question, because in those moments when we find ourselves seized by doubt or discouragement, overwhelmed by the sheer magnitude of the task, it can be reassuring to remember that the Shepherd is the one who calls His sheep into service; we do not call ourselves. And if it is *His* voice that has led us here, it is *His* voice that will see us through.

Listening Well

The purpose of this book is to provide an opportunity for worship leaders to sit awhile with their Shepherd, listening to His voice. Many voices speak to us as we serve our Shepherd: the urgent voices of our congregation, the guiding voices of our church leadership, the raucous voices of our culture, the compelling voices of godly speakers and writers, the diverse voices of the churches around us. Loudest of all may be the fickle, swayable voice that is our own.

But one voice cuts through, speaking truth that is the filter through which all other voices must be heard. This is the voice of our Shepherd. The voice of our Lord God, who draws near to His own and speaks the word, "This is the way; walk in it" (Isaiah 30:21)[1]. The voice of our Savior, who assures us, "My sheep hear My voice, and I know them, and they follow Me" (John 10:27). The voice of the Holy Spirit, who will "guide you into all the truth" (John 16:13).

This is not a how-to book, nor is it a book to be perused quickly for bullet points. It is a book to ponder in the presence of your Shepherd. With this in mind, each chapter is divided into five days of readings. Each reading concludes with a devotional, allowing you an opportunity to sit awhile and converse with Him. Please try to set aside an unhurried space of time to hear what He will say to you.

The questions included in the devotionals are posed directly to your Shepherd. For example: Will You remind me of the ways You've been faithful to me? Or: How do Your words in this Scripture passage speak to me as I lead Your sheep in worship?

The questions in each devotional are divided into four sections, each section approaching the conversation from a different angle:

- *My life.* These are questions to ask your Shepherd about yourself. He may want to show you something about your life that needs addressing. He may want to remind you of something He's done for you in the past. He may want to give you a specific way to apply the day's reading to your life. He may simply want to encourage you.

- *Your Word.* These are questions to ask your Shepherd to speak to you through His Word, the Bible. Read each passage carefully and thoughtfully, asking Him to help you understand what the passage means and how He wants it to speak to your heart.

- *Your thought for me.* After sitting with your Shepherd and listening to His voice, it is possible to rise and promptly forget what He's spoken. One way to prevent this is to ask Him to show you one thought that you can take with you throughout the day. You may want to type this thought on your computer desktop, or write it on a sticky note and place it in an area where you'll see it throughout the day. (I have even written it on my hand from time to time.)

- *My heart before You.* This is your response to your Shepherd. Write a prayer expressing whatever is in your heart. It may be a sin to confess; it may be something you want to praise Him for; it may be a commitment you want to make; it may be a petition for help in applying the things

He's taught you. This is a time to "pour out your heart before Him" (Psalm 62:8).

As you sit with your Shepherd now, may He reassure you that He does indeed speak. His Word is not silent, and His Spirit is not dormant. He is alive and active in each of His children (Hebrews 4:12; Ephesians 6:17), and if we listen with open hearts, we will hear His voice.

A Conversation With My Shepherd

My life

When in my life have I desperately needed You to say to me, "I know the way. I'll show you"? Do I need You to say it now?

Do I believe it is Your voice that has led me to be involved in worship ministry?

Is there any area of my life or ministry where You are saying to me right now, "This is the way; walk in it"?

Your Word

Shepherd of my life, what do the following verses reveal about the types of things You speak to Your sheep?

Isaiah 30:21

Your Word (continued)

John 10:27

John 16:13

According to Psalm 62:8, what do You invite me to do as I talk with You?

As You speak to me through Your Word, what does Hebrews 4:12-13 say You will do in my heart?

Your thought for me

What is one thing You want me to remember from today's lesson?

My heart before You

(Talk to your Shepherd about all or part of the following.) Here's what I need to confess to You; how I want to praise You; what I hope to do with what You've shown me; what I need You to help me with:

DAY 2: THE JOURNEY TO HERE (PART 1)

Each of us called into worship ministry has our own story of how God brought us here. Some of us knew from the very beginning of our walk with our Shepherd that He was calling us to be worship leaders; others of us are only now discovering our calling. Some of us took a direct route to worship ministry, signposts clearly marked along the way; others of us arrived here through a more circuitous route, riddled with false starts and frustrating stops.

I'd like to share how the Shepherd brought me to the unexpected place of becoming a worship leader. As you hear my story, I encourage you to reflect on your own story and remember the ways your Shepherd has led you to the place where you are. I pray this strengthens your faith to believe He will continue to lead you, with a sure and strong voice, along the path He's laid out for you.

My Backstory: A Passion Ignited

I grew up in a pastor's home with parents who loved Jesus, loved their children, and loved the church. My dad's first church was a little Baptist congregation in the tiny desert town of Joshua Tree, California. On Sunday mornings, old, wobbly voices joined with young, vigorous ones, singing the beloved hymns with robust enthusiasm. I stood next to my mom trying to follow her alto harmonies, my eyes tracking her finger along the little black dots and my voice faltering for notes. Sunday evenings we all took turns calling out our favorite hymns, competing with each other to see who could sing them the loudest. After evening church, the congregation often gathered in our living room for root beer floats and more singing, accompanied by laughter and clapping. People in our schools and workplaces probably wondered why all the Baptists arrived on Monday mornings with voices barely able to croak out words.

Evening lights in the desert sky shine in mind-boggling profusion. Gazing through a cheap telescope I'd begged my parents to buy me, I spent timeless nights searching the brilliant Milky-Way sky for falling stars, barely able to breathe as I tried to wrap my heart around the magnificence of God. The same sky that had inspired David to write:

The heavens are telling of the glory of God;
And their expanse is declaring the work of His hands.
Day to day pours forth speech,
And night to night reveals knowledge.
There is no speech, nor are there words;
Their voice is not heard.
Their line has gone out through all the earth,
And their utterances to the end of the world. (Psalm 19:1-4)

Night after night, as the pungent scent of manzanita and the mournful cries of distant coyotes drifted through my open window, the dazzling sky shouted God's glory to me more distinctly than any audible voice.

When my dad accepted the pastorate of a church in Long Beach, California, I felt cheated. Yanked out of the rural life I loved, I was now thrust into a landscape of stark impersonal pavement and garish lights, surrounded by a big-city sophistication that was entirely lost on me.

I was in 6th grade. It was the 60's, the Age of Aquarius encroaching on my wide-eyed wonder. Our church was a haven of white-haired saints and true-hearted believers, but it was also a hiding place for rebellious youth who proclaimed that "love is all you need" yet were blinded to the ultimate Source of love.

I knew that Source. I had loved Him for years. Still, uprooted and out of place, I felt somewhat like the captives in Babylon whose harps hung silent on the willows (Psalm 137:1-4). How could I regain the joy of singing the Lord's song in this harsh, foreign place?

One evening my family and I, along with our youth group, visited a nearby church. Calvary Chapel Costa Mesa had been around for a while, but something different was happening there. Pastor Chuck Smith was preaching that night, and we knew he would feed us well from the Word. But first we sang, and this singing was like none I had experienced before. Was it that these new songs were accessible, reminiscent of the folk and rock I was hearing on my radio? Was it that people were dressed in casual attire I wasn't accustomed to in church? Was it the groove of the guitar or the rawness of the voices? Yes, these things caught me, but they were not what kept me riveted.

What held me in rapt fascination was the intensity of heart and the unity of spirit. It's not that these people were more sincere than the beautiful Christians I had grown up with, but their expression of their love for Jesus was different. It was free and unselfconscious. Some were standing; some were sitting. Some stood with hands raised high overhead; others sat with upturned palms in their lap. Some closed their eyes and bowed their heads; others gazed upward. Smiles radiated from some faces, tears streamed down others. Though not all of these expressions were comfortable for me, the spirit in the room was palpable, and I felt it was something I could enter into wholeheartedly.

I was enthralled. I wanted to stay and never leave. My spirit swelled with the joy and conviction that must have inspired the psalmist to declare with inspired audacity, "For a day in Your courts is better than a thousand outside..." (Psalm 84:10). I knew I would never again be content to sing a hymn or any other worship song without my heart fully engaged. I wanted to cry out to my Savior. I wanted to declare my love for Him with everything in my being.

That night, God anchored in my heart a revived passion for Himself that would drive me from that moment on. And something more: He planted in me a seed of hopefulness for His church, a vision of how things could be every time we believers gathered together to worship Him. Not that the culture of worship or its expression would always look like it did in that worship service; no, this vision went far deeper than that. It went to the very heart of what it means to be a body of believers worshiping together in Spirit-fused unity, responding with unfettered love to the One who loved us first. The beauty of Colossians 3:14-16 seized my imagination and has held me in its grip ever since:

> *Beyond all these things put on love, which is the perfect bond of unity. Let the peace of Christ rule in your hearts, to which indeed you were called in one body; and be thankful. Let the word of Christ richly dwell within you, with all wisdom teaching and admonishing one another with psalms and hymns and spiritual songs, singing with thankfulness in your hearts to God.*

Over the next few years, God tuned my heart and helped me hone my music skills. My friends and I formed a Christian folk band, I played piano for church services, I helped plan worship sets, I wrote some songs, and I earned a music degree. God gave me a husband called to be a pastor-shepherd, and together we served our churches, all the while growing right along with them in our understanding of worship.

As the wife of a senior pastor, I was given countless opportunities to learn patience and grace, sometimes the hard way. So it was that right in the middle of this learning curve God handed me yet another occasion for growth. Isn't this just His way?

A Conversation With My Shepherd

My life

> Have You anchored in my heart a passion for worship? A passion for worship ministry? If so, what aspects am I most passionate about?

> In what ways have You tuned my heart to worship You and lead Your sheep in worship?

> What opportunities for growth are You giving me in this season of my life?

Your Word

> According to Psalm 19:

> If I listen well, what will I hear Your creation saying about You (verses 1–6)?

Your Word (continued)

If I listen well, how will Your Word speak to me (verses 7–13)?

What should be my response to the things You speak to me (verse 14)?

What inspiration can I find in Psalm 84 as I lead Your people in worship?

What are some things that should characterize our worship as we gather in Your name (Colossians 3:14–17)?

Your thought for me

What is one thing You want me to remember from today's lesson?

My heart before You

(Talk to your Shepherd about all or part of the following.) Here's what I need to confess to You; how I want to praise You; what I hope to do with what You've shown me; what I need You to help me with:

DAY 3: THE JOURNEY TO HERE (PART 2)

My Story Continues: A Call Confirmed

It was February 2003 and the most inopportune of seasons, a deluge of activity already threatening to drown me. Our oldest son had left for college, our second son was vigorously wrapping up his senior year of high school, and our sophomore daughter (whom we had affectionately nicknamed "the human vortex") was accepting every social engagement set in front of her. Forty piano students were showing up at my door each week. My husband Greg and I were trying to hold fast, with white-knuckled grip, to the wild-horse ministry of our quickly-growing church. Out of a strong sense of self-preservation, I had made the conscious decision to say "no" to any new opportunity.

In spite of this resolve, I felt the Spirit prompting me one morning to journal this: "Father, I don't want to drown out Your voice as I think of my own plans and agenda. Help me to be so in tune with You that I recognize what *You're* doing, or planning to do, and how You want me to be part of it."

I felt very brave as I scribbled these words. Much like Peter must have felt when he told Jesus, "Lord, if it is You, command me to come to You on the water" (Matthew 14:28). It made no sense for me to consider leaving the safety of my carefully protected schedule and open myself up to an unknown sea of opportunity. Not *now*. But I also knew that my Shepherd had said:

"For My thoughts are not your thoughts,
Nor are your ways My ways …
For as the heavens are higher than the earth,
So are My ways higher than your ways
And My thoughts than your thoughts." (Isaiah 55:8-9)

A few days after I wrote that prayer, our church's part-time worship pastor told us he was leaving to accept a full-time position at another church. Greg and I met with the worship leadership team to pray and seek the Lord. Through this process, the team felt certain that they should ask the elders to consider hiring me as director of worship ministry, at least on a temporary basis until they found someone else.

I was honored. I was afraid. My spirit soared at the possibilities; it sank at the improbability. In the fifteen years we'd been serving our church, God had endeared these people to us as we had all grown together. But this particular area—the redeemed gathered in grateful praise to their Redeemer—this was my passion! And to be given an official leadership role in this ministry, even for a short time, was something I had never dared to dream.

However, several obstacles hindered me from seeing this position as a viable option: I was the senior pastor's wife, and this could create a conflict of interest or, even worse, smack of favoritism. Accepting a staff position had the potential to add stress to my relationship with Greg, who would now be my boss. I was a woman, and in our church there was some reticence to placing women in visible places of leadership. I was a capable musician, most often participating from the piano or keyboard, but my voice was neither strong nor suited for leading worship. I liked to be one of the group, not the one in charge.

Finally, there was the very practical consideration that I had no time to add even the smallest additional thing to my life.

On the other hand, I'd always found great joy in planning worship sets. I loved to see people grow in their faith. I took great satisfaction in helping them reach their full potential with the gifts God had given them. I could see the big picture, and I could come up with a plan to accomplish it. My heart's pulse was to help our beloved church family worship together with humbleness before the Lord and grace toward each other.

God had confirmed this heart pulse years earlier: It was 1992, and I believed He was leading me to follow a course of songwriting. I had entered some (what I thought were) promising songs in a songwriting competition at the Christian Artists Music Seminar in the Rockies. In addition to these songs, I had also entered a worship song, almost as an afterthought. The songs I had expected to place were soundly dismissed, but my worship song "Draw Me to Your Throne" received an award.

After the conference I did much prayerful soul-searching because I knew this was a watershed moment of sorts. Just as Paul and Barnabas learned that their calling was not primarily to the Jews but to the Gentiles (Acts 13:46-47), my Shepherd soon confirmed to me that my primary calling would not be professional songwriting but serving in worship ministry in my local church. In the years following, my little worship song became somewhat of a theme song for our congregation, and each time we sang it, I was reminded that the Lord had called me to *these* people, to serve in *this* place as I worshiped side by side with them.

So it was that, years later, as I was trying to discern whether God was asking me to say yes to the worship director position, I kept thinking about the lesson He had taught me through the music seminar experience: "The mind of man plans his way, but the Lord directs his steps" (Proverbs 16:9). It reminded me of something I had heard George Mueller always did when he was trying to discern the will of God: "I seek at the beginning to get my heart into such a state that it has no will of its own in regard to a given matter."[2] As I faced this new crossroads, I intentioned to keep an open and receptive heart as I looked to my Shepherd for direction.

It proved to be more intensely difficult than I could have imagined, but through careful listening on my part and patient communication on His, He finally gave me the clarity and the peace to say yes to this improbable calling.

Why, then, did obeying His voice exhaust every reserve of my courage? As I ask myself this question now, nine years later, it reminds me of a couple of summers ago when Greg and I traveled with our friends, Mike and Karen, to Zambia. Never a fan of flying, and violently averse to being in confined places, I found myself one sunny morning folding myself into the back seat of a Cessna 210. As I took my place next to Karen, I was instantly seized by the panic of claustrophobia. Awash in a gush of unstoppable tears and fighting an overwhelming urge to escape, I prayed fervently that I would have the strength to stay on that plane.

By the grace of God and the sweet encouragement of my husband, I remained strapped in place, and incredibly, I even found the wherewithal to re-board the plane for our return trip. At the end of the day, Karen said, "Jeanelle, I was so stinkin' proud of you for staying on that plane." I didn't feel proud, only deeply grateful. Because it was a day I wouldn't have missed for the world: flying low over herds of zebra galloping across the plains; being greeted by colorfully-arrayed crowds of people who had walked up the road and gathered on the runway; meeting faithful saints who had given their lives to follow

Jesus in an obscure yet vibrant corner of the world. I would have missed it all had I given in to my fear.

This is how I felt when I became director of worship ministry for our church: frightened, vulnerable, and tempted to bolt. But I would have missed *everything*—all the relationships that were forged through the toil, all the faith-building evidences of His strength showing through my weakness, all the scraping off of my own rough edges as His image emerged more clearly, and all the joys of being one of the joints that Christ has fitted together in His body for the building up of itself in love (Ephesians 4:16). Indeed, I would have missed out on countless gifts God had in store for me:

> *"Things which eye has not seen and ear has not heard,*
> *And which have not entered the heart of man*
> *All that God has prepared for those who love Him."*
> (1 Corinthians 2:9b)

A Conversation With My Shepherd

My life

Will You remind me of a time when I've had to trust that Your ways and Your thoughts were higher than mine?

Are there aspects of this ministry for which You are asking great courage of me?

Help me recall some of the gifts You've given me in this ministry that I might have missed had I not followed Your voice here.

Your Word

What does Isaiah 55:3, 6, 8-9 teach me about the heart posture I should have as I listen to Your voice?

What can I learn from Proverbs 16:9 about making plans as I serve You in this ministry?

Your Word (continued)

How will You encourage me through the following verses as I serve You in worship?

Ephesians 4:16

1 Corinthians 2:9

Your thought for me

What is one thing You want me to remember from today's lesson?

My heart before You

(Talk to your Shepherd about all or part of the following.) Here's what I need to confess to You; how I want to praise You; what I hope to do with what You've shown me; what I need You to help me with:

DAY 4: WHY WE NEED OUR SHEPHERD TO SPEAK

Whether lost at night on a California freeway, belted into the crammed back row of a Cessna six-seater, or committed to leading a ministry for which "inadequate" seemed far and away too generous a designation for my felt level of competence, my compelling need was to hear a knowing Voice speak truth to my quavering heart: "Take courage, Child. I am with you. I know the way. I will lead you there." I needed the voice of my Shepherd.

We all are sheep who lose our way sometimes, the worship leader no more and no less than anyone else. This is why the writer of Psalm 119 prayed,

With all my heart I have sought You;
Do not let me wander from Your commandments. (Psalm 119:10)

We are beset by the enemy of our souls. This is why Jesus commanded us to pray,

And do not lead us into temptation, but deliver us from evil.
(Matthew 6:13)

We are susceptible to counterfeit voices—even our own. This is why Paul warned the Christians in Colossae,

See to it that no one takes you captive through philosophy and empty
deception, according to the tradition of men, according to the elementary
principles of the world, rather than according to Christ. (Colossians 2:8)

But those of us called to lead worship ministries are not only sheep. We are shepherds too, serving under the leadership of the Head Shepherd:

Shepherd the flock of God among you, exercising oversight not under
compulsion, but voluntarily, according to the will of God; and not for
sordid gain, but with eagerness; nor yet as lording it over those allotted to
your charge, but proving to be examples to the flock. And when the Chief
Shepherd appears, you will receive the unfading crown of glory.
(1 Peter 5:2-4)

As His *undershepherds*, we do not listen to the voice of our Shepherd merely for our own sake. We also listen for the sake of the sheep in our charge with whom we serve side-by-side in this ministry, knowing full well the unique spiritual challenges they face because we face them too. And we listen for the sake of our brothers and sisters in the congregation who are lifting their voices along with ours. This is *their* time of refreshment, the weekly sheep-gathering time when we are given the solemn and glorious responsibility of leading these precious ones into soul-sustaining worship of the One who gave His life for them.

For the sake of His sheep, as well as for our own sakes, it is imperative that we cup our hands behind our ears and filter out every other voice so that we can hear what our Shepherd is speaking to us. Since He has created each of us with unique strengths and flip-side weaknesses, enmeshing our lives with one-of-a-kind congregations of applaudable accomplishments and deplorable deficiencies, He speaks to each of us the word *we* need to hear, according to the need of the moment.

He speaks in tones of tenderness or tones of gracious sternness; with a "well-done" or a "you can do better." He coaxes us with the gentle pull of His staff or prods us with the slight sting of His rod. His voice comes like thunder on the mountain and it comes like the wisp of a breeze through pine branches. He alternates between prose and poetry, and He communicates one day with crystal clarity and the next day in shadowed mystery.

But speak He does. And He speaks to us personally, calling us by name (John 10:3). We are promised this. We are gifted this. We would be undone without this. We don't deserve such tailor-made attentiveness, but our kind Shepherd knows that in its absence we would wander aimlessly, spirits shriveled, resolve quashed. If we allow the full import of His voice to saturate our hearts, we will be driven to gratitude of infinite depths.

I pray this book helps worship leaders grow in their ability to listen to their Shepherd. I pray it helps *me* learn to listen better. So let's lean in close, not missing a single word. Because as we drink from His river and reside in His meadow, staying well within earshot of His voice, we "shall be sure to have good nurture and admonition, and shall be taught to walk in right paths, and *that* you know is a favour of no small account (emphasis mine)." [3]

A Conversation With My Shepherd

My life

Will You show me if there has ever been a time when I've lost my way as a worship leader?

Are there any voices speaking to me louder than Yours right now?

As a worship undershepherd of Your sheep, are You saying "Well done" in any area of my ministry? Are You saying "You can do better" in any area of my ministry?

Your Word

According to the following verses, what are some pitfalls I can avoid by listening well to Your voice?

Psalm 119:10

Matthew 6:13

Your Word (continued)

  Colossians 2:8

  What does 1 Peter 5:2-4 tell me about my calling as a worship undershepherd?

  What does John 10:3-4 tell me about the type of relationship You have invited me into as Your sheep?

Your thought for me

  What is one thing You want me to remember from today's lesson?

My heart before You

  (Talk to your Shepherd about all or part of the following.) Here's what I need to confess to You; how I want to praise You; what I hope to do with what You've shown me; what I need You to help me with:

DAY 5: WHAT WE NEED TO HEAR FROM OUR SHEPHERD

What *is* that nurture and admonition we worship leaders find ourselves needing to hear? To what waters need we be led, from what pitfalls coaxed away? Our fellow sheep might think, "But you get to dwell by these waters all day, sitting there as the brook bubbles up its joy songs and the sun lights up the face of your Shepherd." We may even have hoped this happy picture for ourselves right up until the day we took up this calling. But each of us who has been in the ministry any amount of time knows that these waters can be more elusive than we had imagined.

I write this book as one who has often sensed a profound need to hear my Shepherd speak as I've led our church's worship ministry. In the chapters that follow, I will talk about some of the spiritual challenges worship leaders face and the word we need to hear from Him as we encounter each one:

- When our spirit runs dry, the word that will *refresh* us
- When we falter, the word that will keep us *persevering* in worship
- When we are too weak to do what He asks of us, the word that will bring us *strength*
- When we seek our own honor, the word that will show us the way of *humility*
- When we wrestle with our inadequacy, the word that will *reassure* us with His all-sufficiency
- When we are confused about who we, our congregations, and our teams are called to be, the word that will clarify our *identity*
- When we balk at how long it takes to move forward, the word that will help us remain *patient*
- When we elevate our own agenda, the word that will bring us back into *submission* to Him and others
- When we get caught up in ourselves, the word that will remind us to delight in *community*
- When we shudder under the weight, the word that will encourage us to seek *help*

- When we fail to remember God's faithfulness, the word that
  will draw us back to a *thankful* heart

Without the wise voice of our Shepherd leading us along, we would be fools to try to lead His people in worship. We would wander in utter futility. We would fail to grow, and our churches would suffer. Furthermore, we would miss out on being part of the astounding miracle that occurs when He takes all of us bleating and hobbling sheep and turns us into a people for His glory.

Do you want to miss out on this? I know I don't.

So let's listen well, together.

A Conversation With My Shepherd

My life

What words do I need You to say to me today?

What are some of the greatest spiritual challenges I've experienced as I've served You in worship ministry?

What would I like You to do in my heart as I read this book?

Your Word

As I prepare my heart to consider the spiritual challenges discussed in the remaining chapters of this book, how can You encourage me with each of the following words?

Spiritual refreshment (John 7:37)

Perseverance (Acts 16:23-25)

Strength (Isaiah 41:10)

Humility (Philippians 2:5-8)

Reassurance (2 Corinthians 3:4-5)

Identity (1 Corinthians 12:14-18)

Patience (Psalm 37:5)

Your Word (continued)

Submission (Ephesians 5:19-21)

Community (Hebrews 10:24-25)

Help (Exodus 18:17-18)

Thankfulness (Psalm 92:1-2)

Your thought for me

What is one thing You want me to remember from today's lesson?

My heart before You

(Talk to your Shepherd about all or part of the following.) Here's what I need to confess to You; how I want to praise You; what I hope to do with what You've shown me; what I need You to help me with:

A PRAYER TO PRAY

Each chapter in this book concludes with a prayer for you to pray. Each prayer provides a way for you to converse with your Shepherd about what you have read in the chapter that precedes it. My hope is that these prayers will be a means through which you can come before Him in worship, inviting Him to bring your heart to where it needs to be as you continue leading His sheep with gladness.

Good Shepherd, here I am, all bowed and helpless, hands laid open and ears fine-tuned. I take in wide-eyed the calling before me, and its immensity can tempt me to trepidation. But I have YOU. Isn't it You who have brought me here? Aren't You the one who stands ready to guide me? Isn't Yours the voice, strong and sure, that I will hear along the way?

So let this familiar voice, so graciously made known to me and calling me by name, remind me of those things You know I most need to hear.

You've invited me to proceed along these paths and to work hard in these fields. As I persevere, will You please convince me again of my need for You? Will You stop me in my tracks to listen? Will you train my ears to hear all the nuances of Your voice? My greatest reward will be to hear that voice speaking to me in tones of joy and pleasure. This is what I live for. So keep me faithful to hear and to follow.

Even when I am not faithful, You are. Day in and day out. May the thought of this cause my heart to overflow with thankfulness and my lips to pour forth praise. May it build in me a heart that longs for nothing more than to bring You glory and honor, Good Shepherd.

Here I am. Waiting. Listening. And trusting You to speak.

CHAPTER 2

OUR SHEPHERD SPEAKS REFRESHMENT

DAY 1: WE GET THIRSTY

Greg and I love to hike. Rocky crags and panoramic views and the promise of new beauty around each bend exhilarate us. But sometimes we become so caught up in rapturous anticipation of the journey ahead that we neglect to take the time to prepare as we should. We will be driving along, catch sight of an enticing trail and exclaim to each other, "How hard can this be? Let's do it!" We are not *seasoned* hikers, nor are we always *wise* hikers. We just love to hike.

One day we were cruising along a highway in central Idaho, taking in the beauty of the surrounding Sawtooth Mountains. We stopped at a ranger station to inquire about any day hikes that might provide spectacular views. One hike caught our attention: Alice Lake. We were lured in by the ranger's description of great cliff views and a gorgeous waterfall on the way to one of the most beautiful lakes in the region (neglecting to consider his use of the word "strenuous"). Five and a half miles of glorious grandeur—what could be more perfect?

We took a moment to calculate how long it would take us to get to the lake. Figuring that we walk through our own neighborhood at a pace of about 3.5 miles an hour, we cut that pace in half and decided it would take us two hours to climb to the lake. (First problem: It had been a while since we had studied basic division and multiplication.) We tossed a water bottle and some trailmix into Greg's backpack and headed off. Or, more accurately, up. Straight up. (Second problem: We didn't consider how much more difficult it would be to walk up a mountain at 8,000 feet than to stroll along flat suburban streets).

For the first half hour we exulted in the adventure before us, with a song in our hearts and a spring in our steps. But then as the trail steepened and the terrain became rockier, our progression slowed considerably. With every step our feet slipped on the shale-strewn path, forcing our eyes to stay glued to the trail. Our calves burned. Our bodies ached from exertion. Our hearts pounded out of our chests. Our mouths were cotton-dry. We made a valiant effort to ration out the water, but by the time we were within a half mile of the lake, our bottle had run dry.

Overcome with exhaustion, we finally made a sensible (though disappointing) decision: Turn around and head back down the trail without seeing the lake. Defeated, we began working our way carefully back through the dusty shale, aware that any misstep could send us careening down the mountain. With each switchback, our thirst grew until we could think of nothing else. The majestic magnificence of our surroundings was lost to us. All we could see was the drinking fountain waiting for us back at the trailhead.

Many hours after we had begun our trek, we stumbled back into the clearing where our car was parked, only to realize that the drinking fountain had been a cruel figment of our imaginations. Consumed with thirst, we fell into the car and drove the longest twenty-one miles of our lives to the first restaurant we could find. Before we ordered, we drank one large carafe of water. By the time our food arrived, we had guzzled down two and a half more, and the server was looking at us with jaw-dropped disbelief.

Since that day, I have never read Psalm 42 without being transported directly back to that experience:

As the deer pants for the water brooks,
So my soul pants for You, O God.
My soul thirsts for God, for the living God;
When shall I come and appear before God? (Psalm 42:1-2)

When I think of my soul thirsting for God, I remember what real thirst feels like. It eclipses every other desire. There is no room for any other thought.

Thirst Can Be A Good Thing

As a worship leader, I certainly have experienced spiritual thirst of this intensity. I have found myself wandering far from the Shepherd's good streams, my soul parched and listless. Ministry demands—administrative, relational, creative, and technical—steal my time and sap my energy so that the one thing I most love to do—worship my Savior—gets marginalized. Even when I am putting together worship sets and immersing myself in Scripture and praying for those who will worship with me, I can find that worship itself has become more a program to plan than a passion to pursue. Pragmatism has replaced praise. So I end up thirsty, and I need my Shepherd to speak refreshment to my jaded soul.

Experiencing spiritual thirst can be a very good thing. If we did not thirst, we would not know our need to drink; we would wither and die. Thankfully, our Good Shepherd is well acquainted with our frailties (Psalm 103:14) and knows what we need far better than we do. With grace and tenderness, He allows the parched seasons. He knows it is these that will drive us back to Him to receive the sustenance He is holding out to us.

With sympathetic compassion, Jesus reassures us: "Blessed are those who hunger and thirst after righteousness, for they shall be satisfied" (Matthew 5:6). And, because He *is* our righteousness (Jeremiah 23:6; 2 Corinthians 5:21), He offers this gracious invitation: "If anyone is thirsty, let him come to Me and drink" (John 7:37).

A Conversation With My Shepherd

My life

> Will You remind me of some times in my life when I have felt spiritually dry? Am I feeling spiritually dry now?

> Am I able to see times of spiritual thirst as a good thing in my life?

Your Word

> In Psalm 42, what are some things that can happen to Your sheep when they are in need of refreshment?

> In Psalm 42, what words of encouragement do You give Your sheep when they are needing refreshment?

Your thought for me

What is one thing You want me to remember from today's lesson?

My heart before You

(Talk to your Shepherd about all or part of the following.) Here's what I need to confess to You; how I want to praise You; what I hope to do with what You've shown me; what I need You to help me with:

DAY 2: SPIRITUAL DESERTS IN THE LIFE OF A WORSHIP UNDERSHEPHERD

I have this ideal of how I want my life to be lived with my Savior: I long to be vibrantly alive in Him, living in a continual rhythm of breathing in His presence and breathing out His praise. He didn't create me to be an earthworm crawling in and out of dirt, never looking up to see the sky. He made me to behold Him in everything, to let His beauty hallow all I do and say and think.

Yet this vision of perpetual spiritual vitality can be painfully elusive. Why, I ask myself, don't I live in constant awareness of Him? Why don't I always experience the fullness of joy that is promised in His presence (Psalm 16:11)? As Ann Voskamp puts it,

*Isn't it here? The wonder? Why do I spend so much of my living hours struggling to see it? Do we truly stumble so blind that we must be affronted with **blinding** magnificence for our blurry soul-sight to recognize grandeur?* [4]

It is a very human experience to miss the wonder. God has placed eternity in our hearts (Ecclesiastes 3:11), but He has also housed our souls in bodies that weaken and tire, with minds that get easily distracted and emotions that can sound louder to us than the truth. Though our Shepherd leads us by still waters (Psalm 23:2), we can neglect to stop and drink. We can forget how indispensable it is to our existence. We become dry; we become thirsty.

Had Greg and I recognized how quickly our water was running out and how desperately thirsty we would become on that Sawtooths hike, we would have turned around much sooner. But we were so intent on putting one foot in front of the other that we never saw the crisis coming.

What It Looks Like When We Are Spiritually Dry

As worship leaders, we can at times become so enmeshed in the requirements of our calling that we don't realize we are becoming spiritually depleted. Furthermore, we can remain in this dry place for quite a while before we even recognize we have arrived there.

What this dry place looks like for me may be different from what it looks like for you. In my own life, I've come to recognize some of the following conditions as signs that I need spiritual refreshment:

Apathy: Life may be running smoothly, and I may not feel particularly discouraged, but there is just lethargy, a lack of zeal. My eagerness to sit at Jesus' feet has waned. I neither rejoice exceedingly about the things God is doing nor mourn over the things that break His heart.

Academic worship: I sing the songs and pray the prayers, but rather than allowing them to renew my mind and soften my heart, I stand back, detached. I mouth the lyrics while analyzing the song arrangements. I pray the prayers while evaluating their wording. I do not fully engage my heart.

Inability to focus: I find it difficult to keep at a task without my mind wandering. I am unable to provide the cogency of thought that worship ministry deserves. Details and concerns whirl around in my head, unsettled and refusing to be quieted.

Ministry fatigue: I feel overwhelmed by the requirements of the job. My eyes glaze over when people talk to me. I procrastinate opening my email because I don't have the energy to answer. The thought of mustering the creativity to plan one more service paralyzes me. Quite simply, my spirit and mind are depleted.

Lack of perspective: I have a hard time acknowledging the good fruit the Lord is producing. Instead, I dwell on the discouragements. All I can see are my own inadequacies, the negative responses of others, the slowness of progress, and the failures.

Sin: My heart easily goes to places of pride, bitterness, or selfishness. I lack grace in my responses to people. I make poor choices that don't honor my God. I neglect confession and recoil at correction. I seek my own way.

Physical symptoms: Sometimes I am slow to recognize that my body is tied to my spirit. But over time I've learned that, for me, things like sleeplessness, drowsiness, heart palpitations, or upset stomach can be signs that I am in deep need of spiritual replenishment.

Why Worship Leaders Run Dry

All Christians find themselves in spiritual deserts sometimes, the worship leader no more and no less than anyone else. However, worship ministry does come with its own set of challenges that can make us particularly susceptible to landing in these desert places.

Responsibility For The Flock

Probably the thing that weighs on us most heavily is the responsibility we feel for the spiritual well-being of our congregations as they grow in their heart of worship. Paul knew it well: "There is the daily pressure on me of concern for all the churches. Who is weak without my being weak? Who is led into sin without my intense concern?" (2 Corinthians 11:28-29). We understand that God is the one who does the deep-down work in people's hearts. He is the one who causes the spiritual growth. But He does ask us to plant; He does ask us to water (1 Corinthians 3:6-9). Week after week He calls us to stand up with our teams and bring our congregations along with us as we lead them into pure and authentic, God-honoring worship. "What if they don't follow?" we wonder. "What if we are not in the right heart-place to lead them?" we ask ourselves.

Satan will do anything he can to rob God of the glory He is due. He works very hard against us, lashing out in desperate anger, striking at every vulnerable spot in our heart to shake our confidence and wear us down. He will take the slightest discouragement and try to twist it into the lie that what we are doing has no impact on people's lives. Our Shepherd provides the armor we need to fight off our enemy for the good of the flock (Ephesians 6:11), but as we take it up, the energy expended and the sweat poured out can leave us dried up, gasping for water.

Ministry Demands

If our struggle was only in spiritual realms, that would be exhausting enough. But before Paul speaks of the daily concern for the flock, he prefaces it with: "Apart from such external things." What external things? What are those other things that can bring us to spiritually dry places? We may not face beatings and shipwrecks like Paul did, but sometimes the daily demands of our calling can make us *feel* beat-up and tossed onto a rocky shore. It's not that the requirements of the job are unreasonable as they arrive one by one, but as a whole, they can feel oppressive. Planning fresh and creative services, keeping up with administrative details, building relationships, attending countless meetings, and training up worship volunteers can have a cumulative effect on our spirit. As ministry demands tumble into our lives one upon the other, we can easily find ourselves "weary in well-doing" (2 Thessalonians 3:13, KJV[5]).

The Nature Of Our Calling

What empties us of spiritual vitality is not simply that we *have* a lot to do; what can sap us dry is the very *nature* of what we are called to do. Our *job* is worship, but we can work so hard at helping others pour out their hearts in worship that we fail to notice that the worship in our own heart has slowed to a trickle.

Or, perhaps even worse, we don't recognize that it is being poured out on the wrong object. Years ago God placed in me a passion to worship Him with my whole being and to help the congregation join together in the same pursuit. He also gave me a love for music and a vision for its potential to help bring us into worship. Unfortunately, the sheer joy of *music* can sometimes supplant my joy in *God.* Before I know it, I am delighting in harmonies and rhythms and riffs so much that I forget to delight in the Lord Himself. I start valuing the *gift* more than the *Giver.* As singer and songwriter Matt Maher says, "We lose heart when we look to music to satisfy our hunger and thirst for deeper knowledge of God."[6]

Our Shepherd understands these spiritual deserts we worship undershepherds can find ourselves in. On Day 3, we will listen to some of the encouraging words He speaks to us there.

A Conversation With My Shepherd

My life

What are some of the symptoms I experience when I'm in need of spiritual refreshment from You?

Will You help me be aware of some of the things in worship ministry that can make me feel spiritually depleted?

When is the last time I let You speak to me?

Your Word

According to Psalm 16:11, what happens when I am living in awareness of Your presence?

How can 1 Corinthians 3:6-9 encourage me when the spiritual welfare of Your sheep lies heavy on my heart?

When Satan tries to make me doubt that You are at work in Your sheep, what help do You give me to fight him off (Ephesians 6:10-17)?

Your thought for me

What is one thing You want me to remember from today's lesson?

My heart before You

(Talk to your Shepherd about all or part of the following.) Here's what I need to confess to You; how I want to praise You; what I hope to do with what You've shown me; what I need You to help me with:

DAY 3: HIS WORDS, OUR REFRESHMENT (PART 1)

When responsibility for the flock, ministry demands, and the nature of our calling have depleted our spiritual reserves and brought us to a desert place, this is when our Shepherd's voice often sounds the sweetest. Our desperation can make us hang onto His every word, which, of course, is exactly the attentiveness He wants from us. When we listen to Him and hear Him well, He promises to bring refreshment to our weary bones (Proverbs 3:1-8).

So, what are some of the words we need to hear from our Shepherd in the desert places?

What Our Shepherd Speaks To Us When We Are Spiritually Dry

Our Shepherd's Voice: "Do not be surprised by this dry season."

The thing that reassures me most when I come to my Shepherd, desperate to be revived, is His reminder that my experience is a natural part of the Christian life. I should not be surprised by it, nor should I be dismayed. I need not default to the conclusion that I have done something wrong for this to have happened (though it is possible that as I listen, He may show me places where I have gone off-course).

In His Word, God graciously and unreservedly paints the whole-truth picture of His children in all their infirmities. Noah, Abraham, Isaac, Jacob, Sarah. They were strangers and exiles on the earth, fully subject to the very real effects of the Fall. They became weary and weak, as do all God's children. But they knew something different was coming. A better country where someday all their longings would be fully realized. They held heaven in their hearts (Hebrews 11:13, 16). Holding this hope fast, they walked with their God and "*from* their weakness they were made strong…" (Hebrews 11:34).

What this says to me is that when I find myself in spiritually impoverished places, having succumbed to fatigue or apathy or distraction or sin, unable to see things quite through His eyes, I can know that this happens to the Shepherd's sheep. It just does. But I can also know that He holds out better things for me. My Savior, who is preparing a place for me, is also preparing me for that place, and He will provide the needed nourishment along the way. All He asks of me is that I come to Him in my thirst and let Him fill me.

Such humble acknowledgment of my need will never make Him ashamed to be called my God (Hebrews 11:16). He welcomes it, and He welcomes me. This is the place where I find Him.

Our Shepherd's Voice: "Wait in this dry season."

Our friends Carolyn and David decided recently to take a drive to watch sheep that were trailing down through a mountain pass. They drove until they came upon a flock grazing in a grassy meadow alongside a rippling stream. As they sat and took in the idyllic scene, they noticed two sheep wandering off, moving farther and farther away from the flock. Our friends looked around to see who was watching over the sheep, but they saw no one. Then they heard a whistle far away but distinct. Their eyes followed the sound, and high up on a bluff, they could barely make out the image of the man who had whistled. Just as their eyes found him, two dogs came bounding toward the wayward sheep. They barked and headed them off, skillfully prodding them until they returned safely to the flock.

This is how our Shepherd is. He sees everything, but He may let us wander away from green pastures and quiet waters for a while. Eventually, He will show us our need to return and help us get there. Then He will whistle, and the sheepdogs will come at His command: a timely word of encouragement from a friend, a lyric that stops us in our tracks, a familiar Scripture that we see with new eyes, a forced rest because of illness. The dogs may nudge quietly or bark vociferously, but they will bring us back if we let them.

The way back may not always be clear or easy or quick. Furthermore, when we find the streams again, we may have forgotten how to drink. It could be that we will sit there a while, begging our Shepherd to teach us again, and the only response we will receive is, "I will. Just wait."

I often feel like the Psalmist who cried, "I opened my mouth wide and panted" (Psalm 119:131). I want refreshment *now*. But sometimes the only answer I receive in my desperate panting is, "Wait."

There is much accomplished in waiting. It's in the waiting that I gain strength. It's in the waiting that God's Spirit breaks through to mine. As my son reminded my daughter some time ago when she was discouraged about the lack of forward movement in her life: "This season is not a parentheses to the rest of your life. This *is* life, right now."

Why did God give Joseph a hopeful dream and then allow him to languish for years in an Egyptian prison? Why did God, through Moses, promise Caleb the hill country only to have him wait forty-five years for the promise to be fulfilled? Was it because it's only in the waiting that some of the deepest soul-work is accomplished? Was it because there are blessings found in the waiting that are found nowhere else? Was it to grow a thirst and longing so strong that nothing short of God Himself would ever satisfy it? If so, wasn't it worth it for them, this waiting? And isn't it worth it for us? If all our waiting brings us back to the only true source of refreshment, no moment of it is wasted.

A Conversation With My Shepherd

My life

Will You show me why it is that sometimes I feel surprised by seasons of spiritual thirst?

Here's why it can sometimes be hard for me to wait for You to answer my prayer for refreshment:

Will You show me some ways You are graciously bringing me refreshment right now?

Your Word

According to Hebrews 11, what are some of the hard things Your people went through, even when they were being faithful to seek You?

Your Word (continued)

How can the following Scriptures encourage me when I am waiting for You to bring refreshment to my spirit?

Psalm 25:3

Isaiah 40:31

Isaiah 64:4

Your thought for me

What is one thing You want me to remember from today's lesson?

My heart before You

(Talk to your Shepherd about all or part of the following.) Here's what I need to confess to You; how I want to praise You; what I hope to do with what You've shown me; what I need You to help me with:

DAY 4: HIS WORDS, OUR REFRESHMENT (PART 2)

<u>Our Shepherd's Voice:</u> "Keep seeking Me in this dry season."

It is good for us to wait with expectation, cup held out, eyes fixed dependently on Jesus, no matter how long it takes or how difficult the waiting. The refreshment we seek is Christ Himself. He invites us to seek Him, and there is a sure promise attached to the seeking: "Come to Me, all who are weary and heavy-laden, and *I* will give you rest" (Matthew 11:28, emphasis added).

The Psalmist went through a dry season, but it did not deter him from the search for water:

> *When You said, "Seek My face," my heart said to You, "Your face,*
> *O Lord, I shall seek."*
> *I would have despaired unless I had believed that I would see the*
> *goodness of the Lord in the land of the living.*
> (Psalm 27:8, 13)

Worship leader and author Rory Noland writes, "If you're going through a dry spell, whatever you do, don't give up. Even though it doesn't feel as if you're moving forward, your roots are still being planted in the Word." He then references Hosea 6:3: "As surely as the sun rises, he will appear; he will come to us like the winter rains, like the spring rains that water the earth."[7]

The spring rains from our Father's storehouses of grace fall generously in their refreshing. James 4:8 provides all the encouragement we need in our quest to find these rains: "Draw near to God and He will draw near to you." We do not have to wrest refreshment from a tight-clenched fist. God opens wide His hand, and from the palm on which each of our names is engraved, He pours out every spiritual resource we need. All we have to do is ask, trusting in His magnanimous heart (James 1:5, 6). Not just once, but again and again, because one spring rain does not keep the garden growing all summer.

Psalm 34:8 invites us, "O taste and see that the Lord is good." The first taste of coffee in the morning, warm and cream-infused, wakes up and delights my taste buds. I don't put the cup aside, sated, after just one taste. One good swallow inspires another, until the cup is empty. Once the cup is drained, I don't smash it and say, "I am satisfied and will not need this cup again."

Jesus calls Himself the "Bread of Life" (John 6:35). Like the manna in the wilderness, He is our *daily* bread. Fresh and new and nourishing, every day. We must come to Him continually for refreshment because, as Ann Voskamp writes, "I am beset by chronic soul amnesia. I empty of truth and need the refilling. I need come again every day—bend, clutch, and remember—for who can gather manna but once, hoarding, and store away sustenance in the mind for all of the living?" [8]

The old hymn expresses this same need for our spirits to be replenished:

> *Guide me, O Thou Great Jehovah*
> *Pilgrim through this barren land*
> *I am weak, but Thou art mighty*
> *Hold me with Thy pow'rful hand*
> *Bread of heaven, Bread of heaven,*
> *Feed me till I want no more*
> *Feed me till I want no more* [9]

We cannot possibly conceive of all the spiritual riches our Shepherd has in mind to give us. We will never own a cup big enough to hold them. "Oh the depth of the riches both of the wisdom and knowledge of God!" (Romans 11:33). Who could ever say they have plumbed these depths?

Our magnificent God has shown His majesty in the heavens. He has demonstrated His mercy on the cross. He has shown us again and again glimpses of His glory. But do we always heart-see it? I don't.

One morning I sensed that the eyes of my soul were dimming. I prayed, "Lord, *You* are the author of all graces, including the grace to melt my heart to love You all the more. Show me a fresh glimpse of You today. Let me know when You are saying, 'Here, this is your glimpse,' and let it stop me in my tracks to worship You."

I waited all day. Nothing cleared before my dull eyes. That evening my friend texted me a photo of a glorious sunset. I threw on my jacket and walked out the door into a world awash in shades of amber and pink. As I walked, I listened. In the calm air I could almost hear the words, "Here. This is your glimpse." My heart became lighter, and I began singing and clapping out rhythms. Then I found myself skipping, arms thrown open in worship. Was it the night sky or the fresh breeze or the peaceful stillness that brought such worship? Those certainly helped. But the real rejoicing, deep in my soul, was because I knew the Shepherd Himself was with me in a way tailor-made for this moment. I was reassured that He is true to His promise to draw near, though it may take a day or much longer.

Our gracious, generous God means it when He says, "You will seek Me and find Me when you search for Me with all your heart" (Jeremiah 29:13). When the time is right, He will be faithful to pour refreshment into our cup. We are wise to keep bringing it back for the filling.

Our Shepherd's Voice: "Refreshment is not just for your own sake."

As worship leaders, we must not take lightly this promise of finding refreshment, as if it were only one of many gifts our Shepherd offers to us and we can take it or leave it at will. Everything we are must flow from our relationship with Him. Drawing near to Him is the most important thing we'll ever do.

We are asked by our Shepherd to lead His beloved sheep into worship. How can we do this if our own cups are not being filled? Nothing else we might pursue—putting together good music sets, running tight meetings, polishing up our skills, attending inspirational conferences, training our teams—even comes close to the mandate to pursue Christ Himself. If we are to lead with authenticity and integrity, setting an example of sincere worship for our congregations, we must be able to say, with Paul, that we count all these things as loss in view of the surpassing value of knowing Jesus Christ (Philippians 3:8).

I once went through an eight-week season of ravenous seeking and sponge-like receiving of spiritual refreshment from the Lord. One morning I woke up and realized that even with all this refreshing, I still felt empty. As I asked the Lord why, He impressed on me this thought:

"The nourishment you've received was not only for you; it was also meant to be shared with others." I began thinking of the people I was called to serve in my family, in the world, in my congregation. I realized that the question I should have been asking was not, "Am I filled?" or "Why don't I feel filled?" but rather, "How can this filling I've received be extended to others?" I saw that the more I had grasped for myself the less I had kept. I was being invited by my Shepherd to extend an open hand to others, and I knew that in doing so my own heart would not be emptied but filled all the more.

Christ, our Shepherd, has called us to be His undershepherds, loving His flock, nurturing them, living humble lives of worship before them. If we can learn to delight in the presence of our Good Shepherd, drinking thirstily from His cup, our fellow sheep will be encouraged to do the same.

A Conversation With My Shepherd

My life

Good Shepherd, do I come to You often enough for spiritual refreshment?

How can I "taste and see that You are good" today?

Will You please bring to mind the names of some of my fellow sheep who seem to be going through a dry spell and could use my encouragement?

Your Word

What encouragement regarding spiritual refreshment do You give me from the following Scriptures?

Matthew 11:28

Psalm 27:8, 13-14

Hosea 6:3

James 4:8

Psalm 34:8

1 Corinthians 2:9

Jeremiah 29:13

Your thought for me

What is one thing You want me to remember from today's lesson?

My heart before You

(Talk to your Shepherd about all or part of the following.) Here's what I need to confess to You; how I want to praise You; what I hope to do with what You've shown me; what I need You to help me with:

DAY 5: RECEIVING REFRESHMENT FROM OUR SHEPHERD

Do you ever find yourself in a really wonderful place of joy and hopefulness and awareness of the Lord's presence, and yet the beauty of the moment is tainted by this thought: "What if it doesn't last"? You try to capture the moment as long as you can, only to find that it can be as temporal as a snowflake melting in your hand, as elusive as a dandelion floating free in the breeze?

In John 3:8, Jesus tells the seeker Nicodemus, "The wind blows where it wishes and you hear the sound of it, but do not know where it comes from and where it is going; so is everyone who is born of the Spirit." Though we know that our Father *will*, through His Spirit, answer our deep cries for spiritual refreshment (Luke 11:9-13), we cannot know *how*. We cannot predict whether, in His gracious wisdom, He will show us yet another shining facet of His glory and flood us with a profound awareness of His presence or whether this same merciful God will allow the fog to roll in and the deserts to encroach for a while. For this reason, we must use every means available to keep seeking Him. We must believe all the while that He *will* "satisfy the weary ones and refresh everyone who languishes" (Jeremiah 31:35).

The Means To Refreshment

When my husband and I returned to the trailhead in the Sawtooths that day, desperate for water, we would have happily quenched our thirst by any number of means: a drinking fountain, a concession stand, a forgotten water bottle in the car. But the only option at our disposal was to drive a grueling twenty-one miles to the nearest restaurant and wait several long minutes to be seated and given a carafe of water.

Quenching our spiritual thirst is similar to this: the means may vary, but we must use to full advantage whatever means are available to us.

Some of the means for our refreshment are laid out clearly in our Shepherd's Word. They include:

Prayer: Prayer is what keeps our hearts soft to the voice of the Spirit. The admonition to "pray without ceasing" (1 Thessalonians 5:17) is neither extravagant nor overstated; it is *everything* to the Shepherd's sheep.

God's Word: Scripture reveals the heart of God so we can be better attuned to it. No word from our Shepherd is an idle word; His Word is our very life. (Deuteronomy 32:47)

Fellowship: There is no concept of a solitary Christian in the Bible. Hebrews 10:24, 25 tells us to never stop meeting together, because the encouragement we receive from each other is irreplaceable.

Worship: Worship brings us awestruck to our knees, placing everything in perspective and filling us with profound thankfulness. The Spirit of God searches the whole world over to find such worshipers, people whose hearts are completely His (2 Chronicles 16:9).

Sabbath rest: God rested on the seventh day, and He gave the gift of rest to man who is created in His image. The command to set aside time to rest and remember who we are in Him is a gift to us. In fact, Jesus tells us that the Sabbath was *made* for us (Mark 2:27).

Time alone at Jesus' feet: Nothing can replace time alone, sitting quietly, listening to the heartbeat of our Shepherd and pouring out our heart to Him. Jesus' friend Mary did this, and He said, "Mary has chosen the good part which shall not be taken away from her" (Luke 10:42).

These are indispensable practices for any of the Shepherd's sheep that long to be refreshed by His streams. It is necessary for us to sit at His feet each day, breathing in His Word, hearing His voice and pouring out our hearts to Him. We are called to worship Him with our whole being every moment of our lives. We must have fellowship with other believers as an integral part of our existence.

But there are many different ways to incorporate these spiritual disciplines into our lives: going for a walk with our Shepherd; singing songs to Him; praying over coffee with a friend. The list is endless. (See Appendix A for a few ideas.)

The Means Of Refreshment Vary From Person To Person, Season To Season

There is no all-encompassing formula for seeking spiritual refreshment. Our creative God invites us to seek Him in creative ways. How you drink from His streams will look different from how I drink. How you receive refreshment today may look different from how you receive it tomorrow.

Each of us is created as a unique, very-loved child of our Father. He knows how we are formed, because He is the one who has skillfully made each of us into a creation uniquely crafted to reflect Him (Psalm 139:13-15). Some of us are Type A; others of us are Type B. Some of us are reflective and introspective by nature; others of us are gregarious and energized by social situations. Some of us are straight-ahead analytical thinkers; others of us are free-flowing and creative. How we each listen to and receive from the Lord is filtered through the way He has made us.

Our Father not only knows how we are made, He also knows each day and each season of our lives before it happens (Psalm 139:16). In each day and in each season, He may show us new and fresh ways to quench our spiritual thirst. We must continually ask Him to show us how.

Author Charles Ringma writes, "In our busy serving we often attempt to live off the memory of God's presence and grace, and not out of the present reality of God's nurture and care."[10] I don't want to live off memories, content to stay in the same place, letting His nourishment become old and stale. I want to live a life of fresh relationship with my Father, delighting in the creative ways He chooses to constantly replenish my heart.

Ears To Hear

Before our worship team goes out to lead our congregation in worship each Sunday morning, we gather in the music room to pray. Across one wall of the room is stenciled this prayer from the hymn

"Come Thou Fount"[11]: *Tune my heart to sing Thy grace.* These words were placed there to remind us that it is of far greater value to have hearts tuned to God's heart than voices and instruments tuned to one another. Andy Park states it well in his book *To Know You More*: "Becoming a worship leader involves far more than developing a set of skills—it's all about developing a life in God."[12]

Thomas à Kempis, the medieval author credited with writing the classic devotional, *The Imitation of Christ*, inspires me with these hopeful words: "Blessed are the ears that catch the accents of divine whispering."[13] Can we have ears like this? Even above the deafening roar of a flood of spiritual responsibilities, ministry demands, and the nature of our calling itself? It won't be easy, but we will find that it is worth it. Once we have sat by His still waters and rested awhile, we will find out for ourselves that what the Psalmist says is true: The words our Shepherd speaks *do* restore our souls; they *do* rejoice our hearts (Psalm 19:7, 8). They *do* bring refreshment.

A Conversation With My Shepherd

My life

> Of the six means of refreshment listed in this day's lesson, which one do I resonate with the most? Which one is most difficult for me?

> How can I tune my heart to sing Your praise today?

Your Word

What do I learn about You from Luke 11:9-13, and how can this encourage me when I find myself in a spiritually dry place?

What do the following Scriptures say about seeking You through:

Prayer (1 Thessalonians 5:17)

Your Word (Deuteronomy 32:47)

Fellowship (Hebrews 10:24-25)

Worship (2 Chronicles 16:9)

Sabbath rest (Mark 2:23-27)

Time alone with You (Luke 10:42)

Your Word (continued)

How can Psalm 139:13-15 explain why Your means of spiritual refreshment may vary from person to person and season to season?

What do You promise me as Your child, no matter what season I am in (Jeremiah 31:25)?

Your thought for me

What is one thing You want me to remember from today's lesson?

My heart before You

(Talk to your Shepherd about all or part of the following.) Here's what I need to confess to You; how I want to praise You; what I hope to do with what You've shown me; what I need You to help me with:

A PRAYER TO PRAY

Generous and Wise Shepherd, how I long to live by Your streams, drinking deeply and soaking in the sweetness. But for reasons I can't always know, You allow me to wander away at times. You let me become parched. You build in me a strong thirst that drives me to You as the only source of my refreshment. Thank You.

*In You alone is fulfillment, joy, repose. Yet sometimes I forget. Sometimes I'm not sure how to locate Your waters. How grateful I am that You did not say, "**Find** Me." You said, "**Seek** Me and I will be found by you." This promise is the one word I need to hear; the one encouragement that will keep me running after You, eyes fixed.*

*As I go about each day (**this** day!), help me to seek You in all of it. Keep my heart open, holding out my cup so You can fill it. If anything threatens to knock the cup from my hand, let me tighten my grip and determine all the more to keep coming to You. As I come, I am trusting that Your Holy Spirit will breathe into my soul the fresh breezes that will enliven me to keep coming back again and again.*

CHAPTER 3

OUR SHEPHERD SPEAKS PERSEVERANCE

DAY 1: WHEN IT'S HARD TO WORSHIP

We went to bed praying hard one Saturday night, my husband and I, exhausted and spent. I was wearily asking God for the elusive heart of worship I longed for amidst the onslaught of ministry details with Easter just around the corner. Greg was helplessly begging for strength to preach the next morning, body and spirit succumbing to the worst flu he'd had in years.

Heads sinking down like deadweight onto our pillows, we drifted into fitful sleep. When the phone rang, it sent our hearts racing and our thoughts scrambling to reorder themselves.

My brother's voice: "Mom has had a stroke and she's being life-flighted to the hospital."

"Wait... *Our* mom...? Aren't she and Dad spending the night in Jordan Valley so he can fill that pulpit tomorrow? Wait. What are you saying?"

I hung up, stunned. My kind, so-sick guy held me in his arms and croaked out a prayer for all of us. I stumbled to the closet, threw on a pair of jeans and a wrinkled T-shirt, grabbed the keys, and drove to the hospital, trying to assimilate this alarming news.

My mom. At seventy-one years of age, she was effervescent and energetic, constantly engaged in creative and artistic endeavors. She served each person in her life out of a spirit overflowing with generosity and graciousness. She possessed an inquisitive mind and a teachable heart. As the center of our family, her presence infused our gatherings with love and laughter. Best of all, she was a worshiper of Jesus.

Not that any of these thoughts manifested themselves in the form of words. My mind was all impression and anguish, questions and doubts piling themselves up, one upon the other.

My brother and his wife greeted me at the hospital, and we fell into each others' arms, tears mingling. Then we waited—for the rural volunteer ambulance driver to find my mom and dad; for the dispatcher to inform them that the helicopter could not land because of fog; for the ambulance to transport them the forty-five minutes to the waiting helicopter; for them to fly the remaining forty miles to the hospital where we anxiously paced and prayed.

Hours later, we heard the whir of helicopter blades, then muffled voices as Mom was wheeled into the emergency room. Soon, Dad's stricken face greeted us, and my heart broke to see it.

The night lengthened into a marathon of tests and procedures, medical terminology and paperwork. Hospital personnel patiently explained medical jargon as they looked into our blank and dazed faces. We experienced moments of hopefulness and endured a seeming eternity of grief. We knew, intuitively, that life would be different for us now.

The next morning I remained at the hospital while life went on at church. God strengthened Greg to whisper out his sermon, and our dear worship team friends led the congregation in worship, all the while their own hearts breaking on our behalf.

I spent much of the next ten days and nights at the hospital, the full impact of my mom's condition crushing down, grief stone upon grief stone, until I felt I could bear it no more. CT scans of her brain showed the damage to be so extensive that, if she survived at all, she would never be the same. She would probably not be able to speak, walk, or perhaps even understand.

In the weeks that followed, through all the chord charts and instrumental arrangements and phone calls and emails and meetings and rehearsals and planning that accompanied the preparations for Easter, my one prayer, the only prayer I could think to pray was, "Lord, have mercy on us. Whatever that means—and only You know—have mercy on us."

Each Thursday night as I led the worship team rehearsal and each Sunday morning as I sat at the piano, I had to ask myself in a way I had never been forced to before: "How do I persevere in worshiping through raw pain?"

Portrait Of A Worship Undershepherd

All believers experience seasons of pain, grief, temptation, failure, and discouragement. We worship leaders are not uniquely spiritual or particularly brave, yet for some reason God has given us the serious responsibility of encouraging our brothers and sisters to persevere in worship through these seasons. Even when our own season of trial causes us to cry out, "But I can't do this today. I can't!"

Psalm 34 paints a compelling portrait of what it looks like to be both a lifelong worshiper and a worship undershepherd in the most difficult of circumstances. As David writes this psalm, he is hiding in a cave. He has recently fled for his life from King Saul to take refuge under Achish, king of Gath, only to realize that his life is in jeopardy from Achish as well. Coming up with a creative if not humiliating plan, he has decided to act like a madman, writing on doors and letting spit run down his beard so that Achish will not feel threatened by him. The plan has worked, and now he has taken up refuge in a cave where a group of outcasts and malcontents has gathered, looking to him as their captain.

David has just come through a frightening and undignified experience. Still in grave danger, he takes the time and has the heart to write a psalm of worship. A psalm to encourage the strugglers and stragglers around him to worship as well.

Today's devotional will give you an opportunity to look closely at Psalm 34 and discover on your own how it reveals the heart of both a worshiper and a worship undershepherd. On Day 2, we will look at this psalm together to view David as a lifelong worshiper. On Day 3, we will delve more deeply into this psalm to see how David moves beyond worship to leading others in worship.

A Conversation With My Shepherd

My life

> Have You ever asked me to persevere in worshiping You through raw pain? If so, was I able to do so?

> Has there ever been a time when circumstances in my life have made it difficult for me to lead Your people in worship?

Your Word

> What phrases does David use in Psalm 34 to show that he is a lifelong worshiper of You?

> What phrases in Psalm 34 show that David has a heart to encourage *others* to worship You?

Your thought for me

What is one thing You want me to remember from today's lesson?

My heart before You

(Talk to your Shepherd about all or part of the following.) Here's what I need to confess to You; how I want to praise You; what I hope to do with what You've shown me; what I need You to help me with:

DAY 2: PERSEVERING AS A WORSHIPER

We live in a fallen world. I know it; you know it. Yet, when hardships and tragedies crash down upon us violently and unexpectedly, the threads that hold trust firm in our hearts can be stretched to their limits. As I drove back and forth from home to church to hospital in the days following my mom's stroke, eyes blinded with tears, worship melodies did not flow out of me in joyful profusion. Sometimes I did not feel capable of persevering as a worshiper at all. I was only aware of a desperate need to know that my Shepherd was with me in the car. My spirit numbed by sadness, I had few words to speak to Him. But I was hanging onto every word He might speak to me.

What Our Shepherd Asks Of Us As Worshipers

Our Shepherd's Voice: "Worship Me at all times."

As David writes Psalm 34, it is evident he has been listening to his Shepherd even in his dire circumstances. He understands that, no matter how defeated his spirit may feel, he has been created to be a worshiper in all of life. The first words he utters are: "I will bless the Lord at all times; His praise shall continually be in my mouth." He not only worships quietly in his heart, which would be challenging enough; he also takes it a step further and summons the energy to speak praise out loud in front of others.

The first thing our Shepherd asks of us as worship leaders when we are in a difficult season is: "Keep worshiping Me." We are the sheep of His pasture, called out to be His own, way before we are ever called to be His undershepherds. As this psalm reminds us, we are created first and foremost to bless the Lord.

There is an aspect of worship that can be particularly troublesome for those of us who take joy in the way that lyrics can convey what's in our hearts: because we see them not as throwaway lines but as deeply-felt expressions of what's inside of us, we can feel almost hypocritical when they do not express our current heart condition.

For example, when "Satan buffets and trials come," I *want* to be able to sing with confidence that "it is well with my soul."[14] But I often catch myself praying smack in the middle of that boisterous chorus, "Is it *really* that way with me, Lord?"

In these moments of dilemma, I can wonder, "Is it honest for me to sing these lyrics today?" Yet, singing to the Lord can be the very vehicle He uses to show me my weakness so that He can strengthen my heart.

God's Word paints vivid full-color portraits of worshipers who, though they may have been quaking and flailing inside, fought through and worshiped anyway:

Habakkuk, trembling with fear at the horrific discipline his people were about to experience, proclaimed: "Yet I will exult in the Lord, I will rejoice in the God of my salvation" (Habakkuk 3:16, 18).

Jonah, confined in the putrefying belly of a fish, knowing his own rebellion had driven him there, still cried: "But You have brought up my life from the pit, O Lord my God" (Jonah 2:6).

Jesus Himself, His soul anguished by the knowledge that the following day He would suffer more painfully than any human ever had, sang a hymn with His disciples (Matthew 26:30).

When we sing the words,

> *Take my moments and my days*
> *Let them flow in ceaseless praise…*[15]

we must remember that not all those moments, and not all those days, will be easy. Just as Paul and Silas, chained in a pitch-dark prison cell, chose to sing songs of praise to Him (Acts 16:23-25) so, too, must we. It will take a won't-be-denied resolve to keep worshiping through some of them. Yet this is what our Shepherd calls His sheep to do.

A Conversation With My Shepherd

My life

> What types of situations might arise this week that could make it difficult for me to worship You?

> Is it difficult for me to worship You with songs that do not reflect where my heart is in the moment?

> Do I need Your help in saying with confidence today, "It is well with my soul"?

Your Word

> In what ways will You use the following Scriptures to encourage me to persevere in worship through difficult circumstances?

> Habakkuk 3:16-19

> Jonah 2:1-9

> Acts 16:22-26

Your Word (continued)

> Matthew 26:20-30

Your thought for me

> What is one thing You want me to remember from today's lesson?

My heart before You

> (Talk to your Shepherd about all or part of the following.) Here's what I need to confess to You; how I want to praise You; what I hope to do with what You've shown me; what I need You to help me with:

DAY 3: PERSEVERING AS A WORSHIP UNDERSHEPHERD

My mom and dad are well-known and loved by our church family. If you were to visit our church, chances are my dad would be one of the first people to greet you and make you feel welcome. Before my mom's stroke, she would have been purposefully engaged in conversations with people who needed encouragement or befriending. Her stroke deeply affected our entire congregation, and as a worship leader, I knew I worshiped through this difficult time not only for myself but for the benefit of my brothers and sisters as well.

As we continue to look at Psalm 34, it becomes clear that David is aware not only of his calling to be a worshiper but also of his calling to be a worship leader. His relationship with his Shepherd is not being lived out in some isolated pasture; his conversations with his Shepherd do not revolve only around himself. His Shepherd has given him some pointed directives, and David has been listening.

What Our Shepherd Asks Of Us As Undershepherds

__Our Shepherd's Voice:__ "Come alongside My sheep."

As one under whose leadership the Lord has placed many hurting people, David knows he is being called to come alongside them with empathy. He is being asked to speak strong truth with a gentle heart so that their faith will not falter. "The eyes of the Lord are toward the righteous," he reassures them, "and His ears are open to their cry." He then reminds them of a God who is "near to the brokenhearted and saves those who are crushed in spirit." He coaxes them to "taste and see that the Lord is good," and he tells them a truth that probably seems almost too wonderful to believe: "They who seek the Lord shall not be in want of any good thing."

On any given Sunday, we worship leaders do not know the story of all of our brothers and sisters sitting in the pews. Some will have had a victorious week, living in fruitfulness and righteousness. Others will have given in to temptation and may be feeling the crippling effects of shame. Some will have received surprise joys; others will have endured unforeseen sorrows.

One week as I sat at the piano, ready to begin worshiping with my church family, my heart was overcome with the poignant dual emotions of grief and thankfulness as I remembered a visit I had had earlier that week.

On the aisle to my right sat Terry and Cecilia. The previous Monday, Greg and I had gone out to dinner with them. Terry, in the last stages of his 3 1/2-year ordeal with bone cancer, had begun our visit by asking *us*, "How is it with your soul?" From there, the conversation had journeyed to what life looked like from their point of view. As we had listened to their words and helped them wrestle with what God was asking of them, we had felt humbled and honored to come alongside them in this excruciating season.

If Jesus in the Garden asked His disciples to sit with Him and keep watch, we know that our brothers and sisters need no less from us. As we come before His people on Sunday mornings, they need to know that we are *with* them.

Though we can't personally dissolve their hurts and struggles, we can let them know that we walk with them. We can make it clear that, even though we stand up front, our hearts stand right next to them, singing with them and caring for them just as our Shepherd cares for us.

Our Shepherd's Voice: "Lead My sheep in worship."

As we read David's psalm, it is clear that he is not content to simply be a sympathetic presence to those who are struggling around him. He also wants to help them take courage and worship their God. In this role, he is no mere motivational speaker pumping up his listeners with inspirational one-liners and shoving them out into the fray. He hunches beside them in the trenches, urging them to come along with him on this counterintuitive journey of worship: "Oh magnify the Lord with me, and let us exalt His name together." His own soul boasts in the Lord in the worst of circumstances so that the humble around him "will hear it and rejoice." While he is fearing for his own life, he models true courage for those quaking by his side: "Come, you children, listen to me; I will teach you the fear of the Lord."

In our weaker moments, we may not feel any better qualified to lead worship than our fellow sheep are—and in truth we may not be. But we are the ones our Shepherd has asked to do it. If our congregations see that we genuinely desire to worship our Savior in all circumstances, and if they know that we are with them as they strive to do the same, then they will more readily trust us to lead them.

In one of the most dramatic displays of courageous leadership imaginable—think Shakespeare's Henry V or Tolkien's King Theoden, except this is no rewriting of history and it is no fiction tale—Scripture tells of another man who led God's people to worship in an extreme moment of paralyzing fear (2 Chronicles 20). Brutal enemy hordes had amassed against Judah, and the enemy was bearing down hard. The people were terrified. The king was terrified. But King Jehoshaphat knew he had a choice to make. He could either trust in his own wisdom and lead the charge in a futile battle, or he could admit his fear and turn to the only One who could save them. He chose well.

Imagine fears being quelled when the people heard their king pray, "O Lord, the God of our fathers, are You not God in the heavens? And are You not ruler over all the kingdoms of the nations? Power and might are in Your hands so that no one can stand against You."

Envision insecurities being simultaneously validated and relieved when their king turned to the Lord and humbly admitted, "Nor do we know what to do but our eyes are on You."

Picture courage and hope on faces as this directive took hold of their hearts: "Stand and see the salvation of the Lord on your behalf!"

Put yourself and your congregation in the scene when the king and all the people fell down before the Lord, worshiping. And then join them in the moment when they all sang and praised the Lord, thanking Him for His lovingkindness, even as the Lord Himself routed their enemies before them.

This event in the history of God's people could very well describe what is going on in our congregations, and what is going on inside of us, when we come together to worship on Sunday mornings. You and I may be quaking with fear. We may be reeling from setbacks and sadness. We may be exhausted from the effort of fighting off sin. We may be dealing with enemies who would try to defeat God's purposes in us. So may our brothers and sisters standing before us. Nevertheless, we are called to lead them in worship, and by God's grace, we will persevere.

Our Shepherd's Voice: "Be transparent as you lead My sheep."

In all of Psalm 34, David never pretends to be something he is not. He knows that for the sake of those around him he must allow them to see his struggle. He neither wears it on his sleeve nor masks it on his face; he simply tells them that he has had very real fear; that he has needed saving from many troubles; that he is a poor man who has had to cry out for help. Perhaps it was this very vulnerability that helped them to trust his leadership all the more.

However, if this was *all* they saw, they would not have sought him out to lead them. They also saw that here was a man who believed in a God who remained strong and good and wise in every situation. Here was a man, like them, who recognized his own limits but trusted in a God of infinite ability.

One Easter weekend, my friends Jon and Melissa had been preparing to join me in leading worship for our Good Friday service. A few hours before the service, Jon received news that his dad had been diagnosed with a very serious form of cancer, and the prognosis did not look encouraging. In spite of deep sorrow, they decided to lead as planned, postponing until the following day Jon's flight to visit his dad. I will never forget the picture of my two friends fervently and wholeheartedly worshiping with our little team that Good Friday evening.

I will also never forget the servant-hearted worship Melissa demonstrated that Easter morning when she (without Jon) helped lead the congregation in joyful singing. (I may have been the only one who knew that, minutes earlier, she had been dissolved in tears.)

Good Friday and Easter that year showed two very different pictures of how to lead worship through pain. One worship service was led with vulnerability and tears, the other with bravery and a joyful countenance. Sometimes we cry in front of our congregations; other times we set aside our tears. Sometimes we show up; other times we let someone else take over for us.

Do we share everything—all the emotions and struggles and details of our current situation? Probably not. Do we put on a smile and camouflage the emotions we are feeling inside? That's a tricky question, because sometimes this is what the sacrifice of praise as a worship leader requires. But there are other times when we can best minister to our church family by cluing them in on the fact that this morning, this season, our commitment to worship the Lord is taking a special degree of perseverance.

We need to be transparent for both our own sake and the sake of our congregations. There will be times when *we ourselves* need our congregations to minister to us. Sometimes I have shown up on a Sunday morning feeling like I've been tossed under and around a rogue wave all week, salt up my nose, trying desperately to find the solid bottom. I arrive at church dizzy, waterlogged and wrung out, barely able to stand upright. On mornings like this, I may ask my worship team to pray for me. I may choose to give a forthright answer when someone in the hallway asks how I am doing. It may even be helpful for me to share with the congregation that this has been a hard week.

We also need to be transparent with our brothers and sisters for *their* sakes, because they need to know that they are not the only ones who struggle to persevere in worship through hard times. We do our fellow Christians a disservice when we find ourselves in the fray of battle and refuse to acknowledge it, acting as if every word of praise flows effortlessly out of a carefree heart. How much better to admit our struggle, confessing our utter dependence on the Lord for every breath of praise we offer and inviting our brothers and sisters to join with us in the brave pursuit of steadfast worship.

A Conversation With My Shepherd

My life

Will You remind me of difficult situations some of the sheep in my congregation are facing right now?

Is there a brother or sister You want me to encourage this week? How?

What are You leading me to do to show Your sheep that we are together in struggles and the pursuit of steadfast worship?

Your Word

In the response of King Jehoshaphat to a difficult situation (2 Chronicles 20), what courage can You give me as I try to persevere as both a worshiper and a worship leader?

Verses 3-4

Verses 5-7

Your Word (continued)

  Verses 8–9

  Verses 10–11

  Verses 12–13

  Verse 18

  Verses 20–21

Your thought for me

What is one thing You want me to remember from today's lesson?

My heart before You

(Talk to your Shepherd about all or part of the following.) Here's what I need to confess to You; how I want to praise You; what I hope to do with what You've shown me; what I need You to help me with:

DAY 4: ENCUMBRANCES THAT MIGHT KEEP US FROM PERSEVERING IN WORSHIP (PART 1)

We know from Scripture that good and godly people suffer hardships that can threaten to keep them from worshiping wholeheartedly. Hebrews does not flinch from telling us of lions and fire, torture and chains, stonings and wanderings—trials that have afflicted God's people and could have robbed them of their intention to worship (Hebrews 11). Thankfully, Hebrews also enheartens us with the hope-bringing admonition to "lay aside every encumbrance" (Hebrews 12:1). This admonition brings hope because it acknowledges that there *will* be encumbrances, but, by God's grace, these encumbrances will not hobble us. Whether they come in the form of earthquakes that knock us off our feet or the much-more-common tremors that unsteady us a bit, by His strength we can persevere in bringing Him glory.

One morning recently, I read these words from Psalm 5:3: "In the morning I will order my prayer to You and eagerly watch." I meditated on this for a while as I sipped my coffee, then rose from my chair with a heart of anticipation. What wonderful things would the Lord show me in this day as I kept an eye out? I drove to the YMCA for my morning workout, heart expectant, and arrived back home energized and ready for a day of worship.

However, I had forgotten to put away my coffee cup. Buddy, our cute but incorrigible little Schnauzer, a coffee lover himself and ever alert for opportunities, had knocked my mostly-full cup of coffee all over the carpet. But not only the carpet—he had also splattered it across my journal, my Bible, and Bonhoeffer's *Life Together*. Furthermore, Buddy was now highly caffeinated.

The rest of the day descended into an unceasing barrage of events that were most certainly not what I had expected to see as I "eagerly watched." My stomach gave me trouble all morning. I was late for our weekly staff meeting. My husband and I got into a quarrel. Upon arriving home from work that evening, Buddy happily greeted me at the car, never a good thing. His cheerful disposition is often a cover-up to distract me from some obvious truth, this time the truth that he had enjoyed a jaunty afternoon excursion through the neighborhood. After giving him an ineffective scolding, I started in on dinner, distracted. A short while later I simultaneously detected the disturbing scent of dinner burning in the oven and heard the unsettling sound of Buddy throwing up all over the kitchen floor.

And with this I wondered: How do I see God in this day?

[I long for the day when mishaps and messes, trials and tragedies, will cease to exist. But that day is not yet here. While I wait for it, a relentless parade of challenges marches through my life threatening to trample my heart of worship. With each challenge, I have a choice: will I worship, or will I not?]

For purposes of this discussion, I will divide encumbrances to our worship into three categories: personal hardship, sin, and opposition. Each category comes with both its own challenges and its own remedies as we seek to persevere in our calling as worshipers and as worship leaders.

Potential Encumbrance #1: Personal Hardship

The Worship Leader's Challenge: How do we persevere in worship when we experience personal hardship?

There are any number of burdens we may carry with us when we come before God's people to lead them in worship. Just today, I received a phone call informing me that my friend who will be leading worship this week injured his back on the golf course. He sits in the emergency room even now as I write.

Sometimes we are given opportunities to praise the Lord literally through our pain. Other times the opportunities are not physical, but they can be just as painful. Some of the burdens I've carried into worship are:

- Grief
- Family concerns
- Difficult relationships
- Financial hardship

- Frailty of spirit
- Unmet desires
- Worry
- Life's challenges, changes and setbacks
- Weariness
- Care for people in the congregation

When we show up on a Sunday morning, weighed down by such things, how do we keep them from making us so spirit-weary that we cannot play music or sing or even speak words that honor the Lord?

The Worship Leader's Choice: Choose songs of truth and listen to them

We worship leaders have been given the privilege of a calling that allows us to immerse ourselves in lyrics that abound with the truth. So, when personal hardship threatens our ability to persevere in worship, we can take advantage of this amazing resource by listening to these truths we sing about. As we do, we can ask our Shepherd to help us proclaim them with a secure heart.

Psalm 105 urges us to:
- Make known His deeds among the peoples
- Sing to Him, sing praises to Him
- Speak of all His wonders
- Glory in His holy name

If we feel too weak to do such a glorious thing, the words that follow can give us courage:
- Let the heart of those who seek the Lord be glad
- Seek the Lord and *His* strength

God's Word abounds with promises that give us strength and make our feet firm. (In Chapter 4, we will take a deeper look into the ways God gives us strength as worship leaders.) If we've chosen our songs carefully, these promises will be the truths that keep us going as we proclaim them along with our fellow believers.

One evening, a few months after my mom's stroke, I was visiting with her and showing her pictures of the family. The last photo was of her with her daughters and granddaughters, smiles on every face. I said,

"Mom, we girls will all get together soon and giggle and giggle and giggle!" A couple of minutes later, she became sad and started crying. In the midst of her tears, she said distinctly: "I don't remember... I don't remember." I reached for her hand, and we sat and wept together.

When I arrived at worship team rehearsal that Thursday night, I was ready to sing truth. I *needed* to sing truth. When I joined with the team in leading our congregation that Sunday, I was craving the encouragement that comes from brothers and sisters lifting their voices together to proclaim truth and draw near to their Strong Deliverer. That morning, the lyrics were a tool in my Shepherd's tender hand to soothe and repair my breaking heart.

Leading our brothers and sisters in worship when our hearts are burdened or breaking requires a certain brave tenacity. Thankfully, the lyrics we sing can instill courage when we have none. We lift up the name of a God who astounds us with His faithfulness. When we cannot see around the bend and there is no respite in sight, His songs sustain us along the way. When there are no quick-fix answers to our prayers, we will sing of something better. When opening our hands may mean He will place something in them that we think we do not want, we will sing with confidence of a generous Father who will not give us a stone when we ask for bread.

A Conversation With My Shepherd

My life

Is there any circumstance in my life right now that might be a potential encumbrance to my worship?

If so, how can I worship through it?

My life (continued)

What are some lyrics that have encouraged me as I've worshiped You through personal hardship?

Your Word

In Psalm 105:1–8, what encouragement can You give me when seasons of personal hardship make it difficult for me to persevere as a worshiper and as a worship leader?

When choosing songs to encourage Your sheep in hard times, what are some truths I should look for?

2 Corinthians 1:3–4

2 Peter 1:3

Philippians 4:6–7

Nehemiah 8:10

Your Word (continued)

Psalm 37:4

2 Corinthians 4:7–10

Philippians 4:19

Luke 18:1

John 16:33

Your thought for me

What is one thing You want me to remember from today's lesson?

My heart before You

(Talk to your Shepherd about all or part of the following.) Here's what I need to confess to You; how I want to praise You; what I hope to do with what You've shown me; what I need You to help me with:

DAY 5: ENCUMBRANCES THAT MIGHT KEEP US FROM PERSEVERING IN WORSHIP (PART 2)

Potential Encumbrance #2: Sin

The Worship Leader's Challenge: How do we persevere in worship when we struggle with sin?

We all sin. If we say we don't, we are deceiving ourselves, and the truth is not in us (as the Apostle John bluntly reminds us in 1 John 1:8). After the writer of Hebrews instructs us to lay aside every encumbrance, he adds, "and the sin which so easily besets us." Sin should not surprise us.

What should surprise us, however, is that we sinners are also called to be worshipers. Worshipers of the Holy God against whom every single one of our sins is ultimately aimed. Sinful as we are, He gives us a remarkable invitation: Come boldly before My throne in spite of your sin, and receive My grace and mercy. (Hebrews 4:14-16)

Sin may well be the most discouraging of all the encumbrances to worship, because it is an encumbrance of our own doing. While our minds may nod a hearty yes to the theology of grace, our hearts may still condemn us. We can become consumed with guilt over our sin— or so afraid of guilt's hurt that we hide it instead.

We worship leaders have an added challenge as we struggle to rest in God's grace: We, all frail and sin-ridden, are called to come before His people and direct *them* to the throne of grace. We might be tempted to approach this sacred trust from a place of defeat. After all, who could argue against the irrefutable fact that we are not worthy, and perhaps less worthy than many, to lead others in God-pleasing worship?

The Worship Leader's Choice: Admit our unworthiness to lead, and accept His grace

The irony is that coming to grips with our unworthiness is the very thing God uses to bring us to the right heart to lead His people. One of the best definitions of worship I've heard is that it is a response of the rescued to the Rescuer. The more we understand our constant need of being rescued from our sin and its hold on us, the more humbly and gratefully we will be able to come before our Shepherd, right beside His other sheep, and worship Him with the pure heart He provides.

As we lead our Shepherd's sheep in worship, we *should* be aware of our unworthiness. We *should* be bowed down by our sin. At the same time, the sweetest worship follows when He lifts us from this place of brokenness and sets us in a place of grateful awareness of the forgiveness and grace in which we stand.

Such grace-inspired worship is the reason why our enemy tries to keep our eyes away from our Savior and onto our sin. He wants us to be so distracted by our sin that we will find it impossible to worship in spirit and in truth. He wants us to feel disqualified as worshipers. But Scripture exposes this ploy. It reminds us that when we come to God through the cross, contrite and repentant, our worship is always acceptable to God. We can counter this attack of Satan with the truth that we have an Advocate with the Father, Jesus Christ the righteous one (1 John 2:1).

Satan also tries to deceive us into believing that our Shepherd cannot use imperfect undershepherds like us to lead His sheep in worship. But unless our sin is of the sort that scripturally requires us to step down from leadership,[16] we are to persevere through times of brokenness and lead our congregations from a humble, grace-aware heart.

None of us is perfect. David, Israel's worship leader, wasn't. John, Christ's beloved disciple, wasn't. Nor were any of the other kings or warriors or apostles or prophets. Yet, inexplicably, God uses fallible people to accomplish His work on this earth. The best thing we can do when we face our congregations, deeply aware of our sin, is to fix our eyes on the only perfect One, the One who perfects our faith (Hebrews 12:2). He is more than able to take broken servants and use them to build His church into a temple of worshipers for His glory.

Potential Encumbrance #3: Opposition

The Worship Leader's Challenge: How do we persevere in worship when we are being opposed by others?

Have you ever noticed that sometimes the big, cataclysmic things that happen to you are actually things that you can gear up for, straightening tall and grabbing your armor, forging ahead with fortitude? In the great grief over my mom's stroke, I knew from the first moment that this was a big one, something I needed resources for that were well beyond my own strength.

But sometimes it's the smaller things that can knock us off our game and sideline us. One of those things that can slam us, unsuspectingly, is opposition from our brothers and sisters whom we worship alongside.

There are people, even in my own congregation, who do not approve of the work that we in the worship ministry believe God is calling us to carry out. Sometimes I can look up from the piano at my brothers and sisters in the congregation, and there will be one or two of these faces that loom especially large, obscuring all the others from my view. It is at these moments that my thoughts can migrate to any number of places: distraction, defensiveness, denial, bitterness, disillusionment, insecurity. How do I corral these thoughts and prevent them from overtaking me when I am trying to worship and lead God's people in worship?

The Worship Leader's Choice: Believe that God can be trusted with His church

There is so much that could be said here about how to persevere as a worship leader when the direction you believe God has given the worship ministry is threatened. There is much to be said about how to keep a pure heart that is free from pride, defensiveness, insecurity, fear, and stubbornness. In later chapters we will talk at length about these things. But for now, there is one Scripture that addresses all of that:

For you have been called for this purpose, since Christ also suffered for you, leaving you an example for you to follow in His steps, who committed no sin, nor was any deceit found in His mouth; and while being reviled, He did not revile in return; while suffering, He uttered no threats, but kept entrusting Himself to Him who judges righteously.
(1 Peter 2:21-23)

Opposition comes in varying forms. Sometimes we find ourselves personally being reviled; other times, the opposition is less personal. Sometimes people are correct when they accuse us of impure motives; other times they are not. Sometimes opposition causes us great suffering; other times it does not. No matter the type of opposition we face, the phrase in this Scripture that speaks loudly to our resolve to worship is this: *"kept entrusting Himself to Him who judges righteously."*

Everything stems from this. Do we believe that God's plans for our church are greater than our own? Do we trust Him to accomplish what will glorify Him? Will we stand up in front of God's people and say, "The Lord is worthy of our worship" when we are struggling to have faith ourselves? If we trust the One who judges righteously, we *will* stand up before them with integrity and humility, resting in His plan for all of us.

Worship For A Lifetime

We did not see my mom's stroke coming. It caught us off guard and slammed us hard. Almost four years later, most of her words are still unintelligible, and she cannot walk or move her right side. She lives in a care facility where my dad keeps her company several hours every day. Each time I walk up the hall to visit her, passing nurses' charts and IV drips, inhaling the faint scent of ammonia, I grieve. But when I walk up to my mom and catch her eye, our faces break into smiles. Sometimes I'll tell her about my day, or we'll look at photos of her great-grandchildren. Other times I'll sing worship songs, after which she often smiles and says one of the few words I can understand: "Beautiful."

Only our Shepherd knows the difficulties we will face in our lifetime. What deeply sad things will remain with us? What dreams will have to be abandoned? What sicknesses and interruptions and criticisms and setbacks and failures will punctuate our days? What pruning will we endure as He forms us into His likeness? As the character Honest says in *The Pilgrim's Progress*:

> *It happens to us, as it happeneth to wayfaring men; sometimes our way is clean, sometimes foul; sometimes up-hill, sometimes down-hill; we are seldom at a certainty. The wind is not always at our backs, nor is everyone a friend that we meet with in the way. ... A good man must suffer trouble.* [17]

We do not know what trouble we will suffer; only our Shepherd knows these things. But it is enough to know that *He* knows. As the road unfolds before us, let us have hearts intent on worshiping Him along with His people. It is His job to direct our steps; it is ours simply to persevere in worship along the way.

> *Our days are number'd, let us spare*
> *Our anxious hearts a needless care—*
> *'Tis thine to number out our days,*
> *Ours to give them to thy praise* [18]

A Conversation With My Shepherd

My life

Will You search me and show me any sin that is hindering me from worshiping You with a pure heart?

Where have I seen Your unfathomable grace this week?

Will You remind me of a time when You accomplished something good in my life or ministry because of (or in spite of) opposition?

Your Word

When I have been struggling with sin, how can following the instructions of Hebrews 4:14-16 embolden me to worship You?

From 1 Peter 2:21-23, what can I learn from Your example about worshiping You through opposition?

Your thought for me

What is one thing You want me to remember from today's lesson?

My heart before You

(Talk to your Shepherd about all or part of the following.) Here's what I need to confess to You; how I want to praise You; what I hope to do with what You've shown me; what I need You to help me with:

A PRAYER TO PRAY

Sovereign and Sympathetic Shepherd, You reign in absolute perfection, and I long to pour out praise to You with every breath.

You've called me to be a lifelong worshiper, a sheep in Your pasture who never ceases to lift up Your worthy name. In seasons where joyful proclamations flow easily from my lips, and in seasons where profuse tears flow silent down my face.

You've also called me to be a tenacious and transparent undershepherd, coming alongside Your sheep with truth and empathy, helping them to worship through whatever seasons they find themselves in.

I understand full well that, in difficult seasons, I could neither worship You nor lead Your people in worship if You did not help me. Sometimes I don't understand why You've given me such a responsibility. It seems too much. It is at these times that I embrace the prayer of King Jehoshaphat when he and Your people faced what seemed certain defeat: "We don't know what to do, but our eyes are on You."

I trust You, Lord. Please help me to worship You with all my heart, mind, and strength even when I face hard times. Please give me the courage and the sensitivity to lead Your people during such times. By Your grace, and for Your glory, I will persevere.

CHAPTER 4

OUR SHEPHERD SPEAKS STRENGTH

DAY 1: WHEN WE ARE NOT STRONG ENOUGH

As a worship leader, there are times I don't know how I will find the strength to persevere in leading my Shepherd's sheep; the obstacles to worship seem insurmountable. I feel all at sea, bobbing along in an ocean of emotions and fears, moving quickly from joy to emptiness, faith to murkiness—lost and untethered—sometimes tossed about by storms, sometimes languishing in doldrums.

I *know* I am called to persevere in worship even in these unsettling waters. I *know* the choices He asks me to make in the face of such challenges. I *know* all these things we discussed in Chapter 3, yet I *still* can have trouble finding the inner resources I need to actually *do* them.

There is a particular weekend that stands out in my mind as one of those times when (a) I had no strength to lead worship, yet (b) I had no choice but to do so. It was our church women's retreat, and I was involved in leading worship for two of the sessions. I had also been asked to lead our Saturday evening time of Communion, the pinnacle of the retreat where we were asking the Holy Spirit to bring women's hearts to repentance, open their hearts to receive the gospel, and work whatever reconciliation and healing was needed.

The spiritual responsibility weighed heavily on me. But weighing even more heavily was what was going on behind the scenes in our church leadership. Greg and the elders were meeting that weekend to discuss issues that would ultimately decide the future of our church worship ministry. I had great respect for these godly leaders of our church, but some of them held a different philosophical view of worship than my husband and me.

There was a war within my spirit. I fought fiercely to hold the results of the meeting loosely and trust God to work His perfect result; but every few minutes, wild thoughts stampeded my emotions as I thought of the ramifications. My stomach was tied up in knots, my body was shaky, and try as I might, I could think of little else. Several times I cried out loud to the Lord, "I cannot do this. I am not strong enough!"

That weekend was simply one occasion among many that have proved to me that I can do nothing in my own strength. In my years as a worship leader, my weaknesses have appeared with appalling frequency; each time, my desperation has driven me to my Shepherd. I may not always run to Him first; but I run to Him at last.

Isaiah 40 describes the plight of desperate people who run to Him neither first nor last. Their futile attempts at self-help would be comical if they weren't so tragic. Isaiah speaks of nations whom God regards as mere drops from a bucket, specks of dust. Rulers of nations upon whom the Lord of creation simply lets out a whiff of breath and they wither, carried away like stubble. The people of these nations—whether out of pride or desperation or both—rely on their skilled artisans to provide them with their source of strength:

As for the idol, a craftsman casts it,
A goldsmith plates it with gold,
And a silversmith fashions chains of silver.
He who is too impoverished for such an offering
Selects a tree that does not rot;
He seeks out for himself a skillful craftsman
To prepare an idol that will not totter. (Isaiah 40:19-20)

Isaiah goes on to describe how the people try to reassure one another that these idols are strength enough:

> *Each one helps his neighbor*
> *And says to his brother, "Be strong!"*
> *So the craftsman encourages the smelter,*
> *And he who smooths metal with the hammer*
>   *encourages him who beats the anvil,*
> *Saying of the soldering, "It is good";* (Isaiah 41:6–7a)

We can hardly blame these nations for resorting to ridiculous measures to find their strength. They do not acknowledge the God who is over all, so His strength is not theirs to be had. However, for God's people it is very different:

> *But you, Israel, My servant,*
> *Jacob whom I have chosen,*
> *Descendant of Abraham My friend …*
> *Do not fear, for I am with you;*
> *Do not anxiously look about you, for I am your God.*
> *I will* **strengthen** *you, surely I will help you,*
> *Surely I will uphold you with My righteous right hand.*
> (Isaiah 41:8, 10, emphasis added)

God's children, just like any other people of the earth, often find themselves at the end of their strength. It is the wise child who recognizes the situation for what it is and listens to the One who says, "Look to Me. I will strengthen you."

Our Shepherd knows how weak we are. He doesn't ask us to make our way through disheartening waters only to leave us flailing on our own. Whether drowning, capsized, or lost at sea, His voice will direct us to the resources of strength we need to keep afloat, stay upright, and continue on course. During these times, when our strength is gone, we will discover that our Shepherd is not only our guide to still waters; He is our strength in troublesome seas.

A Conversation With My Shepherd

My life

Will You remind me of the ways You've strengthened me when unsettling waters have left me feeling too weak to worship or too weak to lead Your people in worship?

Do I sometimes run to other places for strength before I run to You?

How do I need You to strengthen me right now?

Your Word

What do the following verses say about Your strength, and about mine?

1 Samuel 30:6

1 Chronicles 29:12

2 Chronicles 14:11

Your Word (continued)

Psalm 73:26

1 Peter 4:11

How does Isaiah 40:19-20; 41:6-7 contrast with Isaiah 41:8-10 to show that Your strength is greater than any other form of strength I could rely on?

Your thought for me

What is one thing You want me to remember from today's lesson?

My heart before You

(Talk to your Shepherd about all or part of the following.) Here's what I need to confess to You; how I want to praise You; what I hope to do with what You've shown me; what I need You to help me with:

DAY 2: OUR LIFELINE (OUR SHEPHERD'S WORD)

As I waited to hear the outcome of the elders' meeting that weekend of our women's retreat, apprehensions washed over me, wave upon wave. Drowning in a sea of anxiety, I had no strength to do what my Shepherd was asking of me. I didn't even have the energy to fake it. The women needed me, but I had nothing to give them. As unruly worries pounded over my spirit, they left me floundering and sinking fast.

Have you, too, experienced this sort of helplessness at the most inopportune of moments? Have you found yourself wondering at the irony of God's timing? The longer I walk with my Shepherd, the more convinced I am that He times things this way to drive me to His Word. God's Word is our lifeline, and we can entrust our lives to it. This is no lifeline tossed randomly on the waters, at the mercy of the waves; this lifeline is always near us, never beyond our grasp:

> *"For this commandment which I command you today is not too difficult for you, nor is it out of reach. It is not in heaven, that you should say, 'Who will go up to heaven for us to get it for us and make us hear it, that we may observe it?' Nor is it beyond the sea, that you should say, 'Who will cross the sea for us to get it for us and make us hear it, that we may observe it?' But the word is very near you, in your mouth and in your heart, that you may observe it."* (Deuteronomy 30:11-14)

If we listen intently, our waterlogged ears will catch our Shepherd's voice as He holds out the lifeline:

Our Shepherd's Voice: "Grab the lifeline and hold tight."

I am constantly in awe of how the Lord speaks just the right word at just the right time—when I'm listening. And sometimes, in His mercy, even when I'm not.

There was the time an issue in our worship ministry held me in a vice grip of inner turmoil. After a night of tossing and turning, I stumbled into the living room and opened my Bible to that day's reading. Here is the lifeline I found:

The Lord is my light and my salvation;
Whom shall I fear?
The Lord is the defense of my life;
Whom shall I dread? (Psalm 27:1)

As I continued reading, I felt air coursing through my spirit, strengthening me. Not only because of the reassuring words on the page but also because of the attentiveness of my Shepherd to toss this lifeline to me right when I needed it.

Another time, I had gone to bed late after a heart-wrenching conversation with a good friend. It was the fourth week of a season of mixed emotions over an upcoming change that would affect both of us. Though I knew this change was necessary, I had wept that night. With each tear, a little bit of joy had seeped out. I woke, exhausted in spirit, and opened my Bible to this:

My tears have been my food day and night …
I used to go along with the throng and lead
    them in procession to the house of God,
With the voice of joy and thanksgiving. (Psalm 42:3a, 4b)

I was stunned by its timeliness. I could have written those words myself. I journaled, "*Really*, Lord?"

Yet another morning, I was overcome with a feeling of malaise. As I tried to discern what was going on in my spirit, I realized that my despondency stemmed not from one source but from many. Some of them were large in their own right, but most of them were just little annoyances that had congealed into a hefty lump pulling down my heart. On that morning, I opened my Bible to this long-familiar passage of truth:

Trust in the Lord with all your heart
And do not lean on your own understanding.
In all your ways acknowledge Him,
And He will make your paths straight. (Proverbs 3:5, 6)

I stopped to consider the phrase, "with all your heart." What did that mean? My heart, so stagnant and dead in the water, tied up and tangled by myriads of worries; was it even possible to free it from their grip and summon enough energy to trust?

In my depleted state, I sensed that here was a lifeline worth hanging onto. As I clung to it, I turned my thoughts to things I knew to be true of my Shepherd:

- You are faithful to every promise
- You will do what's best for Your children
- You complete the works You start
- You are perfectly wise
- You withhold no good thing from us
- You will provide our every need
- You love us, every one of us
- Nothing can thwart Your plan
- You keep us in perfect peace when we trust in You

With each truth, fresh breezes of hope soothed me.

We worship leaders can find ourselves serving in unfavorable waters, bereft of all strength and struggling to keep our head up: too distracted to think through a service flow; too weary to run another meeting; too shaky to lead our congregation in worship. If God's Word is not the lifeline that keeps us afloat in these times, what is? Wishful thinking? Platitudes? A season that happens to be going well? How blessed we are that we do not need to entrust our lives to such slippery and capricious wanna-be rescuers. Our lifeline is truth, hand-crafted by our Rescuer and held firmly in His grip. When our weary hands cling to the rope, He will haul us to safety.

When all around my soul gives way
He then is all my hope and stay [19]

A Conversation With My Shepherd

My life

Will You please bring to mind a Scripture You have used as a lifeline to give me strength when my strength was gone?

What are some truths about You I can cling to in this season of ministry?

Are my ears hearing You, or have they become waterlogged?

Your Word

How does Deuteronomy 30:11-14 reassure me that I can rely on Your Word at all times, even in times when my own strength is gone?

In Proverbs 3:5-6, how can each of the following phrases be a lifeline to me in times of weakness?

"Trust in the Lord with all your heart"

"Do not lean on your own understanding"

Your Word (continued)

"In all your ways acknowledge Him"

"He shall direct your paths"

Your thought for me

What is one thing You want me to remember from today's lesson?

My heart before You

(Talk to your Shepherd about all or part of the following.) Here's what I need to confess to You; how I want to praise You; what I hope to do with what You've shown me; what I need You to help me with:

DAY 3: OUR BALLAST (REMEMBERING OUR SHEPHERD'S FAITHFULNESS)

Greg's dad used to own a sailboat. A generous and trusting man, he would often let us borrow this prized possession.

One day my sister Denise and her husband Thom joined us on the boat. They, too, are trusting souls. The day was perfectly calm. The water had not a ripple in it, lying smooth as glass, sunlight dancing off its surface. We motored out of the harbor and into the open sea, warm, salty air caressing our faces. We switched off the motor, unfurled the sails, and bobbed along in the water. We saw no other boats.

Which should have clued us in.

The Coast Guard is kind enough to hoist flags in the harbor indicating weather conditions and safety warnings. There are different kinds of red flags that contain varying degrees of warnings. I do not know which red flag was flying that day because I am also trusting and did not feel the need to check for myself, but I'm pretty sure it was the one that meant, "Dangerous waters ahead, and unless you are very, very foolish you will not sail out there."

Our husbands saw the flag but chose to ignore it. (Please understand, I do not hold onto any bitterness; I am just stating the facts. Which are indelibly marked in my memory so that they can be sprinkled into future conversations as needed.)

Denise and I climbed out onto the bow and lay there, lulled into reverie by the sound of water lazily lapping against the boat. We hadn't been in that idyllic state for more than 30 minutes when we heard a whipping sound as a sudden wind caught the sails and the boom swung hard. The boat lurched violently, and we grabbed the side ropes in a desperate attempt to save ourselves from careening off the boat and into the waves. Hanging on with heroic resolve, we heard the guys yelling instructions back and forth to each other as they tried to control the erratic boom. Sails thrashing fiercely, hearts pounding wildly, we each prayed fervently that the boat would stay upright.

The wind never died back down that day. After what seemed an eternity, we made it safely back to harbor without being thrown into the ocean or destroying the boat. We came to appreciate three things that day: The extent of God's mercy, the significance of red flags, and the importance of ballast.

Our Shepherd's Voice: "Let the ballast right you."

Ballast is what gives a boat stability. It helps the boat have strength to right itself and stay true to its course in the roiling waves. On our particular sailboat, the ballast was the keel hanging under the hull of the boat.

As worshipers of our God, and as His worship undershepherds, we sometimes struggle to stay on an even keel. Life can send us reeling, and even the strongest resolve to worship can be thrown off-kilter by the battering waves.

In such situations, our kind Shepherd offers us a valuable word of advice: Rest in the ballast of His faithfulness, and let it keep us upright. He understands human nature, and He knows that we can have a hard time applying His past faithfulness to our current situation. This is why He invites us to stop and take the time to rehearse the ways He has proven His love to us over and over again. In doing so, we will remember that our changeless God will remain faithful until our last breath.

In old seagoing vessels, the stabilizing force was ballast stones placed in the bottom of the boat to add weight. As Christians, the ballast stones that stabilize us are made up of days, weeks, and years of God's faithfulness, each one adding substance to the ballast that will keep us upright in the most violent of seas.

When the people of Israel crossed the Jordan River at the end of their forty-year detour through the wilderness, it marked the beginning of a series of fiercely fought battles to claim the land the Lord had promised them. It would take audacious strength of heart; strength that would not crumble; strength fed by faith in a God who had already proved Himself mighty to save. In order to steady their hearts, the Lord directed their leader, Joshua, to make sure they would never forget His power and His presence with them:

and Joshua said to them, "Cross again to the ark of the Lord your God into the middle of the Jordan, and each of you take up a stone on his shoulder, according to the number of the tribes of the sons of Israel. Let this be a sign among you, so that when your children ask later, saying, 'What do these stones mean to you?' then you shall say to them, 'Because the waters of the Jordan were cut off before the ark of the covenant of the Lord; when it crossed the Jordan, the waters of the Jordan were cut off.' So these stones shall become a memorial to the sons of Israel forever." (Joshua 4:5-7)

The Lord knows we have short memories. He understands our need for reminders. For the people of Israel, there would for years to come be a pile of stones, standing silent and persuasive, assuring every faltering heart: "God has *been* faithful to us. God will *remain* faithful to us."

As I faced the challenge of serving the women at our retreat that weekend, bereft of my own strength and struggling not to panic about the results of the elders' meeting, I was in danger of capsizing; I needed to be set right again. This meant intentionally remembering the ways God had shown Himself faithful up to that point. If I neglected to do this, the memories of His mighty acts would be in danger of slipping quietly away into oblivion. Would I choose to gather these stones of remembrance and build them into a monument to my Shepherd's faithfulness, or would I leave them back in the Jordan River, submerged and forgotten?

There were many ways He had shown Himself to be faithful:

- He had preserved our church's unity through disagreements in the past
- He had given us humble worship team volunteers who were able to worship from a sincere heart even when they suspected potential controversies
- In all the times I had felt faint from fatigue, my Shepherd had seen to it that services were planned and teams prepared so that our church had an opportunity to worship

Each day, no matter what it brings, God gives us gifts that evidence His faithfulness. These gifts are meant to be remembered, not flung into the ocean and forgotten. Every moment, we are given the opportunity to remember, along with Isaiah:

> *O Lord, You are my God;*
> *I will exalt You, I will give thanks to Your name;*
> *For You have worked wonders,*
> *Plans formed long ago, with perfect faithfulness.* (Isaiah 25:1)

When we feel the boat being tossed one way and the other, these remembrances are the ballast that will bring it back upright so that we are not ditched over the side. As we lead our Shepherd's sheep in worship, this ballast will keep our vessel strong even in the most challenging of waters, allowing us to sail forward with trust and confidence.

A Conversation With My Shepherd

My life

Are there evidences in my life that I am relying on Your faithfulness to steady me in troublesome waters? If so, what are they?

How are You showing me Your faithfulness right now?

Will You help me make a list of "stones of remembrance" right now?

Your Word

How does Joshua 4:1-7 show me the importance of intentionally remembering the times You've been faithful to me?

How does Your past faithfulness described in Isaiah 25:1-5 set the stage for Your future faithfulness described in Isaiah 25:6-9?

Your thought for me

What is one thing You want me to remember from today's lesson?

My heart before You

(Talk to your Shepherd about all or part of the following.) Here's what I need to confess to You; how I want to praise You; what I hope to do with what You've shown me; what I need You to help me with:

DAY 4: OUR NORTH STAR (OUR SHEPHERD'S ETERNAL PERSPECTIVE)

Waiting for a connecting flight in the Portland airport one afternoon, I found myself pondering some of the hopes I carried in my heart for my grown children, wondering when and if these hopes would come to fruition. I opened the book I had brought with me.[20] The Scripture on the page astounded me with its timeliness:

The counsel of the Lord stands forever,
The plans of His heart from generation to generation. (Psalm 33:11)

The question that followed sobered me: "Does knowing that God might thwart your plans frustrate you or frighten you, or does it bring you comfort?" As I read this question, I realized that honesty compelled me to acknowledge that I am not always comforted by this thought. For example, during the weekend of our women's retreat when the elders were discussing the future of our worship ministry, I, quite honestly, was frightened. The possibility of being asked to relinquish my vision was sending me to a fearful place. I was not at all sure I had the strength to uncurl my tight-clenched fingers from my carefully protected ideas of what our worship ministry should look like.

Where does such reluctance come from? I can draw no other conclusion than that I don't fully rest in God's goodness and power and wisdom. If I really believe, without reservation, that He loves me and will accomplish what is best for me and for those I care about, then I will not have to think twice about entrusting myself and them into His perfectly capable hands.

As worshipers, the way we answer the above question will determine whether we worship our Shepherd with a stout heart or with an unstable one. As worship undershepherds, it will establish whether we lead the Shepherd's sheep with confidence or with constraint.

Our Shepherd's Voice: "Look up!"

The lifeline of God's Word has been thrown to us, and we are kept afloat by its truth. The ballast of His continual faithfulness has kept us strong and steady in the water. What remains now is for us to lift our eyes up, up, up to the heavens and follow the One who sees the whole wide world. He takes in the oceans and the land and the moon and the sun. He cuts through the mists and rides above the waves. He remains forever as a light in the darkness, for even the darkness is not dark to Him. He is our North Star, permanent and true, and He orders everything well. With our eyes riveted on this luminous beacon, we need never fear falling off the edge of the world.

Every passage of Scripture is a beam that sheds light on this ocean we travel. But certain passages just seem to cast a wider glow, allowing us a more expansive bird's-eye view of the journey. It's as if our North Star is saying to us, "Here's a snapshot of what I see from up here. Come, take a look."

Romans 8 is one of those passages. Christians throughout the ages have drawn strength from the elegant truths penned here; even when they have felt lost at sea, their courage melting and their sea legs quavering, these words have emboldened them with the knowledge that their Shepherd sees all and will guide them surely to safety.

Before proceeding further in this chapter, I encourage you to pause here and read straight through Romans 8. Out loud if possible.

As you absorbed the truths of Romans 8, did you notice the opening blanket statement of freedom in Christ, this beautiful remedy that nothing can undo? Did you absorb the assurance of life and peace for those who set their mind on the Spirit? Did you rejoice in the promise of heaven, our mortal bodies raised to life? Did you settle into the closeness of your Father, the one who invites you to come close and call Him "Abba"? Did you take comfort as you read of sufferings not worthy to be compared with the glory to come? Did you feel the groaning of all creation as it waits with us for this glorious hope? Did you find new resolve to pray as you read that the Spirit prays for you even when you don't know how? Did your faith strengthen when you read the familiar and abiding truth that God causes all things to work together for good for you? Did you fill with gratitude for His predestining you to be conformed to the image of His Son? Did you bow your head in humility to think that He did not spare His own Son for you and that all things are yours through Him? Did you take courage in hearing that no one can bring a charge against God's elect? Did your heart soar as the chapter crescendoed into a victorious declaration that nothing in heaven or on earth will ever separate you from the love of God?

I had just finished writing the second sentence of that last paragraph when my husband came home and asked if I would come with him to visit some friends of ours. Greg had married Justin and Kristi nine years earlier, and they had since adopted two little boys. Kristi was now in the last days of a long and difficult ordeal with cancer.

We drove to their house, unsure how to comfort these dear friends. Their faith was strong, but one of them had a body that was failing and the other a heart that was breaking. All we knew to do was to give hugs, pray with them, and sit for a while; to talk a little of the eternal perspective, the hope of heaven. Greg read out loud from Romans 8:

> *But in all these things we overwhelmingly conquer through Him who loved us. For I am convinced that neither death, nor life, nor angels, nor principalities, nor things present, nor things to come, nor powers, nor height, nor depth, nor any other created thing, will be able to separate us from the love of God, which is in Christ Jesus our Lord.*
> (Romans 8: 37-39)

As we sat in the quietness of the room, absorbing the tragedy and the truth, few words could be added. No song was sung. But there was worship, because each heart was silently looking upwards to our North Star, shining strong and sure in the darkness and beckoning us toward home.

This is the grand view that our Shepherd takes in: the whole world groans and eagerly awaits the day when all will be made right. Until then, He sees when His sheep are too weak to worship; He notices when His undershepherds quail at the impossible journey ahead.

He not only sees these things; He masterminds the entire voyage. He will bring it all to a glorious end, and a glorious new beginning. And He will strengthen melting hearts along the way.

When I think of how I might answer the question I considered that day in the Portland airport—"Does knowing that God might frustrate your plans bring you comfort?"—I know I won't always get the answer right. But, as a worshiper and as a worship leader, I believe that my all-knowing Shepherd will keep directing my eyes upward. Little by little I will see my way more clearly, and I will have the strength to journey on.

A Conversation With My Shepherd

My life

Does knowing that Your plans may be different than mine frighten me or reassure me?

Have my hands become clenched around things that are not from Your hands?

What are You wanting me to help others look up and see?

Your Word

How can Psalm 33:11 help me lift my eyes above my present situation and trust You?

In Romans 8, what are the forever-true things that should strengthen me to worship You at all times?

Your thought for me

What is one thing You want me to remember from today's lesson?

My heart before You

(Talk to your Shepherd about all or part of the following.) Here's what I need to confess to You; how I want to praise You; what I hope to do with what You've shown me; what I need You to help me with:

DAY 5: HIS STRENGTH, ALL WE NEED

I have known anguished moments of ministry when I believed I had no strength to carry on. The weekend of our women's retreat was one of those times. The Lord was faithful that weekend, as He always had been. He is faithful, even when we are not (2 Timothy 2:13).

He used this weak and vulnerable vessel to accomplish His purposes at the retreat. He also guided our church leaders to decide what was good and right for our church. I rejoiced in the results of that meeting. But even before I knew how it would turn out, I knew what my Shepherd was teaching me: I must find my strength in Him, and Him alone.

Our Shepherd's faithfulness to give strength in troublesome waters propels me as I write this book. My constant prayer has been that He would help me put on paper the truths He has spoken to my heart so that you, too, will be encouraged in your calling, and your church will be blessed as a result. I resonate with the prayer Paul prayed for his beloved brothers and sisters in Christ. I pray it for you:

For this reason I bow my knees before the Father … that He would grant you, according to the riches of His glory, to be **strengthened** *with power through His Spirit in the inner man, so that Christ may dwell in your hearts through faith.* (Ephesians 3:14–17a, emphasis added)

Worship ministry will require strength beyond our reserves, but in times of paralyzing weariness and debilitating weakness, our Shepherd will be all the strength we need. I pray that you and I will listen to His voice and learn from Him how to receive the strength He gives when our strength is gone. I pray that, in such times, we will reach out and feel the tug of the lifeline—His Word—pulling us surely through the waters. I pray that we will stand secure in the boat as it is steadied by the ballast of His faithful ways. I pray that we will feel our eyes drawn upward to the North Star, where the One who sees the grand view of our voyage will strengthen our hearts and lead us safely to a good end. Finally, I pray that each of us will be able to say with confidence:

He sent from on high, He took me;
He drew me out of many waters...
For who is God, but the Lord?
And who is a rock, except our God,
The God who girds me with strength
And makes my way blameless? (Psalm 18:16, 31–32)

A Conversation With My Shepherd

My life

Do I really believe Your Spirit will give me strength when I need it?

In what ways do my brothers and sisters need to be strengthened by Your Spirit this week?

Of the three forms of strength discussed in this chapter (Your Word, remembrances of Your faithfulness, and Your eternal perspective), which is the easiest for me to apply to my life? Which is the most difficult?

Your Word

In Ephesians 3:14–17, what are some of the results of being strengthened by Your power?

In Psalm 18, what are some of the ways Your strength is shown to those who rely on You?

Your thought for me

What is one thing You want me to remember from today's lesson?

My heart before You

(Talk to your Shepherd about all or part of the following.) Here's what I need to confess to You; how I want to praise You; what I hope to do with what You've shown me; what I need You to help me with:

A PRAYER TO PRAY

Mighty Shepherd, Strong to Save, You are my only strength.

When trials roll over me and suck the breath from my lungs so that I have little strength to bless Your name, You speak the Word of truth to my gasping heart and give me courage to lift my head in worship.

When I am staggering and reeling from raging seas that have tossed me on high waves and threatened to carry me into the abyss, You steady me with reminders that You have always been faithful so that my mouth fills with praise again.

When I have lost my way and falter in my faith, You raise my eyes to the heavens where the One who sees it all casts light on my voyage and pours hope into me so that I sing yet another new song.

Oh Lord, You have given me every resource of strength I need to worship You and lead Your people in worship for the long haul. It is an indescribable privilege, and I do not deserve it. Let me never forget that I cannot do it without You. And let me look to You, every day, to strengthen me so that I bring honor to Your name.

CHAPTER 5

OUR SHEPHERD SPEAKS HUMILITY

DAY 1: HUNTING FOR HUMILITY

Humility. Who can ever be qualified to speak about it? As I pick up this pen, I am painfully aware of the pride that resides deep in me. I stare at the blank page and see it filling up with a litany of self-incriminations before my pen moves:

Have you *ever* gone through an entire worship service without some thought for what others were thinking of your skill or your heart?

Have you *ever* left the stage without a care for how you or the team had been perceived?

The answers to these rhetorical questions prove to myself that I am not qualified to speak about humility. Even so, I am asked to exhibit it in my life. As are you.

The problem is, humility hides, and we must hunt for it. To complicate matters, sometimes we don't even want to find it. Furthermore, the enemy to humility—pride—can walk around *disguised* as humility so that we don't recognize we have a *need* to find it.

Who then is qualified to speak about humility? Only our Shepherd. He is qualified not only to speak about it but to strip us of pride's cloak and drape us with attire far more fitting for those He calls His own. On Days 2 and 3 we will take a close look at the humility of Jesus, but first let's consider some of the reasons it can be difficult for us to keep a humble heart.

Humility Can Be Elusive

Every one of the Shepherd's sheep has particular areas of weakness where pride raises its haughty head, obscuring (or even obliterating) all signs of humility. Worship ministry comes with its own particular set of vulnerabilities.

Threats to humility during the service

One moment we are standing up front, all prayed-up and honestly desiring to glorify the Lord alongside His people, eyes laser-focused on Jesus. We strike the first chord, sing a line, and look into the faces of our brothers and sisters with a heart to serve them. But then we notice that some of them seem sleepy; others are looking through their bulletin; a few seem reluctant to leave off their conversations. We wonder, "Are they with us? Are they going to allow God to lead them to a place of worship today?" We square our shoulders and rise with determination to the task. "Well then, we will persevere and show them what it looks like. We will persuade them to join us!"

We survey the room, adopting an expression of what we hope comes across as invitational, and belt out the lyrics: "*Come*, Christians [oh please!], join to sing!"[21] We glance at the faces before us and ask ourselves, "Can't they see that there is worship going on here?"

At this point, we enter a wilderness of no easy return. "Are they paying attention? Why are his arms folded? Why is her expression blank? Are they noticing the thoughtful way the lyrical themes are woven together? Did they catch the artful musical transition on that last song?"

Though we may be too spiritually sophisticated to insert the word "I" into our musings ("Can't they see that *I* am worshiping?"; "Are they appreciating that *I've* put a lot of thought into this service?"), it is there, looming large and ugly if we are honest enough to admit it.

Sometimes the Spirit will stop us short in the middle of such thoughts. Gratefully, we shoot up a quick prayer: ["Thank You for showing me I've gone off-track and for bringing me back to a heart of worship."] This freshly-humble heart may last until we miss the next entrance, and our thoughts are diverted once again. Our noble response to this misstep may be: "Please don't let my mistakes distract anyone from worshiping." But it's a short hop off the path to: "I just totally made a fool of myself up here." It can be hard to recover from *that* thought.

Threats to humility after the service

I am dismayed by how quickly pride can present itself in my life. Ironically, it often shows up in my spirit, unexpected and uninvited, after a deep and heartfelt time of worship.

Pride can be prompted by a variety of encounters. For example, it can trickle into my thoughts during a conversation in which nothing at all is mentioned about the worship set. Even the most innocuous comment can trip a switch in my brain that makes me wonder, "Did they notice anything our team did this morning?" Perhaps someone will tell me of a new song they heard at another church they visited, never once referring to the music we sang that morning. I *love* to hear of wonderful new worship songs. Why, then, does joy over another church's worship music become tinged with prideful thoughts of, "What about *our* worship service?"

Another way pride can intrude on my thoughts is when a well-meaning person compliments the team or me but their observation seems to miss the point. There is a man in our church family who will often say to me after a church service, "I just *love* watching your hands tackle those piano keys!" I believe his motive is kind, but my immediate inner response is, "I'm not performing a solo; besides that, I've worked really hard to perfect the art of blending well with the band." I feel invalidated as a musician and as a worship leader. My pride feels the blow.

There is another type of comment that can uncover the pride that lingers in my heart. This is the comment that masquerades as a compliment but holds a possible hidden agenda. It might be a comment like this: "Today was one of the best services we've ever had! Aren't those hymns wonderful?" Granted, such statements might simply be guileless expressions of pleasure over a meaningful time of worship; I must guard my heart from assuming otherwise. However, I do know that behind such words *can* lie a negative critique of my song choices. When I suspect this to be the motive, I can bristle inside.

Then there are the blatant criticisms. No mistaking these. No veiled complaint here: The drums were too loud; the bass wasn't loud enough. We didn't sing enough songs from the hymnal; we sang too many songs from the hymnal. The lyrics were trite; the lyrics were too hard to understand. The vocalists lacked passion; the vocalists were too expressive. We repeated choruses too many times; we didn't linger long enough on the lyrics.

Oh, how I would love for my heart to respond every single time with deep gratitude for the opportunity to learn from these criticisms and excel still more. Yet, pride often finds a way to worm itself into my spirit and bore holes into the humility Christ is so painstakingly building in me. It appears in many forms: defensiveness, hurt, deflation, rationalization, a false smile. Whatever form it takes, pride, by any other name, is still pride.

The final type of encounter that can threaten a humble spirit is the genuinely encouraging comment given by a brother or sister who understands how to give affirmation in a meaningful way. These encouragers will say things like:

"Thank you for the thought you put into the flow of the service."

"I love how the lyrics of that one song reminded us of God's greatness."

"That creative musical interlude just exploded with joy for our Savior."

"It's okay that you messed that entrance up because everyone makes mistakes and we know you're doing this for God's glory and not your own."

"You'll never know how much God used the worship time this morning to draw me close to Him just when I needed it."

Such comments are gifts from God's heart to ours, pure and simple, but any good gift can be distorted because we are human. For me, a well-spoken word of encouragement from a kind soul is *always* welcome; however, as I savor it, I can let it linger a little too long in my mouth. I can become enamored with it, attempting to suck the juice out of it way past the point where it has nourished me with its goodness. I can become fat, puffed up; ascribing credit to myself where only God deserves the credit. I can develop a craving for such comments, believing the lie that they are the real food that sustains me rather than the work of my Father.

Threats to humility all the other times

If only the departure point from humility into pride was limited to Sundays! But just around the bend is Monday morning. The long week from Monday through Saturday provides a wealth of opportunities for us to stray onto pride's paths: an email here, a phone conversation there; a drop-in visitor or a scheduled meeting; an overheard comment; a random thought that flits across our mind. One moment we are blithely journeying along, trusting and obeying and so happy to be serving Jesus and bringing Him the glory. The next moment our guard is down, our cackles are up, and the whole world has become about us again.

Such susceptibility to pride shouldn't surprise us. Romans 7:18 makes it clear that the Shepherd's sheep struggle with sins of all kinds: "For I know that nothing good dwells in me, that is, in my flesh; for the willing is present in me, but the doing of the good is not." God's Word spotlights pride in particular as a sin to which we can easily succumb: "Therefore let him who thinks he stands take heed that he does not fall" (1 Corinthians 10:12).

Humility can be elusive indeed.

A Conversation With My Shepherd

My life

Will You bring to mind some of the ways that pride can show up in my life during a worship service?

In what ways have I veered from humility to pride in conversations with Your sheep?

Have I been prideful at any time this past week?

Your Word

How do You remind me in Romans 7:15-24 that any Christ-like character I pursue, including humility, can be elusive?

How can Romans 7:25-8:4 encourage me that all is not lost as I try to have a humble heart like Yours?

What can You show me from 1 Corinthians 10:12 about the way I should approach the hunt for humility?

Your thought for me

What is one thing You want me to remember from today's lesson?

My heart before You

(Talk to your Shepherd about all or part of the following.) Here's what I need to confess to You; how I want to praise You; what I hope to do with what You've shown me; what I need You to help me with:

DAY 2: HUMILITY AS JESUS LIVED IT (PART 1)

The only person ever to live a perfect life of humility was our Savior. As we hunt for this elusive quality, we need an unobstructed view of Him. Philippians 2:5-8 pulls back the curtain between heaven and earth and opens up such a view:

> *Have this attitude in yourselves which was also in Christ Jesus, who, although He existed in the form of God, did not regard equality with God a thing to be grasped, but emptied Himself, taking the form of a bond-servant, and being made in the likeness of men. Being found in appearance as a man, He humbled Himself by becoming obedient to the point of death, even death on a cross.*

Most of us entered worship ministry because we love our Shepherd and because we love His sheep. We took up this call because our heart's desire is for Him to be glorified and for His people to respond to Him with worshipful hearts. We understand that He has given us gifts in music and the arts in order to accomplish these purposes. When we agreed to serve Him as worship leaders, we offered these gifts back to Him to use at His discretion.

Yet if we've been in this ministry any amount of time at all, we know that pride can seep in to even the best of our intentions. In our pursuit of humility, it is imperative that we listen well to what our Shepherd says to us. As we peer through the pulled-back curtain of Philippians 2 for a better view, we will see that His life speaks to us with pristine clarity about what true humility *is* and what it is *not*. In today's discussion, we will let our Shepherd's life speak to us about what humility is *not*. Tomorrow we will learn from His life what humility *is*.

What Humility Is *Not*

Our Shepherd's Voice: "Humility is *not* self-congratulation."

If any man in history had a right to congratulate himself, it was our Lord. Jesus was God from before time. Everything that exists, visible or invisible, able to be imagined or not, material or spiritual, exists because

He created it. If anything endures, it is because Christ holds it together. *All* of it works to His glory and His alone (Colossians 1:15-17).

Yet, the view Philippians 2 affords us reveals something remarkable. In an act the scope of which we will never come close to comprehending:

- He did not regard equality with God a thing to be grasped.
- He emptied Himself.

Jesus did not use His deity to draw applause to Himself. In all of His serving and sacrificing, He never said, "Do you have any idea how much I gave up to be here with you? Can you even begin to understand what a privilege I bestow on you by calling you My friends?"

I get the sense from Scripture that whenever Jesus told people what He was about, it was so that they would know and receive His love, not so that He would receive their kudos. We see this in His patient conversation with the troubled woman at the well (John 4:11-14). We see this in His gracious response to the remorseful Zaccheus (Luke 19:9-10). We see this in His reassurance of Martha before He raises her brother Lazarus from the dead (John 11:23-26). We see this in His statement that He came in order to seek and save the lost (Luke 19:10).

A few weeks ago as my friend and I were walking, we came upon a mother duck trying to corral her eight ducklings. We watched as four of them made it safely to her side. But the other four, in their scramble to keep up, did not notice the drainage grate that stood between them and their mother. One by one, each of the stragglers disappeared from our view as they fell between the iron bars of the grate.

For the next hour, my friend and I devoted ourselves to saving the little ducklings. Through creative use of a ladle, towel, and cardboard, we were able to draw three of them up to safety. However, the fourth duckling hid himself far up into the drainage tunnel, too fearful to make an appearance. Oblivious to how we must have looked to passers-by, we remained there on our stomachs, heads peering down into the grate, hair dangling in the mud, arms brushing against the dirty cement walls, waiting patiently for the duckling to come out so that we could save him. To our dismay, he never did.

Through this whole rescue mission, we never said, "Little duckling, do you have any idea how we are having to rearrange our schedule to spend this hour trying to save you? Do you have any clue how ridiculous we look? Do you feel profoundly thankful for the sacrifice we are making?" No, our only thought was to save him.

This is how it was when Jesus humbled Himself for us. Yes, He knew that worship would follow for any one of us who came to understand the immensity of God's love and the lengths He was willing to go in order to secure our relationship with Him. But He also knew that, first, we would need to see what love looked like. So, with the greatest display of humility imaginable, He willingly delayed the glory He was due in order to show us.

Our Shepherd's Voice: "Humility is *not* self-belittlement."

Jesus lacked nothing: no skill, no strength, no gift. Our Shepherd was God incarnate, possessing all the attributes that had been His from eternity. Yet, He willingly limited Himself in the use of them, shackling Himself with the constraints of humanity. Philippians 2 tells us:

- He took on the form of a bond-servant.
- He was made in the likeness of men.

Where He could have satisfied His very-human hunger by commanding rocks to become bread, He chose to remain hungry (Matthew 4:2-4). Where He could have called ten thousand angels to rescue Him from crucifixion, He chose the cross (Matthew 26:52-54). He was at peace with His limitations.

We, too, are limited, though not by our own choice. None of us possesses *every skill* or *every* strength (though maybe we would like to). Not one of us has the ability to execute to perfection even the gifts we *have* been given.

Coming to grips with these limitations can trouble us. We do not want to be found lacking in anything, whether in the eyes of others or God or ourselves. This is why, when we perceive that we fall short of some imagined ideal, we can be hard on ourselves, dismissing the gifts and strengths we *do* have. This belittling, in turn, will wreak havoc on our humility.

My husband and I were first drawn to the church we now serve by two things: the love the people had for each other and the love they had for the Lord. It was magnetic, irresistible. Greg felt honored to be considered to lead such a congregation; I felt honored to come alongside him.

However, I soon discovered an inherent danger in coming alongside people I respected so deeply: In trying to emulate their Christlikeness, I found myself forming a mental picture of the ideal Christian and trying to make myself fit into that picture. Ruth K. opened her home in selfless hospitality to everyone who came across her path. Ruth W. served tirelessly and made generous use of her resources. Judy effusively embraced all those around her. Henry led worship with a joy that was palpable. Donna spoke with grace and wisdom. I longed to carry each of these qualities in my person, blessing and bearing fruit in every way possible.

I became exhausted. Defeated. I found myself focusing on my shortcomings instead of rejoicing in my callings, my eyes on myself rather than on serving Jesus and His sheep.

To further hamper my goal of becoming like Christ, another equally humility-killing phenomenon was happening in me at the same time: Perhaps in an effort to console myself about the gifts and strengths I lacked, I became overly-introspective about the ones I *did* possess. This, at times, manifested itself in a form of condescension toward others who did not possess the same gifts and strengths I did, or did not possess them to the same degree (the self-congratulation mentioned above). At other times, however, it manifested itself in a subtler form of pride: I adopted a false humility where I was reticent to rejoice in what I had been given for fear of *looking* prideful.

These two flip sides of pride—belittling myself for the gifts I lacked and belittling the value of the gifts I did possess—resided concurrently in my heart. But rather than deal with either of them effectively, I vacillated between the two. I tried to make up for each by overcompensating in the opposite direction. I had no clue how to still the pendulum.

Then, one day I read these words of Paul:

For through the grace given to me I say to everyone among you not to think more highly of himself than he ought to think; but to think so as to have sound judgment, as God has allotted to each a measure of faith. ... Since we have gifts that differ according to the grace given to us, each of us is to exercise them accordingly. (Romans 12:3, 6a)

I found great freedom in these words, and great help. Nowhere in them is there grounds for belittling of any kind, no hint of berating ourselves for what we have *not* been given or minimizing the value of what we *have* been given.

When we understand this, we will not belittle ourselves for lacking certain gifts and abilities. Nor will we belittle the gifts and abilities we do possess, downplaying their importance in some ill-advised attempt at appearing humble.

Jesus had self-imposed limitations; we have limitations we would not have chosen. As we look to Jesus, He will show us how to live a life of humility in light of our limitations. As we keep our eyes on Him, we will see that He simply asks us to go about the Father's business, as He did, graciously accepting our limitations and offering Him our gifts with joy.

A Conversation With My Shepherd

My life

When I first became involved in worship ministry, were my motives based on humility or pride? Can You show me what they are based on now?

Will You show me if there is any aspect of worship ministry that I am taking the credit for, even if just in my own private thoughts?

Am I content with the gifts and strengths You've given me?

Your Word

In Philippians 2:5-8, what are some of the ways You exhibited the humble attitude I am to have?

In Philippians 2:3-4, what are some of the ways humility can be lived out in my own life?

Your Word (continued)

Colossians 1:15-20 paints a vivid portrait of who You are and why You are worthy of all praise. What are some of these things that will help me humbly worship You?

How can Romans 12:3-6 help me have a correct view of the gifts and strengths You've given me, and the gifts and strengths You have not?

Your thought for me

What is one thing You want me to remember from today's lesson?

My heart before You

(Talk to your Shepherd about all or part of the following.) Here's what I need to confess to You; how I want to praise You; what I hope to do with what You've shown me; what I need You to help me with:

DAY 3: HUMILITY AS JESUS LIVED IT (PART 2)

There is only one place where we can behold the sterling quality of humility in all its beauty, untainted and unhidden: in the heart of our Shepherd. Like a jewel gleaming in the light, humility is reflected in His life at every turn.

On Day 2 we looked at the person of Jesus to see what humility is *not*. Now, we'll continue to fix our eyes on Him and listen to His voice to discover what humility *is*.

What Humility *Is*

Our Shepherd's Voice: "Humility *is* a stalwart determination to honor God."

One facet of the shining jewel of humility we see in our Savior is His absolute determination to bring glory to His Father. Jesus said, "For I have come down from heaven, not to do My own will, but the will of Him who sent Me" (John 6:38). There is no more poignant picture of humility than Jesus kneeling with undaunted submission in the Garden of Gethsemane, agonizingly breathing out the words "Father, if You are willing, remove this cup from Me; yet not My will, but Yours be done" (Luke 22:42).

When we decide to live a life of worship and lead others to a life of worship, we must know that it will take a lifetime of relinquishing our own pride. It will demand some intense wrestling matches with our flesh. It will require a vigilance that confronts the slightest twinge of self-promoting with immediate and unflinching ferocity. This is no mere nice-to-have quality of a worshiper; it is the essence of what it means to be a worshiper. Self-promoting and worship cannot reside in the heart at the same time.

Four years after becoming worship director for our church, a decision was made about my salary that I perceived to be a lack of respect for my position. I may or may not have been accurate in my perception, and I do not believe it was the intent of the decision-makers to minimize the importance of my role; however, in the moment, it was a hard pill to swallow. The morning following the decision, the Holy Spirit impressed on me that this was a make-or-break moment. I could either dwell on the decision and allow discouragement to turn into bitterness, or I could subjugate my pride and move forward with openhanded humility.

Aware that this was a moment of testing, I posed a hypothetical question in my prayer journal: "If I received *no* praise and *no* monetary compensation, would I *still* serve You with joy?" And then I willed the following words out of my pen: "Lord, I will *not* be irritated. I will *not* feel used. I will *not* lose my passion for serving You and Your church! By Your grace I will serve all the *more* faithfully and joyfully."

Paul, too, asked such probing questions of himself: "For am I now seeking the favor of men, or of God? Or am I striving to please men?" His answer shows that here was a servant committed to doing whatever it took to bring honor to God rather than to himself: "If I were still trying to please men, I would not be a bond-servant of Christ" (Galatians 1:10).

It is good for us to ask our Shepherd whether we are committed to living out the humility He modeled for us. His prayer in the garden shows a heroic resolve to humbly submit to the Father's will. If we are to glorify God in our calling, such resolve will be required of us as well.

Our Shepherd's Voice: "Humility *is* a resting resignation to the will of God."

The second facet of humility we see in the life of Jesus is a peace-infused trust in the ways of the Father that kept Him at all times receptive, unhurried, deliberate, and fully present. An absence of striving after His own agenda. A willingness to endure the disapproval of others so that, in the long run, they would see the bigger picture of God's love for them.

We see such deep-seated setting aside of Himself from the outset of Jesus' ministry. He was launched into the public eye with an act of humility: As a prelude to the opus that would sing love to the world and reveal the heart of God, Jesus was led by the Spirit into a wild place far from the reaches of the public eye. It was here that, with humble and yielding trust, He endured forty days of solitary preparation, severe hunger pangs wracking His body, Satan relentlessly pummeling His spirit. When Satan seized on what he apparently believed was a weak moment, brazenly proposing that Jesus fall down and worship him in exchange for all the kingdoms of the world, Jesus' ready response was proof of a heart long settled on humility and unruffled by its ramifications:

"Go, Satan! For it is written, 'You shall worship the Lord your God, and serve Him only.'" (Matthew 4:10)

Even as Jesus neared the end of His life, He continued to walk about in restful resignation to the will of His Father. In those final days, His heart heaving with sorrow for what He would soon undertake, He received a frantic summons: His dear friend Lazarus was dying, and Lazarus's sisters Mary and Martha were beside themselves with grief and anxiety. As they sent word for Jesus to come quickly, He responded with what must have been to them an infuriatingly leisurely approach.

The apostle John tells us, "Now Jesus loved Martha and her sister and Lazarus. So when He heard that he was sick, He then stayed two days *longer* in the place where He was" (John 11:5, 6, emphasis added). He stayed longer *because* He loved them? Yes, because He knew the most loving thing to do for them would be to let them see the glory of God and believe in His Son. This is why, before He ever arrived at the tomb, He stopped to speak with Martha and reassure her: "I am the resurrection and the life; he who believes in Me will live even if he dies." Then He took extra time to be sure she understood: "Do you believe this?" (John 11:25-26). When Jesus did finally arrive at the tomb, He stopped first to pray out loud: "Father, I thank You that You have heard Me. I knew that You always hear Me; but because of the people standing around I said it, so that they may believe that You sent Me" (John 11:41-42).

The story of Jesus' life, characterized by these acts of resting resignation—the wilderness, the raising of Lazarus—is not the story of a man seeking His own good; it is not the tale of a man scurrying to complete a personal agenda. It is the witness of a calm and deliberate

Deliverer intent on glorifying the Father. It is the saga of a selfless Savior who, with a composed and gracious spirit, received whatever His Father required of Him in the moment so that others would come to know the God who loved them.

Our Shepherd's Voice: "Humility *is* a heart that shows mercy."

The third facet of humility we see in Jesus is the one that shines the most profoundly: *His merciful heart.* God in the flesh died for those who did not love Him (Romans 5:8). Can humility present itself any more poignantly than this?

> *"Died He for **me**, who caused His pain?*
> *For **me**, who Him to death pursued...?*
> *'Tis mercy all, immense and free,*
> *For O my God, it found out me!"* [22]

Hear mercy pouring out from our Savior's humble heart, generous and compassionate:

> *"Friend, your sins are forgiven you."* (Luke 5:20)

> *"Go home to your people and report to them what great things the Lord has done for you, and how He had mercy on you."* (Mark 5:19)

> *"I feel compassion for the people, because they have remained with Me now three days and have nothing to eat."* (Matthew 15:32)

> *"I do not condemn you, either. Go. From now on sin no more."* (John 8:11)

> *"Father, forgive them; for they do not know what they are doing."* (Luke 23:34)

If we are to exhibit the mercy of Jesus, we must first receive the mercy He's poured out on us, letting it overwhelm us and bring us to our knees. Wherever our Savior's mercy is received, all traces of entitlement are obliterated. In such mercy-receiving hearts, we find the humility Jesus commended in this story:

"But the tax collector, standing some distance away, was even unwilling to lift up his eyes to heaven, but was beating his breast, saying, 'God, be merciful to me, the sinner!' I tell you, this man went to his house justified rather than the other; for everyone who exalts himself will be humbled, but he who humbles himself will be exalted." (Luke 18:13–14)

Did this man rise from his prayer with pride, his nose looking down on anyone who was not in the same spiritual place as him? Jesus tells us he went home justified because of his humility. I am convinced that he rose from his prayer deeply grateful for the mercy he had received and eager to extend it to others.

A Conversation With My Shepherd

My life

Here are some of the ways it has been my joy to honor You with my life:

If I received no praise or reward of any kind, would I still serve You with joy?

Is there a person on my team or in my congregation that You want me to show mercy to?

Your Word

Jesus, how does Matthew 26:38-45 show Your stalwart determination to honor Your Father?

How does John 11:1-44 demonstrate Your resting resignation to the will of Your Father?

How does Romans 5:6-8 show me Your merciful heart?

Your thought for me

What is one thing You want me to remember from today's lesson?

My heart before You

(Talk to your Shepherd about all or part of the following.) Here's what I need to confess to You; how I want to praise You; what I hope to do with what You've shown me; what I need You to help me with:

DAY 4: FINDING HUMILITY

Whether we're leading worship, talking with people after services, or interacting with them throughout the week, this process of acquiring the humble heart of our Savior will always involve a learning curve, and sometimes a very steep one. We will not arrive there the first week we accept the call of worship leading; we will not arrive there fully until the moment we see Jesus face-to-face. But, if we let Jesus' life teach us, we will find that humility is growing little by little inside of us.

On Day 1 we looked at the places pride can invade the life of a worship leader. Today, let's visit these places again and see how humility can grow there.

Finding Humility During The Service

The thing we want most, if we are pursuing our ministry out of love for our Shepherd, is to help others see Him. Yet the most difficult thing to do is to lead in such a way that they *can* see Him. I like the insight Andy Crouch brings to this challenge. He says that leading worship is like being a pair of glasses—a lens so to speak—that our congregations look through. The lens itself is not the focus, but a good, clear lens helps them to focus on what they are trying to see.[23]

As we keep before us the goal of helping the Shepherd's sheep worship Him, a right understanding of our calling will allow us to lead without apology. He's asked us to do this thing, and we can accept His commission with joy and confidence.

At the same time, we know very well the struggle that can take place inside us as we strive for the right heart. Whether it's prideful self-awareness of how well we are coming across or prideful self-consciousness about how poorly we are performing, there can be a battle within ourselves as we fight to quell such thoughts.

There is no easy, quick-fix solution to this. But there is one thing our Shepherd says to us that, if we hear Him well, will help us keep a humble heart when we come before His sheep:

"The mouth speaks from that which fills the heart." (Luke 6:45b)

What are we filling our hearts with during the week? How much time are we spending at Jesus' feet? Are we including moments of worship where we simply sing to Him out of pure and simple adoration? Are we asking often for His Spirit to search us and show us hidden sins? What efforts are we putting into studying and memorizing and meditating on the Word? Chapter 2 discussed our need for constant spiritual refreshment, and this cannot be emphasized enough. If we are living our days in the presence of the Lord, hearts soft and ears open, then when we come before His people, our words and our songs will pour forth from a heart already humming with the sweet music of humility.

For example, perhaps our Shepherd has been speaking to us throughout the week from Romans 15:1-6 (bearing with one another's weaknesses as we glorify God with one voice). When we notice those in the congregation who seem resistant to entering into worship, rather than taking offense, we will be better able to bear with these precious sheep. We will remember that they are being taught by the Shepherd at their own pace, just as He has been teaching us all week.

If we have lived a life of devotion to the Lord throughout the week, we will bring with us on Sunday mornings the heart He requires of us. And people will see it.

It will show on our *countenance*. Not in some disingenuous way, earnestness applied carefully for appearance' sake. Rather, it will bubble up from the fountain of a heart overcome with astounded adoration for our Shepherd, and it will overflow with deep love for His precious sheep.

It will show in our *demeanor*. Our up-front actions will be neither a show we put on so that others will notice nor a guarded cover-up of our true feelings for the Lord we adore. We will simply be ourselves before Him and our brothers and sisters.

Finally, it will show in our *music*. A musician who understands that music is a gift given from the hand of a creative God to be used for His pleasure and for His glory will play with joyful passion and excellence, heart tuned to the Shepherd's direction.

Finding Humility After The Service

Proverbs 27:21 says, "The crucible is for silver and the furnace for gold, and each is tested by the praise accorded him." Perhaps we could also add that each is tested by the praise *not* accorded him.

At the end of our worship service, the worship team plays music as the congregation is dismissed. As we play, I often ask the Lord to lead me to the people He wants me to encourage after the service. I find that when I have the goal of serving others, I am much less susceptible to defensiveness, self-justification, judgmentalism, or any other of the countless things that threaten to erode a humble heart.

If our heart is primed with humility before we enter any conversation, many of our responses will automatically be ones that build up others and glorify the Lord. But, even with the right heart and even with a listening ear, we can still be caught off guard by unexpected comments. This is why it can be helpful to consider ahead of time what would be appropriate responses to certain types of conversations. Taking some of the examples mentioned on Day 1, here are some ideas of what might constitute a humble response for each:

When nothing at all is mentioned about the worship set: "How did the past week go for you? I really liked what the pastor said about... Did the sermon or anything else in the service encourage you today as you face the week ahead?"

When another church's worship ministry is praised: "Thanks for sharing that! It makes me so happy to hear how God is at work in another body of believers."

When a well-meaning person compliments the team or me but their observation seems to miss the point: "It means a lot to me that you took the time to tell me that. Thank you. You know, as I was playing today, one of the lyrics that really blessed me was... Isn't God just so good to...?"

When we perceive that a criticism or hidden agenda is masquerading as a compliment: Take it at face value and say, "Thank you for saying that about the service today."

When we receive blatant criticisms: "I appreciate that you care so much about the worship here to bring that up to me." Then, either "I will think about what you've said [and perhaps discuss it with our worship leadership team]" or, "This is something that I [and perhaps the worship leadership team] have given much thought to, and we believe the Lord is leading us in a different direction. But I will keep in mind what you've said."

When we receive a genuinely encouraging comment: "What you just said encouraged me more than you know. Thank you so much."

No matter what takes place in the conversation, our heart will be helped to stay humble if we filter each comment through the lens of what is true:

 Finally, brethren, whatever is true, whatever is honorable, whatever is right, whatever is pure, whatever is lovely, whatever is of good repute, if there is any excellence and if anything worthy of praise, dwell on these things. (Philippians 4:8)

Not everyone's comments will be true. But, in every conversation, this is always true: Our Shepherd is committed to perfecting us. If we approach each conversation as an opportunity to choose humility, He will use it to glorify Himself and make us all the more like Him.

Finding Humility All The Other Times

As I was thinking about what it means to be humble in all the other times outside of Sunday morning, I asked Greg what wisdom he could offer. His first response? "Don't talk to people during the week." He and I laughed as he spoke these words, because the best humor always contains an element of truth. If I could blissfully stay in my office and immerse myself in lovely worship music all day, practicing and praying and being washed in the presence of my Lord, the opportunities to demonstrate humility would be greatly diminished. But the truth is, we are called into community with others (see Chapter 10). This means there will be continuous opportunities to swallow our pride as we try to faithfully carry out our calling as undershepherds of Christ's beloved sheep.

As discussed on Day 1, the occasions for humility-building are numerous. The week can be very long between Sundays. We cannot blithely wake up on Monday morning still coasting on the wave of worship from the day before, assuming it will carry us through the rest of the week. Nor can we force our heart into humility.

But we do have a Shepherd who can gently bring it there. On Day 5 we will consider what it means to invite Him to build this coveted quality into our lives every day of the week.

A Conversation With My Shepherd

My life

What have You filled my heart with this week that I can take with me into the next worship service?

What is one way I can intentionally open my heart for You to fill it this week?

Have there been any recent conversations where You've given me an opportunity to choose humility? How did I do?

Your Word

What can I learn from Luke 6:45 about preparing my heart to lead Your sheep in worship each week?

As I interact with people after the worship service, what do You want me to keep in mind from Proverbs 27:21?

How can Philippians 4:8 help me filter difficult comments I receive through a lens of humility?

Your thought for me

What is one thing You want me to remember from today's lesson?

My heart before You

(Talk to your Shepherd about all or part of the following.) Here's what I need to confess to You; how I want to praise You; what I hope to do with what You've shown me; what I need You to help me with:

DAY 5: WELCOMING OUR SHEPHERD'S SEARCHLIGHT

Acquiring the elusive quality of humility is only possible as we ask our Shepherd to search us and show us our hurtful ways (Psalm 139:23, 24). It is only possible as we open ourselves up to the Spirit's filling (Ephesians 5:18). It is only possible as we invite His searchlight, opening our eyes wide and unblinking, taking in the blemishes and cracks that are sure signs that we are not yet fully freed from pride.

Being open to the Spirit's searchlight means we will keep our eyes open to His warning signs along the way. These signs will rescue us from pride and return us to humility, if we let them. Isaiah 30:15 speaks to this: "In repentance and rest you will be saved... but you were not willing." Welcoming the Spirit's searchlight means standing ready to make course corrections at a moment's notice, never letting it be said of us that we were not willing.

There are several places we can look for His warning signs. First, we can look for them in *our words*. I am disappointed sometimes by the things that come out of my mouth: little quips and jabs, quick responses motivated by self-preservation, sophisticatedly humble-sounding offhand boasts. If our words belie our pride, may we be quick to confess, willing to apologize, and glad to submit ourselves once again to the skillful work the Spirit wants to do in us.

The second place we can look for the Spirit's warning signs is in *our thoughts*. I love the rubric Darlene Zschech proposes we use as we examine ourselves:

We can tell when our own sense of humility is waning and our hearts are starting to be filled with prideful thoughts, and our questions change from "who me?" to "why not me?" [24]

We did not earn this ministry; God in His mercy called us to it. Our calling is a supreme gift from our gracious Shepherd's hand as He entrusts us with His beloved sheep for whom He died. Keeping this thought in front of us at all times will leave us no choice but to walk in gratitude-infused humility.

The third place we can look for the Spirit's warning signs is in *our behind-the-scenes actions.* Our away-from-view actions are strong indicators of the condition of our heart. Are we stopping on the sidewalk to listen to the complaints of a cranky neighbor? Are we singing with a thankful and joyful heart when we visit a church whose worship style doesn't resonate with us? Are we taking a few minutes to stop in the church hallway and pick up crumbs the children have left behind from their activities the night before?

Unflinching self-evaluation under the Spirit's searchlight can only come in an atmosphere of safety. If we fear that God will reject us or give up on us when we admit our prideful ways, we will be unable to see the truth about the pride that lies in us. But if we believe in a God who has perfect love for His children and only wants to come alongside them in their weakness, we will be able to receive His assessment with a fearless heart, secure in His love and confident in His intention to remake us.

I am often struck by the courage found in the prayers of saints of earlier generations who were willing to submit to any tool the Shepherd wished to use in order to build in them a humble heart. May God give me the courage to pray such prayers as this one:

O Fountain of All Good,
Destroy in me every lofty thought,
Break pride to pieces and scatter it to the winds,
Annihilate each clinging shred of self-righteousness, . . .
Break me then bind me up;
Thus will my heart be a prepared dwelling for my God [25]

Here is a child desperate for his Father to do whatever it takes to make his heart a fit place for Him to reside. Here is a sheep trusting enough to ask his Shepherd to wound him if this is what is needed to gain such a heart.

If God *were not* the "Fountain of All Good," could we ever have the courage to pray such a prayer for humility? Would we even want to?

Oh, but He *is* the Fountain of All Good, and He only desires our good. Our Shepherd possesses great skill, and He owns a great heart. As

He gently works in our hearts over time, we will find that humility no longer eludes our grasp—it pervades our being.

A Conversation With My Shepherd

My life

Am I afraid of Your searchlight, or do I welcome it?

Have You given me any warning signs about pride this week, either in my words or my thoughts or my behind-the-scenes actions?

Is there an area of my life where You need to "break pride to pieces and scatter it to the winds"?

Your Word

How can Psalm 139:1-18 help me feel safe enough with You to let Your searchlight show me hard things about myself (Psalm 139:23-24)?

Your thought for me

What is one thing You want me to remember from today's lesson?

My heart before You

(Talk to your Shepherd about all or part of the following.) Here's what I need to confess to You; how I want to praise You; what I hope to do with what You've shown me; what I need You to help me with:

A PRAYER TO PRAY

Humble Shepherd to whom belongs all the glory, You emptied Yourself for me. You humbled Yourself and died on a cross for me.

How can I ever begin to absorb such an audacious act of love?

You—holy and sovereign God, perfect and full of radiant light, complete and self-contained, existing before time and reigning forever—You gave Your life for me to call me Child. How can I not fall on my knees before You now and cry, "Worthy, Worthy, Worthy!"?

When I am tempted to think well of myself, forgetting that I would be nothing without You, would You please place Your hand gently under my chin and lift my head to see the risen Lamb slain for me? With this precious sight before me, would You overwhelm my heart with such love that my only choice is to worship You with all-consuming gratitude and praise?

You welcome me to Your side with nail-pierced hands on whom my name is engraved. How can I for one moment have any desire but to bring You glory? How can I entertain even a fleeting thought of my own self-worth?

Oh stay in my view, humble Shepherd. Please stay in my view until all pride is erased and humility pervades.

CHAPTER 6

OUR SHEPHERD SPEAKS REASSURANCE

DAY 1: UNEQUAL TO THE TASK

This morning I sit at a local coffee shop staring at a sheet of notebook paper already covered in scrawls, arrows, large X's and false starts. Page 1 of Reassurance. Ignoring the din of whirring machines and lively chatter, I try to bring order to the page. It occurs to me that today I feel especially qualified to write about the need for reassurance: I am rather shaky, remembering last night's worship team rehearsal, and I am not at all sure I am up for what will be required of me on Sunday morning.

A few months ago I segued out of my position as director of worship ministry at our church, and my son Daniel was hired in my place. Since then, one of our two drummers moved out of state to attend a Bible college. I felt the weight that my son must be carrying as he took over the helm of this ministry one drummer short. So I reassured him:

"Son, I've been there. I know how it feels to have to pray and wait for the Lord to fill a key position in the band. It's tough. I will be praying with you."

My son answered:

"Mom, I'm putting you on the schedule as a drummer."

As long as I can remember, I've been a drummer wanna-be. Last year I bought some inexpensive drums, set them up in our upstairs guest bedroom, took a handful of lessons, and began entertaining our neighbors. Sure, in my dreams I imagined it would be fun to get good enough to play on our worship team. One of these years. Not *this* year or anything. Yet here was an opportunity, unsolicited by me, to serve our teams and our congregation by playing drums.

As I linger in this coffee shop today, I replay last night's worship team rehearsal in my mind. It was my first time at drums. I had spent weeks practicing the songs at home, playing along with CD's and metronome clicks. I had penciled out my drum charts. I had met with Daniel to get his input about the drum patterns that he thought would work. I had practiced with the pianist. I had prayed, a lot.

Thankfully, I was surrounded by co-laborers who were good at showing me grace: Kelsey, soft-spoken and kind college student, on vocals; Jon and Melissa, husband and wife vocalists who liked to joke and put others at ease; their sweet high school daughter Alyssa, on piano; Rob on guitar, Ron on bass—brothers in their 30's, confident and helpful; Judy, my dear friend of 26 years, on percussion. And then there was Daniel, so sure of my ability, at the piano. As the team shot me smiles and gave me thumbs-up, we began rehearsal.

On the first song, I found myself impelled to add an extra measure before every single chorus, pounding out loud 16th-note fills as the vocalists tried to sing over me. On the second song, I nailed the drum pattern I had heard on the CD. I was feeling pretty good about it, actually, until I noticed I was following the vocalists' tempo and not the click. The train wreck that ensued sent the whole team into spasms of laughter. A couple of songs later, I tried a snare rhythm that made glaringly obvious my lack of rudimentary skills. On the following song, I heard myself playing crashes and rides that had no business making an appearance where they did.

By the time we took a break for prayer, my confidence was shot and my creativity nonexistent. Yet somewhere buried under all my mortification was the realization that this just might be an opportunity to learn humility. So I had a conversation with my Shepherd: "Lord, I don't know why You're asking me to do this right now. I feel fearful about Sunday, but please don't let my fear be about me losing face. If I embarrass myself, so be it. I just want Your people to worship You this Sunday. But if You don't mind, I'd rather *not* embarrass myself."

Humility must be our starting point when we feel inadequate. The reason the chapter on Humility is included before this chapter on Reassurance is because when we deal with insecurities as worship leaders, we must *first* settle that we are doing this for God's glory and not our own; that we are doing this for His people and not ourselves. If we are motivated primarily by preserving our own reputation, we will be too afraid to acknowledge our weaknesses and our potential for failure.

What It Means To Feel Inadequate

Greg asked me a few days ago what this chapter is about. I answered that it's about those inevitable times in ministry when we feel inadequate to carry out what God is asking us to do. He responded with another question: "When you speak of inadequacy, what do you mean? Not enough *what*?"

In those last three words, he expressed the core of what it means to feel inadequate: we feel that we do not have enough of something. It could be any number of things:

- Talent
- Time
- Energy
- Wisdom
- Experience
- Charisma
- Spirituality
- Creativity
- Intelligence
- Vision
- You fill in the blank: _____

How we fill in that last blank will vary from moment to moment, depending on an assortment of factors:

- How the last worship service went
- The most recent comment we heard (positive or negative)
- Our mood
- The season of life we are in
- How much time we've been spending with our Shepherd
- How practiced-up we are
- The demands of the week
- The last conference we attended

Some of us have a personality that is naturally self-confident. Others of us are riddled with insecurities. But unless we are pathologically self-assured or in complete denial, every one of us will go through seasons when we simply do not feel adequate for the thing that is before us.

These seasons place us in good company. We are familiar with Moses' hesitancy when God called him to lead His people into freedom: "What if they will not believe me or listen to what I say? ... I have never been eloquent ... for I am slow of speech and slow of tongue" (Exodus 4:1, 10). Gideon, upon being greeted by the angel of the Lord as a "valiant warrior," responded, "O Lord, how shall I deliver Israel? Behold, my family is the least in Manasseh, and I am the youngest in my father's house" (Judges 6:15). Jeremiah protested his call to be a prophet with the words, "Alas, Lord God! Behold, I do not know how to speak, because I am a youth" (Jeremiah 1:6). The apostle Paul freely admitted, "For I am the least of the apostles, and not fit to be called an apostle" (1 Corinthians 15:9).

It is common for God's people to feel unequal to the tasks He calls them to. Which is exactly where He wants us. On Day 4, we will find out why. But first, we will spend the next two days delving more deeply into the reasons worship leaders, in particular, can be susceptible to feeling inadequate.

A Conversation With My Shepherd

My life

What inadequacy are You asking me to give You today?

Will You show me in what types of circumstances I am most likely to feel inadequate?

Am I in a season of confidence or insecurity as I serve You in this ministry?

Your Word

Shepherd, what reassurance did You give for each of the following statements of inadequacy?

Moses' statement, "I am slow of speech and slow of tongue." Your reassurance in Exodus 4:11:

Gideon's statement, "My family is the least, and I am the youngest." Your reassurance in Judges 6:16:

Your Word (continued)

Jeremiah's statement, "I do not know how to speak, because I am a youth." Your reassurance in Jeremiah 1:7-8:

Paul's statement, "I am not fit to be called an apostle." Your reassurance in 1 Corinthians 15:10:

Your thought for me

What is one thing You want me to remember from today's lesson?

My heart before You

(Talk to your Shepherd about all or part of the following.) Here's what I need to confess to You; how I want to praise You; what I hope to do with what You've shown me; what I need You to help me with:

DAY 2: WHY WORSHIP UNDERSHEPHERDS CAN FEEL INADEQUATE (PART 1)

When I came home from my worship rehearsal drumming debacle, I was sobered by how deficient my drumming skills had proven to be. Was it just that I did not want to make a fool of myself? To be honest, I did have to wrestle with that motive. But there were considerations far deeper than preserving my self-respect. It was these considerations, ultimately, that most made me question my ability to carry out my calling.

In seeking to serve my Shepherd well, I have found that there are four things inherent in worship ministry that can cause me to doubt whether I am up for the task. Perhaps these have caused you to second-guess your capability as well. In today's discussion, we will look at the first two causes.

We Feel The Responsibility For The Shepherd's Sheep

Before each worship service at our church, our worship team gathers in the music room to pray for those who will be joining us in worship. We pray that their hearts will be ready to glorify the Lord. We pray that individuals who are hurting will be encouraged. We ask God to meet each person where they are. We ask that people will know they are loved by God, by each other, and by us. We ask that those who are far from God will be brought near.

As we walk into the sanctuary, we are met with the sights and sounds of children running up the aisles, youth animatedly socializing, lone individuals praying, elderly saints adjusting their hearing devices, ushers helping visitors find a seat, and people engaged in conversations all throughout the room. We begin the music, people hurry in from the foyer, conversations slowly (ever so slowly) grind to a halt, and we stand together to join in worship.

When I see all these people gathered, many thoughts run simultaneously through my mind and coalesce in my spirit, forming into a—what is it? A weight to carry? A treasure to guard? A sacred mission to accept? I see these sheep whom the Shepherd loves dearly, and I understand this is no trifling time-filler He is calling us to. He is calling this local body here in Boise, Idaho, to come together and pour out our praise with one voice so that He is exalted above every other thing. He is calling this team and this worship leader, unlikely choices though we are, to *lead* this local body into such worship. He is commissioning us to extend to His sheep this invitation:

Come, let us worship and bow down,
Let us kneel before the Lord our Maker.
For He is our God,
And we are the people of His pasture and the sheep of His hand.
(Psalm 95:6-7)

How can we possibly do it? These pews before us are filled with the joyful and the jaded, the flying and the floundering, the resigned and the resistant. These faces looking up at us reflect brokenness and bravado, anticipation and apathy. *We,* of all the people our Shepherd could have asked, are the ones given the charge of inviting them to join voice and heart to glorify our great God.

If this is not a grand and glorious mission, what is? Yet, we struggling servants up here on the platform know very well that we are not capable of grandeur and that our little ragtag team of musicians and vocalists is anything *but* glorious. We recognize that we are incapable of this magnificent endeavor; at the same time, we feel the weight of the responsibility.

If we have true undershepherd's hearts, we *will* feel the weight of leading the Shepherd's sheep into worship. The weight is as inescapable as it is unachievable. We will always care, but we know we will never be able to do it on our own.

What We Do Is So Public

The part of our ministry that our fellow sheep are most acquainted with is the all-church worship gathering. *We* know that the bulk of what we do is behind the scenes: planning, practicing, maintaining relationships, doing mundane administrative tasks, making decisions, attending meetings, praying. But what *they* see is us up front, inviting them to worship.

No one in the congregation, unless they have done it themselves, understands what it feels like to be up front leading worship. (Just as we wouldn't know what it feels like to be led by our worship teams if we never sat out with our congregation.)

One thing the congregation cannot fully understand is the gift it is to see them all before us worshiping and to hear the richness of their combined voices directed toward us. There is nothing like it, and sometimes the beauty of what I'm seeing and hearing catches me off-guard and takes my breath away.

What they also cannot know is how vulnerable it can feel to be so visible. By standing in front of the whole congregation, we are implicitly inviting everyone's opinion and input. As one of my husband's seminary professors used to say: "High visibility means high liability." If your church is like mine, it is filled with people who care very much about what happens during the worship service. At any given moment there will be someone who is taking issue with something we are doing. People have opinions; some have very strong ones. This is human nature, and it's the church family.

As much as we want to be able to receive all of these opinions with grace, if we hear enough of them we can begin to second-guess ourselves. We can chew on these opinions all week. When one opinion joins with a hundred other opinions, it can mess with our minds and erode our confidence. If our security is not rock-solidly anchored in the reassurance only our Shepherd can give, we can become easily shaken.

In my years as director of worship ministry, many opinions about our worship services have been expressed to me. Besides the few mentioned in Chapter 5, here are some others I've heard:

- "My idea of a perfect worship service is two hymns, a sermon, and out the door in 50 minutes."
- "Worship team members should not have tattoos."
- "You ask people to stand for too long."
- "The way we did that song does not sound as good as it does on the radio version."

Some viewpoints I have agreed with; others I have not. Some have included things I had previously considered; others have brought up ideas I had never thought of before. Some have seemed black-and-white to me, but many have entered gray areas where it has been difficult to discern what was right for our church. Time and again, I have been reminded that in accepting this position of responsibility I opened myself up to an array of opinions. I have needed to remember that, though the nature of my calling as worship leader invites evaluation by my fellow worshipers, ultimately my conscience is answerable to God who gave me this ministry:

> *Therefore, since we have this ministry, as we received mercy, we do not lose heart ... commending ourselves to every man's conscience **in the sight of God**. ... For we do not preach ourselves but Christ Jesus as Lord, and ourselves as your bond-servants **for Jesus' sake**.*
> (2 Corinthians 4:1, 2b, 5, emphasis added)

In my weaker moments, when I have forgotten this truth, I have often found myself losing all confidence and questioning all my decisions.

A Conversation With My Shepherd

My life

What are some things You want me to be praying for the sheep You've asked me to serve?

Shepherd, can You remind me why You've called me to this ministry?

My life (continued)

Have I been second-guessing myself because of someone's opinion of me? Is there any truth at all in their opinion, anything You want me to learn?

Your Word

What does Psalm 95:1-8 tell me about the importance of what You call me to as a worship leader?

Shepherd who alone determines what is successful and what is not, as I hear so many different opinions about this ministry, how can You reassure me from 2 Corinthians 4:1-2, 5?

Your thought for me

What is one thing You want me to remember from today's lesson?

My heart before You

(Talk to your Shepherd about all or part of the following.) Here's what I need to confess to You; how I want to praise You; what I hope to do with what You've shown me; what I need You to help me with:

DAY 3: WHY WORSHIP UNDERSHEPHERDS CAN FEEL INADEQUATE (PART 2)

Today we look at two more reasons why we as worship leaders can be uniquely vulnerable to feeling inadequate in our calling.

The Success Of What We Do Is Not Measurable

What do we hope will occur in people's lives during a worship service? Isn't it a moving of the heart, that indiscernible working of the Spirit that compels people to make Him their vision, moves them to cry, "Holy, Holy, Holy!" and convicts them to cast down their idols?

Who can tell if this is happening? God is the one who searches hearts (Psalm 139:23; 1 Chronicles 28:9). We can only look for signs, and even these can deceive us.

A few years ago, our worship team percussionist invited a friend to church. After the service, the friend commented, "The worship at your church seems dead."

"Dead"? Ouch.

This visitor's assessment stung. It stung because we as a worship ministry had been praying diligently that we and our congregation would worship with passion. We and our brothers and sisters in the pews loved the Lord deeply, but sometimes the way we expressed ourselves in worship did not outwardly convey the love our hearts held. We had been praying that we would be better able to express our heart for the Lord, and we felt we had been making strides toward that end.

As the person responsible for the worship ministry in our church, this one comment made me feel the need to go back to square one. I felt that way until a couple of Sundays later. On *that* Sunday, virtually every person I talked with after the service made effusive reference to the worship time that morning and how much it had meant to them.

It is a monumental task to build a worship service that resonates with old and young, traditional and pushing-the-edges, musical and non-musical, uninhibited and reserved. Not everyone will be pleased. People will put labels on the heart things that they perceive are happening. One service alone can receive a variety of evaluations, depending on the perspective of the one evaluating: "Spirit-led." "Dead." "Sincere." "A show."

What we must remember is that no one can truly assess what is going on in the heart of another person. No one can fully comprehend the things God is accomplishing in the congregation as a whole. We worship leaders can (and must) pray for discernment as we seek to encourage our church families to worship with pure hearts. It is good for us to ask our Shepherd to show us signs along the way that His sheep are growing under our watch. But these heart-things can be measured by no human; for those of us who long to know that we are on the right track, this can be unsettling.

We Live In A Competitive Culture

Like it or not.

- Jesus says, "The last shall be first, and the first last" (Matthew 20:16). Culture says, "If you don't watch out for yourself, you will get left in the dust."
- Jesus says, "For many are called, but few are chosen" (Matthew 22:14). Culture says, "The more people you have in your circle, the more credibility you have."
- Jesus says, "Beware of practicing your righteousness before men to be noticed by them" (Matthew 6:1). Culture says, "If you don't promote yourself, no one else will."
- Jesus says, "If you wish to be complete, go and sell your possessions and give to the poor" (Matthew 19:21). Culture says, "The greater your wealth, the greater your worth."

Whether our particular church is culturally cutting-edge, socially out-of-synch, or somewhere in-between, it is difficult to extricate ourselves from the snare of measuring our spiritual success by cultural standards. If we take seriously Jesus' words that we are sent into the world though we are not of the world (John 17:15-18) and Paul's example of becoming "all things to all men so that I may by all means save some" (1 Corinthians 9:22), we cannot simply ignore our culture and proceed blithely along, hoping it won't matter.

I love books. The paper kind that produce a satisfying rustle each time I turn over a new page. I delight in receiving handwritten letters, and I feel I have shown special care for someone when I write one myself. I find great satisfaction in face-to-face conversations and in hearing someone tell me out loud that I am their friend. But I also acknowledge that texts and emails and social media are valuable tools of communication integral to our society; I know that I would miss out on a whole lot of relational opportunities if I pretended they did not exist.

In the same way, I love many of the old hymns, but I also rejoice in the new music God provides as He raises up godly and gifted contemporary songwriters. I warm to cozy small churches where everyone knows everyone else, but I also celebrate the growth God brings and recognize that each church needs to determine which cultural adaptations are appropriate for its numbers and its demographic.

How do we accept (and even embrace) these realities without letting them define us? How do we escape the trap of trying to reassure ourselves that we are doing well by using society's standards as our measuring stick? How do we not equate "good worship" with:

- Contemporary sound?
- A room full of people?
- Top-notch musicality?
- A youthful spirit?
- Sophisticated technology?
- Creative computer graphics?
- The passion of the last worship conference we attended?

In Chapter 7 (Identity), we will consider how to hear from our Shepherd specifically who *we, our teams,* and *our churches* are called to be in His kingdom and in the world. But, no matter what He reveals to us about our specific identity, we worship leaders need to be aware of the role culture can play in our feelings of inadequacy.

I can only speak for myself and my church: we are somewhere in the middle culturally. We are far from cutting-edge, but we also appreciate and try to incorporate new songs, styles, and technology. Our church is nowhere near mega, but we also do not have the same challenges (and privileges) of the smaller rural churches in the towns outside of our metropolitan area. I love the church God has called me to, and I would rather worship nowhere else. Even so, I have experienced many moments of insecurity when I have seen or heard of other churches that are more culturally savvy and better able to draw and keep certain segments of society because of it.

If you serve in one of the cutting-edge churches, your struggle may be even greater than mine as you labor to keep up rather than catch up. If you serve in one of the rural churches, your struggle may be convincing your congregation that culture should have any bearing at all on what happens on a Sunday morning.

For each of us, is there perhaps a whisper of truth in what pastor, author, and songwriter Glenn Packiam says?

> *Christ came speaking the language of his culture, fully intent on undermining it. We come speaking the language of our culture with the secret hope of being loved by it.* [26]

If we worship undershepherds find any shred of this secret hope within ourselves, we will need a strong dose of perspective from our Shepherd. His Word is the only word that will provide the reassurance our wobbly hearts require to move forward in confidence with the tasks He sets before us. On Days 4 and 5, we will look at some of the reassuring truths His Word offers us.

A Conversation With My Shepherd

My life

Have I heard any comments recently to encourage me in my worship ministry?

What signs are You wanting me to see to assure me that You are growing Your sheep?

Is there any area of ministry where I am using society's standards as my measuring stick?

Your Word

As I wonder what work is being produced in the hearts of those I serve, how can I rest in Your truth from 1 Chronicles 28:9?

As I seek to evaluate my ministry by Your standards and not the world's, how can You reassure me through the following verses?

Matthew 20:16

Your Word (continued)

Matthew 22:14

Matthew 6:1

Matthew 19:21

Your thought for me

What is one thing You want me to remember from today's lesson?

My heart before You

(Talk to your Shepherd about all or part of the following.) Here's what I need to confess to You; how I want to praise You; what I hope to do with what You've shown me; what I need You to help me with:

DAY 4: OUR SHEPHERD'S REASSURING WORDS (PART 1)

When I sat in that worship team rehearsal, reeling from the inescapable conclusion that my drum skills were sorely lacking, I did not need a pat on the back. I did not need someone to tell me that it wasn't as bad as I feared. Though these gestures would have been comforting, the reassurance I needed most was strong truth from my Shepherd. Eternal truth. Truth that could be applied to any situation, no matter how capable I felt or did not feel. I needed the following truths, from His heart to mine:

Our Shepherd's Voice: "You are not adequate, but I am."

As the apostle Paul writes 2 Corinthians, he is planning a visit to the Corinthian church, a group of believers in whom he has invested his heart. False teachers have made their way into the church, and they have been telling everyone that Paul cannot be trusted, that he has no right to be called an apostle, and that he has been pocketing some of the charity offerings. In anticipation of his visit, he writes the church a letter. We can only speculate as to whether the accusations have caused Paul to second-guess himself on some level, but in his letter he does hint at some inner struggle. As he considers the monumental task of tending these vulnerable sheep for whom the Savior died, he writes, "Who is adequate for these things?" (2 Corinthians 2:16).

His calling, like ours, is to bear fruit in the hidden places of the heart. "You are a letter of Christ," he writes, "cared for by us, written not with ink but with the Spirit of the living God, not on tablets of stone but on tablets of human hearts" (2 Corinthians 3:3). Indeed, who *is* adequate for such a calling? No one. Our congregations are cared for by us, encouraged through us, brought along with us, but the heart things can only be accomplished by the Spirit. No wonder we feel so inadequate!

Paul goes on to write: "Not that we are adequate in ourselves to consider anything as coming from ourselves, but our adequacy is from God, who also made us adequate as servants of a new covenant" (2 Corinthians 3:5-6). Our commission as worship leaders is epic in its significance! We are called to be servants of the new covenant, leading the Savior's rescued ones into a unified and passionate response of love and gratitude; if they don't do this, the stones will (see Luke 19:40). Our God *will* be glorified in His people, and He has entrusted us with the responsibility of leading them. Worship is no social event: it's the soul of what it means to be a Christian.

We are absolutely *not* adequate for this. Am I insecure about my drumming simply because people may criticize my lack of talent? Do I approach Thursday night rehearsals with trepidation because I am afraid my team will not applaud my leadership skills? Do I approach planning a worship set with apprehension because people might not recognize the brilliance with which I cause the themes and music to flow? If these are the things that make for my insecurity, then I need to (a) go back to the chapter on Humility and (b) get over myself. But if the reasons I feel inadequate are because I want the music to help people enter into worship, because I long for our team to be the servant-leaders our brothers and sisters need, and because I hope for the Word to be implanted clearly and convincingly in the hearts of our congregation—*then* there is an answer to allay my fears: My Shepherd says, "*I* am adequate for this."

We must go into our Sunday morning worship times (and our Tuesday staff times, our Wednesday planning times, our Thursday music prep times, and every other moment of our ministry week) with the unequivocal conviction that we are not adequate. As Matt Redman writes:

> *The point is, whatever our outer posture is, our inner posture must be one of complete dependence. A knowledge deep down inside that the power of God upon us will always be the deciding factor.* [27]

If God has called us to be worship leaders, it's not because of our innate suitability for the job. It is because, for reasons known only to Him, He has chosen to glorify His name and build up His people through our ministry. We dare not approach such a weighty assignment on the strength of our own abilities, gifts, zeal, or personality. He is the one who is adequate, the *only* one. All we need to do is be faithful as we trust in His sufficiency to accomplish His work.

All that is left for each of us to say is, "Thank Christ Jesus our Lord, who has strengthened me, because He considered me faithful, putting me into service" (1 Timothy 1:12).

Our Shepherd's Voice: "Through your weakness, My power will be seen."

The fact that Christ makes up for our inadequacies should not only give us courage to be faithful; it should also bring us joy. Our inadequacy is the very means through which His power will be shown:

But we have this treasure in earthen vessels, so that the surpassing greatness of the power will be of God and not from ourselves. (2 Corinthians 4:7)

The beauty of the gospel is that it allows itself to be carried about in weak and faulty vessels. This is not some valuable art object hanging on the pristine wall of an echoey museum. This is the incalculably precious gift of salvation walking around in the hearts, minds, and bodies of people who make mistakes, who may not be quite as gifted as the next person, who let their eyes wander from the prize, and who quail at some of the things required of them.

Have you ever had moments when you wondered what God was thinking when He placed such a priceless treasure in your care? Have you ever had times when you asked yourself how someone so inept as you could be entrusted with the sacred task of leading the Shepherd's sheep in praising their Redeemer? I have.

Christmas Eve, a couple of years ago, was one such time for me. Our Christmas Eve service is a very simple event where friends and family come together to set the world aside for a while and savor the sweet story of our Savior's birth. As twinkling lights cast their warm glow, the pews fill to capacity and the room comes alive with celebratory expectancy.

I had planned the service carefully, and all the elements were in place: the music, the readings, the individuals and families who had agreed to read passages from the Christmas story as Advent candles were lit.

The reading from Matthew 1:18-23, about the angel appearing to Joseph in a dream, was given to our youth pastor, Rich. When it was his turn, he walked up with his two young granddaughters in tow. The little girls, all ribbons and curls, formed a touching picture of innocence. I sat at the piano and heard Rich begin to read:

A voice was heard in Ramah,
Weeping and great mourning,
Rachel weeping for her children;
And she refused to be comforted,
Because they were no more.

I shrank down on the piano bench, mortified. I had neglected to proof the instructions I had typed up for each of the readers. Unfortunately, the Scripture on Rich's note read "Matthew **2**:18-23."

I will never know why God allowed this mistake to happen. I could not see then, nor am I able to see now, how it added to the encouragement of the people gathered there that night, especially those little girls standing up there with their grandpa.

What I do know is that it was yet another opportunity for me to remember that I am a very flawed jar of clay. In that moment I had a choice: would I dwell on my cracks and leaks and chipped edges, or would I decide to focus on the value of the treasure that resides in this unworthy container? Would I put a stopper over the top of this vessel, refusing to serve anymore for fear of bringing attention to my flaws, or would I let the owner of this clay pot pick me up and pour me out as He saw fit so that the gospel would continue to fill my world with truth and grace?

We can trust our Shepherd's Word when He tells us that God's power will be shown in our weakness. We may not understand *how* this will happen, but we can rest in the promise that it *will*. This is why Paul says twice in 2 Corinthians 4, "we do not lose heart" as we minister through our weaknesses (verses 4 and 16). We are not doing it for *our* glory (how futile would *that* be?). We are doing it for the sake of our Shepherd's sheep and for His glory:

For all things are for your sakes so that the grace which is spreading to more and more people may cause the giving of thanks to abound to the glory of God. (verse 15)

When we take our eyes off our inadequacies and put them onto the eternal things—those things which can only be seen through eyes of faith (verse 18)—then people around us will more easily stop staring at our glaring imperfections and direct their eyes to our Almighty, saving God who can and will show His power in us.

This is why we jars of clay can take great joy: inexplicably, our Shepherd has chosen *us* to display His power. When we are surrendered to Him, no mere crack or leak or chip will ever keep Him from receiving the glory He is due.

A Conversation With My Shepherd

My life

> Am I trusting in myself to accomplish something in this ministry that only You can do?

> In what areas have I seen You be strong in me?

> Where are You wanting me to have eyes of faith?

> Am I serving You with joy, in spite of my weaknesses?

Your Word

When I feel inadequate to do anything of lasting value, what reassurance will You give me from 2 Corinthians 3:2-6?

When I feel that I have too many flaws and weaknesses for Your power to work through me, how will You reassure me from 2 Corinthians 4:6-7?

How can You use 2 Corinthians 4:15-18 to encourage me to see with eyes of faith?

Your thought for me

What is one thing You want me to remember from today's lesson?

My heart before You

(Talk to your Shepherd about all or part of the following.) Here's what I need to confess to You; how I want to praise You; what I hope to do with what You've shown me; what I need You to help me with:

DAY 5: OUR SHEPHERD'S REASSURING WORDS (PART 2)

In the grip of insecurity following my worship rehearsal drumming debut, I was very tempted to say, "We will just have to do without a drummer this Sunday." However, since my son, the worship director, was still convinced I should play, I felt I had no choice. Besides, there was one more truth I needed to hear from my Shepherd. I heard it something like this: "You don't think you have the ability to play as well as you had hoped? So what? I'm asking you to do this thing."

Our Shepherd's Voice: "Offer Me what you have; I will make it enough."

What does our Shepherd ask us to offer Him? Only what He's given us. Nothing more than this. We cannot offer Him what we *wish* we possessed. He has given each of us exactly the gifts, abilities, strengths, and personalities He wants us to have, and He's placed us in our positions of ministry knowing full well our limitations (1 Corinthians 12:4-31). Can we trust that He knew what He was doing when He placed us there? We *must,* or we will not be able to freely and without reservation offer Him all that we have.

The question to ask our Shepherd is not, "What if I don't have the resources within myself to do this thing You are asking me to do?" The question to ask is, "Will You show me *how* to offer these gifts to You so that You can use them however You want?" Do you see the difference in emphasis between the two questions? The first focuses on our own inadequacy, and it hesitates to act. The second trusts in the Lord's adequacy, and it determines to act.

When the young boy offered his loaves and fishes to Jesus (John 6:8-13), I picture him standing there with questioning eyes, arms held out. How could he have known what Jesus would do with his offering? The boy may have only expected it to be divided between a handful of people, perhaps the disciples. Or he may have had a tiny glimmer of hope that Jesus would do something miraculous. It doesn't matter what his expectations were; he gave his paltry offering to Jesus to make whatever use of it He saw fit.

When the widow gave her last two coins to the temple offering (Mark 12:41-44), what thoughts might have run through her mind? If we had been in her situation, wouldn't we have been tempted to think, "What good will this pittance do for God's work? I might as well keep this and buy bread for myself"? If such thoughts did run through her mind, they did not win out; she gave the Lord the last amount of money she possessed to use at His discretion.

I have felt inadequate at just about every step of my worship-leading ministry. I have led worship teams when I believed I didn't have a leading voice, directed a worship ministry when I wasn't sure people would follow, played newly-learned instruments on the team when I knew I wasn't quite ready, initiated conversations I did not feel wise enough to have, and put in long hours when I had no energy left.

Am I promised a specific result for any of these things I offer to my Shepherd? No. But it does not matter, because I am only asked to offer them. I believe that the God who calls me is the one who will bring to pass whatever He wants to accomplish through me (1 Thessalonians 5:24). I believe that, as I do my part, the Lord will build up the local body of believers I am called to serve (Ephesians 4:16). I believe that if my Master entrusts me with five talents, He can take my faithful use of them and multiply them to ten. If He gives me only one talent, I can offer it to Him with the same open hand and trusting heart as if He'd given me five (Matthew 25:14-29).

This is why I can pray this prayer with confidence, for you and for myself:

> *Now the God of peace, who brought up from the dead the great Shepherd of the sheep through the blood of the eternal covenant, even Jesus our Lord, equip you in every good thing to do His will, working in us that which is pleasing in His sight, through Jesus Christ, to whom be the glory forever and ever.* (Hebrews 13:20-21)

His Reassurance, Enough For Us

Sometimes the reassurance I look for is that *I* am enough: *my* art, *my* influence, *my* giftings. But looking for reassurance here is like looking for a sand castle I've built the day before at low tide. My ministry may appear strong and capable today, but tomorrow everything may change. My gifts may wane; opportunities may be given to another; higher standards may be put into place; I may never reach the level of skill I'd hoped for.

Looking to my own abilities for reassurance can also be like quicksand. The more I try to reassure myself that I have what it takes to succeed in this ministry, the more stuck in futile striving I become. I show up on Sunday confident in my ability to persuade hearts; the fruitless effort draws me down a couple of inches. I work hard to please all the people; exhaustion sucks me further in. I flail desperately for some concrete evidence that validates my ministry; deeper in the mire I go.

The Shepherd's answer? Did you catch it in His words to us? "It's all about Me. *I* am adequate. *My* power will be seen. *I* will make it enough." His words are not simply one form of reassurance out of many others we could choose from. His words are the only true reassurance we have. And they are enough.

A Conversation With My Shepherd

My life

What are some abilities (large or small) You've given me to use for Your glory?

What can I offer You today for Your use?

Do I really believe that You can take my small offerings and make them great for Your kingdom?

Your Word

When I feel that I have nothing to offer You, what reassurance will You give me from the following Scriptures?

John 6:8-13

Mark 12:41-44

According to Hebrews 13:20-21, what are some of the things that only You can do?

Your thought for me

What is one thing You want me to remember from today's lesson?

My heart before You

(Talk to your Shepherd about all or part of the following.) Here's what I need to confess to You; how I want to praise You; what I hope to do with what You've shown me; what I need You to help me with:

A PRAYER TO PRAY

Always-reassuring Shepherd who knows my heart, I sometimes wonder why You chose me to lead Your sheep in worship. I see them gathered before me, these precious lambs for whom You gave Your life, and I wonder how You could entrust them to my care.

I know I am not up for this. Sometimes I know it so well it cripples me. I know my talent has limits, my giftedness is narrow in scope, and my wisdom is finite. Some days my energy flags, my creativity dries up, and my communication misfires. I can be void of vision, lacking in drive, and skewed in perspective.

Thank You for showing me these things. I could not be the servant You want me to be if I did not recognize that these things are true. But I also thank You for showing me so much more:

- *You are abundantly adequate. It honors Your great name when I trust You to be enough.*

- *You are perfectly powerful. It magnifies the beauty of Your gospel when I recognize that I am but an imperfect vessel for Your use.*

- *You are the mighty multiplier. It produces fruit for Your kingdom when I simply offer back to You the gifts You've given me.*

How I need You to reassure me of these things again and again so that I do not look on my shortcomings but rather on Your all-sufficiency!

*I am **not** up for leading Your beloved sheep in worship. Yet You have called me to it. Will You please reassure me for this ministry You've given me, Shepherd who knows my heart very well?*

CHAPTER 7

OUR SHEPHERD SPEAKS IDENTITY

DAY 1: SO MANY VOICES TELLING US WHO WE SHOULD BE

The eleven of us entered the auditorium like little kids walking through Disneyland turnstiles, eyes racing to take in the sights, hearts beating with happy expectation. Bold graphics, stunning on the screen; luminous spotlights, iridescent on the stage—all of it spoke excellence and verve. As we took our seats in the midst of a multitude of other worship leaders and teams, the music began. Euphoric guitars and driving drums pounded their rhythms through our chests as passionate vocals drew us into worship. Thousands of voices rose as one, their melodies and harmonies and descants soaring up through the rafters.

For the next two days of the worship conference, we worshiped alongside people of like mind whose worship would not be quelled. We attended workshops whose speakers challenged us to lead with strength and create with abandon. We learned of new and innovative technologies that sparked our imaginations.

We encountered fellow worship teams whose ministries were much more impressive than ours in size and scope; we met lone and weary worship leaders who aspired to find even one or two other like-minded volunteers to come alongside them. Brushing up against the confident and self-assured, the glassy-eyed and confused, we recognized ourselves in all of them. We came home affirmed yet apprehensive; inspired yet sobered.

As the leader of my worship teams, I came away from the conference wanting very much to encourage my co-laborers: The accomplished violinist, eyes reflecting tentative optimism as she talked of expanding her creativity. The hurting bass player, lonely for the company of a wife who had left him, trying to find his place on the team. The percussionist, missing her grown daughters who now attended other churches where the worship resonated better with them.

I sensed these friends might need reassurance. They might need to know that our ministry was just as vital as the ones we had witnessed. They might need help in coming to grips with the disparity between how our congregation worshiped and how the gathering of hundreds of worship leaders expressed their worship. They might need guidance in assessing their strengths and limitations realistically, yet with hope.

In order to encourage them in these things, I also knew that I would need a clear understanding of who our Shepherd was calling *us* and *our* church to be, not what He was calling any other worship ministry or church to be. I realized that without this understanding, I would be tempted to pour time and energy into all the wrong goals, trying to push us toward something we were never created to be. I returned more convinced than ever of the necessity of finding our particular identity as sheep in our Shepherd's fields.

Whose Voice Do We Hear Best?

For the purposes of this chapter, I am using the word "identity" to encompass all of what we as individual worship leaders, worship teams, and congregations are called to do and to be.

There is no shortage of voices volunteering to help us find our identity:

- The voices of our brothers and sisters in the congregation. Most of these voices are well-meaning, but they may not always line up with what our Shepherd is saying to us.

- The voices of our brothers and sisters outside our congregation. These are the voices we hear at conferences or on the radio, the voices we read in books and blogs. At their worst, they promote agendas that are not God-honoring or scriptural; at their best, they hold out inspirational models of truth and beauty. Yet even the most worthy of models can defeat us if we claim as our own an ideal our Shepherd has not given to us.

- The voices of the world and the voice of Satan, who is the god of this world and the father of lies (John 16:11; 8:44). The values these voices promote are antithetical to our humble Shepherd; they are self-promoting and short-sighted, competitive and crowd-pleasing.

- The one final voice, perhaps loudest of all, vying for our attention: our own. We tell ourselves that *we* are responsible to make this ministry all it should be; we assume some self-imposed vision of our ministry, and if we don't see it realized, we believe we have somehow failed our church and our Lord.

When the voices around us clamor to be heard, we must say, along with Peter, "Lord, to whom shall we go? You have words of eternal life" (John 6:68). When our own voice shouts loudly in our ear, we must remember that "the heart is deceitful above all things…who can know it?" (Jeremiah 17:9). It is in these times that we must adopt the wisdom of Proverbs 3:5-6, refusing to lean on our own understanding and trusting His instead.

Our Shepherd promises that His sheep will be able to hear His voice above all the others. He kindly allows us to discern it as He exposes the other voices as imposters:

The sheep hear his voice, and he calls his own sheep by name and leads them out. When he puts forth all his own, he goes ahead of them, and the sheep follow him because they know his voice. A stranger they simply will not follow, but will flee from him, because they do not know the voice of strangers. (John 10:3b-5)

I have always been drawn to my husband's voice; it's one of the things that made me fall in love with him. When he walks in the door at the end of the day, calling out my name in the sweet way that no one else does, I am reminded that we belong to each other. When we walk along the river on Monday mornings, praying for our children, his word choices and phrasing flowing out of a father's tender heart, I am glad he is by my side through life. When I sit at the piano on Sunday mornings, his voice in the congregation rising clear and resonant above all the others in my ear, I am humbled to be married to this worshiping man.

When he and I get to worship side by side, I almost can hear his heart through his voice. I am endeared to his voice even when it chooses its own way. Like last Sunday:

Thou rising morn, in praise rejoice,
Ye lights of evening, find a voice!
O praise Him, O praise Him
Alleluia! Alleluia!
Allelu - IA! [28]

His last syllable rang out loud and clear, soaring in a world all its own, secure to be marching to its own drummer as all the other voices waited to join in on the proper beat. My husband's mistimed exuberance propelled us both to laughter. He leaned down and whispered in my ear: "They held the Alleluia longer that time." Well, actually, honey, no they didn't.

Our Shepherd's voice is like this (though it never races ahead of the music). It speaks to us in intimate tones, drawing us to Him. It whispers close in our ear, revealing His heartbeat. It leads us in worship, gladdening our spirits.

Just as my husband did not stop speaking to me once we were married, our Shepherd did not call you or me into ministry only to stop communicating with us once we got here. He continues to speak, elucidating our call along the way. Our primary job as worship leaders is to keep listening carefully and to hear Him with a willing heart.

The foundational way to discern His voice is to spend time with Him away from the crowd. As we discussed in Chapter 2

(Refreshment), nothing can take the place of sitting at His feet every day, listening to His Spirit speak to us through His Word. Having spent quiet time with Him, we can then take His words along with us through the rest of our day as we carry on in listening mode. He will keep speaking to us; whether through His Word, wise counselors, circumstances, or warnings and confirmations in our spirit, He will speak. If we ask Him to help us discern His voice above all the others, He will do it.

Jesus Himself said it: "The sheep know his voice."

A Conversation With My Shepherd

My life

Will You show me if there are specific areas of my ministry or my church where I have different expectations from Yours?

Are there any voices I need to tune out so I can hear Yours better about the identity of this ministry You've given me?

How can I listen to Your voice better?

Your Word

How does Jeremiah 17:5-10a both warn and encourage me as I try to discern what worship ministry should look like in my church?

According to John 10:2-5, 11-15, 27-28, what is it about Your voice that should cause me to desire to hear it above any other voice?

Your thought for me

What is one thing You want me to remember from today's lesson?

My heart before You

(Talk to your Shepherd about all or part of the following.) Here's what I need to confess to You; how I want to praise You; what I hope to do with what You've shown me; what I need You to help me with:

DAY 2: ASKING QUESTIONS OF OUR SHEPHERD

When I sat down in my office the week after the worship conference, my mind ran rampant with unsettling thoughts: Was I doing a good enough job as worship director? Was I cut out for this? Were my teams as effective as they could be? Was our church's worship pleasing to the Lord? Why did I have this vague sense of falling short one moment, this hopeful surge of meeting the mark the next? What *was* the mark, exactly?

The more I wondered about these things, the more futile it became to reason them out. Distracted by wishful thinking and overwhelmed by unrealistic goals, I needed a good dose of wisdom from above. I needed very much to know what my Shepherd had to say about all of this.

Do you spend much time asking Jesus questions? I don't know about you, but I forget to ask Him questions sometimes. I walk around in this ambiguous state of confusion, knowing I'm missing something, but I can't quite make out what it is. It's like the scene I once saw in the Broadway musical *The Lion King*. The stage was dark as puppeteers waved random bits and pieces of light-reflected objects in the air. To the audience, it was just a jumble of jagged shapes swirling haphazardly in space. As we watched, the objects were drawn ever so slowly toward each other until gradually the face of a lion emerged, majestic and unmistakable.

In times of uncertainty, I need to take all the confusing pieces of my ministry—those nagging doubts and fears that make me second-guess what we are about—and ask the Master Puppeteer to bring them together so that I can see the shape of the work He's creating.

Have you noticed how the disciples were always asking questions? They weren't afraid to sound stupid; they just asked away:

Tell us, when will these things be, and how will we know?
(Mark 13:3-4)

This is a hard teaching. Who can accept it? (John 6:60)

Why then do the scribes say that Elijah must come first?
(Matthew 17:10)

Rabbi, who sinned, this man or his parents? (John 9:2)

Lord, we do not know where You are going, how do we know the way?
(John 14:5)

Why do You speak to them in parables? (Matthew 13:10)

Where would we get so many loaves in this desolate place?
(Matthew 15:33)

Do You not care that we are perishing? (Mark 4:38)

Then who can be saved? (Mark 10:26)

Shall we strike with the sword? (Luke 22:49)

Lord, who is it that will betray You? (John 13:25)

And what about this man? (John 21:21)

The disciples obviously trusted Jesus enough to know that He welcomed their questions. Sometimes He gave them outright answers; other times He met their questions with further questions to think about. This is the kind of relationship His friends had with Him.

Jesus wanted His friends to know what He was about, and what they were about, so that they could fulfill His purpose for them. Listen to what He told them:

> *You are My friends if you do what I command you. No longer do I call you slaves, for the slave does not know what his master is doing; but I have called you friends, for all things that I have heard from My Father I have made known to you. You did not choose me, but I chose you, and appointed you that you would go and bear fruit, and that your fruit would remain ...* (John 15:14–16a)

Jesus makes it clear: we are His friends if we do what He asks of us. But how will we know what He is asking of us specifically if we do not take the time to find out? As we seek to understand His will for ourselves, our worship teams, and our congregations, there are several questions that will help us discern His will. In tomorrow's lesson we will consider the first question.

A Conversation With My Shepherd

My life

Are there any vague, unsettled questions about my present ministry situation that need to be stated to You more clearly?

What "pieces" of my ministry or my church do I need to leave in Your skillful hands today?

Your Word

What kinds of answers did You give Your disciples when they asked the following questions (clear, obscure, another question, admonition, action, etc.)?

Question: Tell us, when will these things be, and how will we know?

Answer (Mark 13:28–31):

Question: This is a hard teaching. Who can accept it?

Answer (John 6:61–63):

Your Word (continued)

Question: Why then do the scribes say that Elijah must come first?

Answer (Matthew 17:11-12):

Question: Rabbi, who sinned, this man or his parents?

Answer (John 9:3):

Question: Lord, how do we know the way?

Answer (John 14:6):

Question: Why do You speak to them in parables?

Answer (Matthew 13:11):

Question: Where would we get so many loaves in this desolate place?

Answer (Matthew 15:34):

Your Word (continued)

Question: Do You not care that we are perishing?

Answer (Mark 4:39-40):

Question: Then who can be saved?

Answer (Mark 10:27):

Question: Shall we strike with the sword?

Answer (Luke 22:50-51):

Question: Lord, who is it that will betray You?

Answer (John 13:26):

Question: And what about this man?

Answer (John 21:22):

Your Word (continued)

As I read Your answers to the disciples' questions, what do they tell me about Your relationship with Your sheep?

Your thought for me

What is one thing You want me to remember from today's lesson?

My heart before You

(Talk to your Shepherd about all or part of the following.) Here's what I need to confess to You; how I want to praise You; what I hope to do with what You've shown me; what I need You to help me with:

DAY 3: THE FIRST QUESTION TO ASK

In the wake of the worship conference that year, I did some personal assessment. There were changes to be made, issues to be addressed, vision to pursue; was I the one to lead the charge?

Should I Be Doing This?

The question we need to ask before any others is: "Should I be doing this?" We must settle this one first. It's a question that may need to be revisited from time to time. It's a question that may beg other questions of our Shepherd. Questions like:

- Will You remind me how You brought me here in the first place?
- How did You prepare my heart ahead of time?
- What fruit have You brought since I've been in this position?
- Is the leadership behind me?
- Is the congregation with me?
- Are those who know me well telling me I shouldn't be doing this?
- Is my family suffering because I'm doing this?
- Are You still giving me a passion for this?
- Are You placing a passion in me for a different ministry?

Our Shepherd may answer with a few questions of His own:
- Have you been spending time with Me?
- Do you remember the things I showed you at the beginning?
- Are you looking for fruit that has lasting value?
- Are you willing to submit to the leadership?
- Do you have relationships within the congregation?
- Have you asked those who know you well what they think?
- Have you asked your family what they think?
- Do you still love Me enough to feed My sheep?

- Are you willing to do anything I call you to, even if it means a change?

It is beyond the scope of this book to explore whether or not we are called to our ministry in the first place, but our Shepherd stands ready to help us answer any doubts we may have. He has also probably placed people in our lives who can help us address those doubts as well.

What We Can Know If We Are Called To This Ministry

If we do believe we are called to the ministry we are doing now, then there are three things we need to hear from our Shepherd as we move forward.

Our Shepherd's Voice: "I have called you *personally*."

Our Shepherd has not called someone else with a different set of skills and gifts and personality traits; He has called *us*. Ephesians 4:7, 16 reminds us:

But to each one of us grace was given according to the measure of Christ's gift... from whom the whole body, being fitted and held together by what every joint supplies, according to the proper working of each individual part, causes the growth of the body for the building up of itself in love.

Do we fail to see how God can use *us* to build our church into a congregation that loves to worship the Lord together? It's okay that we are not able to see the *how*; we only need to know *that* He has called us. *We* are called to serve these precious sheep, with the gifts that *we* have been given, according to the grace He gives *us*. It's His call, not ours, whether or not we serve here. We can trust His call.

Our Shepherd's Voice: "I have called you to *these people*."

Our Shepherd has made no mistake in calling us to our present location. He has His reasons for calling us here rather than to some other worship team or congregation. In His infinite wisdom, He has not called us to serve in a place where the people are more spiritual, more knowledgeable in Scripture, more loving, more passionate, more musical, more hospitable, more fun, more evangelistic, more devoted to prayer, more wealthy, more open to new things, more youthful, or more mature. He has certainly not called us to serve in a perfect church, because no such church exists. As 1 Corinthians 12:18-23 tells us:

> *But now God has placed the members, each one of them, in the body, just as He desired. If they were all one member, where would the body be? But now there are many members, but one body. And the eye cannot say to the hand, "I have no need of you"; or again the head to the feet, "I have no need of you." On the contrary, it is much truer that the members of the body which seem to be weaker are necessary; and those members of the body which we deem less honorable, on these we bestow more abundant honor, and our less presentable members become much more presentable,*

We cannot quibble with our Shepherd about whom He has placed in our church family. There will be weaker members, and there will be stronger ones. We are all His sheep, and it's to *this* sometimes cuddly, sometimes bleating flock that He has called us.

Our Shepherd's Voice: "I have called you *for this time*."

We cannot stand outside of time and see the grand plan of our Shepherd. We can learn from our history, and we can guess at the future, but we cannot see the whole story. Only God sees the beginning from the end.

If we are called to minister to our church body at this time, we can know that something important will happen while we are here. We may not ever comprehend the complete significance of our ministry, but we can know that God's purposes are always at work in every place and in every time. Imagine Esther as she was brought to be part of King Ahasuerus' harem and then elevated to the position of queen. She had no guarantee that she would be the instrument through which God would save His people. She did not know there would be a book of the Bible named after her. Nor did her cousin Mordecai, yet he urged her to risk her life for her people, saying:

> *"For if you remain silent at this time, relief and deliverance will arise for the Jews from another place and you and your father's house will perish. And who knows whether you have not attained royalty for such a time as this?"* (Esther 4:14)

We do not know what kind of work God will do through us. Our ministry may move our church forward in giant strides; our ministry may see our church slide into a slump. Our ministry may be but one tiny link between two greater ministries. *This* is the time we are given, and we can trust our Shepherd to make it count.

Ready To Narrow Down The Questions

Once we have discerned that *we* are called *here* for *this time*, then we can begin to address specific questions pertaining to our identity as a worship leader, as a worship ministry, and as a congregation. On Day 4, we will consider these questions and discuss how they can help us gain a good understanding of who and what our Shepherd is calling us to be.

A Conversation With My Shepherd

My life

Shepherd of my heart, will You remind me how You brought me to worship ministry in the first place?

Are You still placing in me a passion for this ministry?

Are there any doubts about my calling, the people You've called me to, or Your timing that I need to lay at Your feet?

Your Word

How can You encourage me from Ephesians 4:7, 16 to find my identity in this specific worship ministry and church You've called me to?

When I feel discouraged about either my worship teams or my congregation, how can Your truth from 1 Corinthians 12:18-23 encourage me?

Your Word (continued)

When I cannot see why You've called me to minister here at this time, what can Esther 4:14 teach me?

Your thought for me

What is one thing You want me to remember from today's lesson?

My heart before You

(Talk to your Shepherd about all or part of the following.) Here's what I need to confess to You; how I want to praise You; what I hope to do with what You've shown me; what I need You to help me with:

DAY 4: THREE MORE QUESTIONS TO ASK

If we believe that our Shepherd has called us to be in this place, ministering at this time, we can approach the remaining questions about our identity with confidence, filtering out the false voices telling us their ideas of our calling and listening fearlessly to the one Voice that rings clear and true. He will show us who we are; He will show us who we are not. He will show us what He is calling us to do; He will show us what He is not. He will accomplish what concerns us (Psalm 138:8), here, with these people, and in this time.

As worship undershepherds trying to discern our Shepherd's will for us and our particular flock of sheep, there are three more questions to ask Him. These questions are *highly individualistic*; no two worship leaders will answer them the same about themselves or about their ministries and their churches. They are also *interdependent*, and how we apply the answer to one of them will often depend on the answers to the other two. Finally, these questions should be answered based on what we know *now*. It may be that in the future God will show us a new spiritual gift, or our team will be blessed with another drummer, or our congregation's demographic will change. But, according to our current understanding, what is He asking of us?

Who Are You Calling *Me* To Be?

From the outset of my ministry, I knew some things about myself: I was passionate about generations worshiping together. I did not have a strong leading voice. I was energized by helping others recognize their gifts and develop them to serve the church, but I did not like being in charge. I had a strong sense of rhythm, but it was tempered by my unfortunate tendency toward changing tempos during the course of a song. Knowing my passions and strengths, as well as my weaknesses and limitations, helped clarify what God was asking of me and what He wasn't.

Jesus Himself knew the things His Father had called Him to do and the things He had not. In His own words, He came to:

- Do the will of Him who sent Him (John 6:38)
- Serve and give His life a ransom for many (Matthew 20:28)
- Seek and save that which was lost (Luke 19:10)
- Call sinners to repentance (Luke 5:32)
- Testify to the truth (John 18:37)
- Bring light to the world (John 12:46)
- Give sight to the blind (Luke 4:18)
- Preach the kingdom of God (Luke 4:43)
- Preach the gospel to the poor (Luke 4:18)
- Proclaim release to the captives (Luke 4:18)
- Set free those who are oppressed (Luke 4:18)
- Give abundant life (John 10:10)
- Bring division (Luke 12:51)
- Fulfill the Law (Matthew 5:17)
- Suffer (Luke 24:46)
- Rise from the dead (Luke 24:46)

Jesus did not come to appease the religious leaders. He did not come to abolish the evil governments of the day. He did not come to heal every person of their sickness. He did not come to please everyone. He listened to only one voice, and that was the voice of His Father.

If Jesus carried out His ministry with a clear understanding of His Father's will for Him, how foolish would it be for us to serve without seeking to know His will for us too?

Who Are You Calling *My Teams* To Be?

When I began my ministry, our teams were comprised of people who loved our church and loved to worship the Lord. But some of our instrumentalists did not have the skills to play contemporary music; some of our vocalists did not have the vocal style to sing it. Everyone believed that the tempo of a song should fluctuate depending on how the team was feeling it in the moment. As I became better acquainted with my teams over time, I gained a clearer understanding of how to work within the context of their strengths and weaknesses so that we could serve our church as our Shepherd intended us to.

The team Jesus chose to work with had its distinctions as well. There were rugged fishermen and despised tax collectors; impulsive men of action and reticent doubters; busy doers and thoughtful meditators. They were slow to learn and quick to react; weak in faith and strong in ambition. With every conversation and exhortation, Jesus took into consideration who these disciples were, and He used them to build His kingdom. He will show us how to do the same with the teams He has given us.

Who Are You Calling *My Congregation* To Be?

Our church was almost 100 years old when I became our director of worship ministry. It had a long history of multigenerational worship, and the people loved one another. Most of the younger ones and many of the older ones warmed to contemporary music, but not everyone did. Furthermore, the congregation did a decent job of clapping on beats one and three, but beats two and four could be calamitous. Becoming familiar with our church culture helped me to discern and rest in who God had called us to be as a worshiping community.

The apostle Paul understood the nuances of his churches very well. He praised the church at Corinth for holding firmly to his teaching but reprimanded them for being factious (1 Corinthians 11:2, 17-19). He pointed out to the Galatians that, though they *had* been running well, now they were being hindered from obeying the truth (Galatians 5:7). He told the believers at Thessalonica that there was no need to write to them about loving one another, they did it so well; yet in the very next breath he urged them to "excel still more" (1 Thessalonians 4:9-10).

Who are these sheep we are called to serve? Let's see them for who they are, accepting their shortcomings, praising God for their strengths, and urging them all the while to "excel still more."

Taking An Honest Look

As I took an honest look at myself, my teams, and my church following that worship conference, I saw some things that should not change, some things I hoped would change but that I could only pray about, and some things I knew I needed to work to change. The Lord showed me that He was calling me to build on the good foundation of intergenerational worship that had been laid previously, but that, for our congregation, it would take a gentle and patient intentionality as we transitioned into including more contemporary songs and styles. I also came to understand that I was not to be the main leader on Sunday mornings (except on rare occasions), but that I could use the gifts God had given me to help my teams find and hone their strengths in order to serve and lead the congregation better. I learned to be careful about song choices that would be unattainable rhythmically for our teams and congregations, and I also (over time) helped our teams come to accept the necessity of a metronome. I also prayed continually about specific gaps in our teams (drummers, "color" instruments, audiovisual techs, etc.).

As you no doubt have discovered, trying to discern what the Shepherd is asking you, your teams, and your congregation to be is an ongoing process that requires time and reflection. With this in mind, I have included a chart (see Appendix B) to be used as a tool of encouragement in asking Him to show you His perspective.

The sole purpose of this book is to strengthen and encourage worship leaders, not give them tasks to do. Yet, given the importance of the items on the chart, I believe you will find it worth your while to set aside extra time to work through the chart and hear the Shepherd's voice. On Day 5, you will have an opportunity to prayerfully work through the chart. I encourage you to carve out a good space of time during Day 5 so that you can hear what your Shepherd has to say about you, your teams, and your church.

A Conversation With My Shepherd

My life

Will You help me summarize in one sentence what You are calling me to be in this ministry?

Will You help me summarize in one sentence what You are calling my worship teams to be?

Will You help me summarize in one sentence what You are calling my congregation to be, as a worshiping community?

Your Word

As I consider who You are calling me, my teams, and my congregation to be, what encouragement will You give me from Psalm 138:8?

How can James 1:5-8 prepare my heart to ask You some specific questions about myself, my worship teams, and my church in tomorrow's lesson?

Your thought for me

What is one thing You want me to remember from today's lesson?

My heart before You

(Talk to your Shepherd about all or part of the following.) Here's what I need to confess to You; how I want to praise You; what I hope to do with what You've shown me; what I need You to help me with:

DAY 5: HEARING OUR SHEPHERD'S ANSWERS

Today's lesson involves less reading and more listening—to the one Voice that matters. After the worship conference my teams and I attended, I needed to hear from my Shepherd about who He was calling us to be. Had I let the voices of *other* worship leaders, *other* ministries, or *other* churches determine my identity, I might easily have become discouraged or tempted to lead our church down the wrong path. As worship leaders, it behooves us to sit down with our Shepherd at various times in our ministries and listen to Him carefully as He reveals His will for us. Perhaps now might be a good time for you to do this, using the chart provided in this book (Appendix B).

As you work through the chart, briefly consider each topic, asking your Shepherd to impress on you what He wants you to see. The simple purpose of this chart, for *this* chapter, is to hear His voice telling you who He is calling you and your church family to be, and to rest in that.

It may be wise, at a future time, to work through the chart with your church leaders or your co-laborers in the worship ministry. See Chapter 9 (Submission) and Chapter 11 (Help).

As you consider each topic, ask Him to show you specific aspects of this topic that will help you assess yourself, your teams, and your congregation. Then ask Him to help you evaluate each one as follows:

K = Keep (do not change). This is for those items that you believe should not be changed because (a) they seem to be in a healthy place right now, or (b) they are simply the way God has made you and your fellow sheep to be.

P = Pray (ask God to change). This is for those items that you believe should be changed but that you can do nothing about except pray.

W = Work to change. This is for those items that you believe can and should be changed, either now or in the future, as your Shepherd leads you to address them.

Please take some time now to bring this chart before your Shepherd and let Him show you how to fill out the columns.

After completing the chart, it may be tempting to roll up your sleeves and get to work on fixing all the things that could be improved. Please don't go there, not yet. We will talk about how to patiently approach the process of change in Chapter 8 (Patience); for now, I encourage you to simply sit with your Shepherd as you do the following devotional and let the things He has shown you from the chart settle in to your spirit.

Friends, there is such restfulness in understanding the identity our Shepherd has given us as worship leaders, worship teams, and congregations:

- There is *security* as we cease striving to be something we are neither called nor enabled to be and as we walk in step with our Shepherd down the path He is leading *us*.
- There is *contentment* as we set aside comparisons and envy and trustingly keep our eyes fixed on Him alone.
- There is *joy and freedom* as we hand over our meager best efforts and serve Him regardless of the outcome.
- There is *worship* as we come to understand that, of all the things He calls us to be, nothing matters more to Him than our calling to be His children who love Him.

A Conversation With My Shepherd

For today's devotional, simply spend some time talking with your Shepherd about the chart you've filled out:

As you think of all the items you marked with a **K**, celebrate the way He has made you, your teams, and your church to be. Thank Him that in His infinite wisdom He brought you here, in this place, in this time.

Entrust to your Shepherd all the items you marked with a **P**. Tell Him your desire for changes in these areas, and ask Him to help you believe and rest in His power and wisdom to change them in His perfect way and in His perfect time.

Note: We will talk with our Shepherd about all the W's in Chapter 8 (Patience).

If you'd like to write down some thoughts from your conversation with your Shepherd, you may use the space below:

_____

_____

_____

_____

_____

_____

_____

_____

_____

_____

_____

_____

_____

_____

A PRAYER TO PRAY

Eloquent Shepherd with the clear and true voice, give me ears to hear who You are calling me, my worship co-laborers, and my church to be.

I do not ask for musical skills that wow people, worship teams that perform flawlessly, or a church that rivals the ones up the street. I only ask that You make clear what You want from us so that we can be faithful to it. I believe that You will accomplish whatever things, great or small, You want to do through us as we feed Your sheep in this place and in this moment of time.

Yours is the one voice that counts. By Your words my confusion is cleared and my way is made straight.

Please quiet all the other voices so that I can be quieted by Yours alone.

I am listening.

CHAPTER 8

OUR SHEPHERD SPEAKS PATIENCE

DAY 1: PATIENCE—A NECESSITY AND A GIFT

An Undershepherd's Need For Patience

We could barely tear ourselves off this beautiful and evocative Scottish island, Greg and I and our daughter, Amanda. Iona, the ancient center of Celtic Christianity, centuries-old stone crosses and nunnery ruins giving testimony to generations of saints who had come before. Rocky outcroppings adding a wild dimension to the pastoral meadows profuse with butter-yellow wildflowers and dotted with sheep.

Everywhere, the sheep. Some off to themselves intent on their personal tuft of grass, others in friendly groupings of three or four. Woolly ones, shorn ones (we felt embarrassed for those in the latter category). Black faces, white faces; some heads crowned with curly horns, others adorned with pointy ears sticking straight out. A few aware of our presence; most completely oblivious.

And there was the cougher. "Baa-hack-hack-hack-a-hack-baaaaaaaa!" To this day our daughter can do a syllable-perfect imitation, and each time we hear it, we are endeared to this struggling sheep all over again.

As we lingered in this ancient place, we could almost hear the whispers of ages gone by. How many generations of sheep had wandered these green hills? How many generations of shepherds had led them along? How many generations of sheep and shepherds would follow?

As we undershepherds care for our diverse flocks—the loners and the communers, the filled-to-overflowing and the stripped-down, the attractive and the uncomely, the attentive and the preoccupied, the healthy and the sick—we are in a long line of undershepherds who have followed the Head Shepherd. Generations of sheep and shepherds have come and gone; our Shepherd has faithfully accomplished His work in every generation.

Worship leaders in every generation are given a stewardship: we are to nurture and guide the sheep under our care so that they thrive as worshipers of the Good Shepherd. In Chapter 7 (Identity), we discussed how to discern what this looks like for us and for our congregations. As we worked through the chart, we thanked God for the specific things He has called us to be (all the **K**'s), and we entrusted Him with the things we cannot change (all the **P**'s).

But what about all those **W**'s, all those goals He is asking us to work our way toward? The fields our Shepherd asks us to walk can be arduous and disheartening. The growth we had anticipated for *ourselves* can stall as our skill sets hit a ceiling, our recurring sins pop up like whack-a-moles, and our sparkling creativity loses its sheen. The out-of-reach expectations we had fostered for our *teams* can be forced to realign with reality as we learn that we are working with imperfect people much like us. The gargantuan strides of spirituality we had visualized for our *congregations* can all too often turn out to be laborious, mud-slogged baby steps.

More often than I'd like to admit, I have impatiently cried out to my Shepherd, "How long, oh Lord? How long before we get there?!" But He does not tell me. Rather, He brings to mind His gentle words, "Come, learn from Me" (Matthew 11:29).

Who better to learn patience from than the One who has patiently showered His loving attention on every single generation, including our own:

As for man, his days are like grass;
As a flower of the field, so he flourishes.
When the wind has passed over it, it is no more,
And its place acknowledges it no longer.
But the lovingkindness of the Lord is from everlasting
    to everlasting on those who fear Him,
And His righteousness to children's children. (Psalm 103:15-18)

He will accomplish His plans for us and for our beloved congregations, right into the next generation, and the next, just as He always has. Our patience will prove to be well-founded.

The Perfect Work Of Patience

There are many dimensions to the word "patience." In the New Testament there are two Greek words often translated into English as "patience." One word is *hupomone*, which means to persevere, especially when experiencing hardship. This word is sometimes translated "endurance." The other word is *makrothumia*, which means to be longsuffering, especially toward other people.

Even in English there are many meanings of the word "patience." One definition that combines the essence of the two Greek words is "capacity for waiting: the ability to endure waiting, delay, or provocation without becoming annoyed or upset, or to persevere calmly when faced with difficulties." [29]

Taking all these definitions and applying them to this chapter, I define patience this way: [*The ability to rest in God's faithfulness to bring us to where He wants us to be, in His perfect way and in His impeccable timing, no matter how long the process or how circuitous the route.*]

Learning patience is a non-negotiable for any Christian who wants to grow. It is a most effective tool in the capable hands of our Lord as

He fashions us into people who bring Him honor. James 1:4 makes patience sound like one of God's sweetest gifts to us:

> But let patience have its perfect work, that you may be perfect and complete, lacking nothing. (NKJV [30])

Sometimes we worship leaders underestimate the value of patience in our ministries, in our congregations, and in ourselves. We can set up some fairly worthy goals, but it may be that God's goals for us are more worthy still. For example, *we* may think that one of the primary goals of our ministry is for our teams to lead with musical excellence week after week. But if *God* says, "This is going to take a really long time," He may have the better goal of building in us a heart that trusts Him and remains faithful even while the process seems to stall. *We* may believe that God will be most glorified when our congregation learns to enter into corporate worship with passion. But *God* may be saying that, for the moment at least, His name will be most glorified as we learn to show grace to one another while each of us grows at our own pace. "Let patience have its perfect work."

A perusal of Scripture shows that God uses the tool of patience quite effectively to bring His children to the place He wants them to be. What faith was wrought in the heart of Hannah as she waited many years for a son? What soil was prepared in the despairing hearts of the disciples as they grieved in the days between the cross and the empty tomb? What strength of character was forged in David in the long years between Samuel's anointing him and the realization of his kingship? What pride was ferreted out of Moses' heart in the 40 years he worked as a shepherd before God called him to lead His people out of Egypt? And, for the apostle Paul, what understanding of grace was poured into his heart during the years between his conversion and the beginning of his ministry to the Gentiles?

As worship leaders, we have a picture of what we want ourselves, our teams, and our congregations to look like. It is good to have such hopes and to pray toward them, but let's not forget that the work God does *in the process of getting there* may be just as important, if not more so, as the goals we cherish so deeply. Patience may turn out to be His best gift of all.

A Conversation With My Shepherd

My life

Are there any areas in my life or in my ministry where I feel impatient and need to hear You say, "Come, learn from Me"?

What plans for myself, my teams, or my church am I needing to trust You for right now?

Will You show me how You are using patience in my life to produce its "perfect work"?

Your Word

What encouragement can You give me from Psalm 103 as I learn patience with myself, my teams, and my church?

Verses 1-2

Verse 5

Your Word (continued)

> Verse 11

> Verses 15–18

> Verse 19

> Verses 20–22

According to James 1:2-4, why can patience (sometimes translated as steadfastness, endurance, perseverance) be one of Your sweetest gifts to me as I approach the work You've put in front of me?

Your thought for me

What is one thing You want me to remember from today's lesson?

My heart before You

(Talk to your Shepherd about all or part of the following.) Here's what I need to confess to You; how I want to praise You; what I hope to do with what You've shown me; what I need You to help me with:

DAY 2: HOW AN UNDERSHEPHERD SHOWS PATIENCE

What resources of patience did generations of shepherds need as they watched over those flocks on that lonely Scottish isle? Though their circumstances varied, I imagine they all experienced a need for patience to corral wayward sheep, deal with intruders and inclement weather, walk the fields when their own joints ached, and stave off discouragement when the days grew long and monotonous.

We worship leaders also share some common needs for patience. On Days 4 and 5 we'll discuss how patience applies to those **W**'s on the chart, but today and tomorrow we'll look at the aspects of patience that all worship leaders need as they lead their sheep along.

Taking One Step At A Time

I taught piano for many years. Months before a recital, I would play through stacks of music for each student until I found a piece that sparked his or her excitement. Often the piece we chose together was quite challenging, and early in the preparation process the student would question whether it was even possible to learn it. I would ask, "Do you know how to eat an elephant?" Most students had not heard this familiar question before, so I would offer the reassuring answer: "One bite at a time."

One measure, one arpeggio, one passage. One worship service, one rehearsal, one conversation.

Charles Spurgeon taught, "The holy life is a walk, a steady progress, a quiet advance."[31] We worship leaders are called to holy lives that bring joy to the heart of our Shepherd; so are our teams; so are our congregations. We didn't wake up this morning suddenly arrived, nor will we tomorrow. But by His grace, we will be closer to His ideal today than we were yesterday, closer this year than last.

Showing Sensitivity

In our zeal to move things along to where we think they should be, we can sometimes forget to really *see* our fellow sheep. Yes, that one team member may be coming late to rehearsals, but have we stopped to find out if there is an underlying reason? Maybe he is going through a season of discouragement and is finding it difficult to get his act together because of it. Sure, some of the people in the congregation may be resistant to change, but have we spent time getting to know them so that we can understand why? Maybe they've had a previous experience with a church split where change had been introduced too quickly.

As author Tom Kraeuter says, "Jesus didn't die for music. He died for people… With this understanding, it is no longer a matter of pushing and cajoling people to move ahead. Now it becomes a matter of loving them." [32]

Extending Grace

One day as I was mulling over the reticence of some of my brothers and sisters to adopt a heart of worship, I found myself migrating from compassion to condemnation. Before I was allowed to wander too far into these badlands, the Holy Spirit stopped me short with this question: Which is the worse sin—a sin borne out of ignorance or a sin of pride; the slowness of struggling sheep to come to a heart of worship or the quickness of a self-satisfied undershepherd to judge them for it?

I knew the answer. How many times had I read these words:

Now we who are strong ought to bear the weaknesses of those without strength and not just please ourselves. (Romans 15:1)

Christ calls us to love His fellow sheep just as He has loved us (Colossians 3:12-14). The simple fact that He has called us to this ministry of worship—weak, sinful, and inadequate though we are—is just one of the innumerable ways He has shown us grace. If we allow this deluge of grace to saturate our souls, how will it not overflow onto those we are called to patiently lead?

Repeating Yourself

I forget sometimes that I don't live in an ideal world. In an ideal world, we would all hear important truths once and remember them forever. The reality is, we have selective hearing. Sometimes we don't catch what is being said to us until it has been repeated a few times. And even when we do catch it, we may need a few more repetitions to *remember* it and take it to heart.

Jesus, our perfect example of patience, was surrounded by distractible and forgetful sheep. How many times during His ministry had He told His followers that He would die and rise from the dead? Yet, even after His death, they did not immediately understand.

Take the example of the two men walking to Emmaus on the Sunday morning after Jesus was crucified. They had hoped that He was the promised Redeemer, but His death had made them wonder if their hopes had been misplaced. The patience of Jesus toward them is astounding: He sought them out on the road; He joined them; He listened to them. During these hours with the men, Jesus knew the sad state of their hearts: "O foolish men and slow of heart to believe in all that the prophets have spoken! Was it not necessary for the Christ to suffer these things and to enter into His glory?" (Luke 24:25-26). He could have added, "Where have you been all this time? Haven't you heard a word I've said these past three years?" But He didn't. Rather, He painstakingly took them through hundreds of years of prophecy, explaining to them in detail how it all pointed to Him.

If Jesus' followers were slow to internalize what He had told them over and over again, how can we expect our brothers and sisters to hear and grasp everything we say the first time we present it? Patience requires that we will repeat it as many times as necessary, without exasperation and without condescension. Just like our Shepherd does for us.

Choosing To Hope

When the road stretches out of sight and the challenges present themselves in relentless succession, we can lose sight of the hope we have been given. When we cannot see what God is doing, we can forget that He is still active. But our Shepherd's Word reassures us:

Commit your way to the Lord,
Trust also in Him, and He will do it. (Psalm 37:5)

I have often prayed a prayer like this one I wrote in my journal a year ago:

Lord, I know that You are at work in the lives of those around me. Thank You for the glimpses You're giving me. But is it okay to ask for even more? That I would not only see these small seeds planted but buds springing up and flourishing into vibrant lives full of Your Spirit?

It is okay to ask: the Lord has countless times answered such prayers of mine with gracious evidences of His faithfulness. However, there are just as many times when He has veiled my eyes. These are the times when patience has built in me a faith-filled heart of expectancy. In God's Word, patience is always accompanied by hope:

Therefore be patient, brethren, until the coming of the Lord. The farmer waits for the precious produce of the soil, being patient about it until it gets the early and late rains. You too be patient; strengthen your hearts, for the coming of the Lord is near. (James 5:7-8)

Strengthen your hearts, fellow worship undershepherds. Take hope. He *will* bring us all to where He wants us to be, as we continue on with patience.

A Conversation With My Shepherd

My life

Is there a member of my teams or my congregation that I have been insensitive to? Will You show me how I can do better?

Is there any person or group in my church that I am being quick to judge or refusing to show grace to?

What things are You asking me to patiently communicate over and over to my teams and my congregation?

Here is an area of ministry where I need You to open my eyes and help me see more of what You are doing:

Your Word

What reason do You give in Romans 15:1-2 for being patient with my fellow sheep as I carry out my ministry?

Your Word (continued)

What does Your response to the two men in Luke 24:13–30 teach me about being patient when my brothers and sisters seem slow to learn?

What hope do You give me from Psalm 37:3–7 as I seek to have patience with the work that still lies ahead?

Your thought for me

What is one thing You want me to remember from today's lesson?

My heart before You

(Talk to your Shepherd about all or part of the following.) Here's what I need to confess to You; how I want to praise You; what I hope to do with what You've shown me; what I need You to help me with:

DAY 3: PREPPING OUR HEART BEFORE WE MOVE FORWARD

Tomorrow we will begin applying patience specifically to the **W**'s on the chart. Today, let's prepare our hearts for that task.

The volume of work that lies ahead of us may seem daunting. If you are like me, as you stare at all those **W**'s, you may find yourself caught somewhere between hopefulness and fear, eagerness and dismay. I remind you, as I remind myself, that the chart is intended to be a tool of *encouragement*. My prayer is that the chart will not be used as a "how-to" but as a "way to": a way to be; a way to think; a way to position our heart as we consider the work ahead.

Patience is the way we will be able to overcome any fear or dismay as we face these tasks. Do you remember our definition of patience from Day 1? *The ability to rest in God's faithfulness to bring us to where He wants us to be, in His perfect way and in His impeccable timing, no matter how long the process or how circuitous the route.*

Does resting—even as you work, or even as you wait for the Shepherd's go-ahead—feel impossible to you? It often does to me. So how can we ready our hearts for patience as we look toward the work ahead of us? Let's consider three ways, from the mouth of our Shepherd Himself.

Our Shepherd's Voice: "Determine to filter all your plans through My will."

James 4:13–15 instructs us:

Come now, you who say, "Today or tomorrow we will go to such and such a city, and spend a year there and engage in business and make a profit." Yet you do not know what your life will be like tomorrow. You are just a vapor that appears for a little while and then vanishes away. Instead, you ought to say, "If the Lord wills, we will live and also do this or that."

Come now, we worship leaders who say, "Today I will arrive at a good understanding of how to motivate my teams to practice more" or, "This Sunday my team and I will lead worship in such a way that our congregation will have no choice but to enter in wholeheartedly." Come now, these are not *our* goals and plans. Our churches do not belong to *us*.

We do not know how long God will call us to our present ministry. We do not know what He will accomplish through us while we are here. Like those generations of sheep and shepherds on the hills of Iona, seasons and centuries come and go. We have no control over what eternal things are wrought in those spaces of time. But we follow the One who does. We need not fret about the outcome, and we must not presume upon it. He will lead us perfectly, all in His good time.

Our Shepherd's Voice: "Determine to keep your gaze on Me."

2 Corinthians 3:18 reminds us:

But we all, with unveiled face, beholding as in a mirror the glory of the Lord, are being transformed into the same image from glory to glory, just as from the Lord, the Spirit.

This has long been my life verse. I want nothing more for myself than to resemble Jesus more closely at the end of my years than I do now. I want nothing more for my church than to be continually growing into a people who reflect Christ's character as we worship and love and serve.

Sometimes I have trouble seeing the image emerge. I feel like this poet:

Am I new-minted by thy stamp indeed?
　　Mine eyes are dim; I cannot clearly see.
Be thou my spectacles that I may read
　　Thine image and inscription stamped on me.[33]

But God's Word never fails; we can believe He is stamping Christ's image on us even when our eyes are too dim to see it. If we and our churches will keep our eyes on our Lord, He will fulfill His promise to refine us from one glory to the next. As Matt Redman says, our God who blazes with power and holiness also "burns with a heart of love for His people, longing to usher each one of us into deeper levels of glory.

It is there that we are transformed ever more into His likeness." [34] There is no need for discouragement, no need for panic. There is no need to take matters into our own hands. *He* will do the work in us.

Our Shepherd's Voice: "Determine to not lose heart."

Galatians 6:9–10 encourages us:

Let us not lose heart in doing good, for in due time we will reap if we do not grow weary. So then, while we have opportunity, let us do good to all people, and especially to those who are of the household of the faith.

There is much room for improvement in my church and in myself. I know that the need for refinement is a given for any Christian and for any church. Then why don't I readily admit my shortcomings and embrace opportunities to improve? Why is my first instinct often to become downhearted? Is it that I'm afraid I will be "found out," as if it's news to anyone that I am not perfect, or that my congregation has a long way to go?

Downheartedness is an enemy of patience. It ruins resolve and hampers hope; it distorts our perspective and obscures our view; it tempts us to despair of any good outcome and lures us to give up. Servants of Christ have always faced such seasons of temptation. This is why the Holy Spirit inspired Paul to pen the above words to his fellow Christians in Galatia a couple thousand years ago.

"In due time" we will reap, if we patiently work and do not give up. God knew I would need this promise. He knew you would need it too.

The Right Heart For The Right Work

There's hard work ahead, no denying it. I assume your chart does not consist of all **K**'s and **P**'s. Mine doesn't either. There are several things to consider as we delve into those **W**'s:

- Some of the work is heart work, unquantifiable and resistant to a straight-ahead approach. Some of it is more concrete, lending itself easily to goals and timelines and checklists.
- Some of the work cries out for attention *now,* while other parts of it can wait awhile.
- Some of us may be in seasons of vision-casting and global thinking. Others of us may be more in survival mode.
- Our Shepherd will lead some of us to address the work in small pieces, others of us to approach it more globally.
- He will direct some of us to take action on our own, others of us to sit with our pastor or leadership team to determine what the priorities are. (Chapter 11 will discuss at length the value of leadership teams.)

Again, this is not a how-to book. Its purpose is not to give you a list of things to jump up and do the moment you finish reading the last page. The reason I write this book is to remind worship undershepherds to listen to their Shepherd and take heart.

I trust that today's devotional will help you keep in view the three Scriptures discussed above. I urge you to plant them firmly in your heart; they will be an invaluable encouragement to you as you ready your heart for patience in the work that lies ahead.

A Conversation With My Shepherd

My life

Here's how I feel when I look at all those **W**'s I believe You are asking me to work toward:

Is there any goal I have for my ministry where it is difficult for me to say "if the Lord wills"?

Thank You for the image of Yourself You are stamping on me in this area of my life:

What is something You are doing in my church right now that can cause me to take heart?

Your Word

How can Your words in James 4:13-15 help me feel restful even as I plan and work?

What is Your promise I can claim—for myself, my co-laborers, and my congregation—from 2 Corinthians 3:18?

Your Word (continued)

What motivation do You give me in Galatians 6:9-10 to keep pressing on even when I am not seeing immediate results?

Your thought for me

What is one thing You want me to remember from today's lesson?

My heart before You

(Talk to your Shepherd about all or part of the following.) Here's what I need to confess to You; how I want to praise You; what I hope to do with what You've shown me; what I need You to help me with:

DAY 4: PATIENTLY LOOKING TO MY SHEPHERD TO BRING *ME* TO WHERE I NEED TO BE

Today, we begin to look at the patience that is needed as we consider all the **W**'s on our chart—all those things we believe can and should be changed as our Shepherd leads us to address them.

I asked my niece Audrey one day if she had any insight into this subject of patience as a worship leader. Audrey, a worship leader herself, answered: "Aunt Jeanelle, I think it's important to remember that the people in our churches need to have patience with *us* too."

She was absolutely right. Sometimes it's the undershepherd who needs to be brought to the right place. This is where we will start.

Looking To Ourselves First

A couple of days before my husband, my daughter, and I visited the island of Iona, we spent some time in the city of Edinburgh. We had been told not to miss the beautiful little hike up the 822-foot hill in town known as Arthur's Seat. So we set out one afternoon on the dirt path leading to its summit. As we walked, dark clouds began to gather, and a thick fog rolled in. By the time we reached the top, we could not see 20 feet ahead of us. We had hoped to take a photo of the panoramic view to document our successful climb, but the only picture we brought home was of a round stone marker etched with spokes pointing to all the places we *could* have seen had it not been for the unfortunate weather.

Soaking wet from the rain that had begun to fall, we made our way back down the path. This time it seemed much more slippery and steep; less direct, more winding. And grass had sprung up over the path in the time since we had walked up.

This last fact did seem strange to us, but we were too intent on heading back to warm clothes and a hearty meal to stop and ask ourselves what the explanation could be (or whether it would be important for us to know, for that matter).

By the time we passed some ancient ruins we had not seen earlier and a flock of sheep that also had somehow escaped our notice, the sad truth was inescapable: disoriented by the fog, we had worked our way down the wrong side of the hill.

We could swear those sheep were laughing at us.

Sometimes the sheep get to where they need to be sooner than we do. This can be quite sobering to someone who is trying very hard to lead them well. It can be embarrassing (I found myself blushing a bit in front of those sheep). It can also be time-consuming, as it might force us to backtrack and regroup. But pretending all is well with us will not make us better undershepherds. We will never be the leaders our Shepherd is calling us to be if we're not willing to stop and check our own progress along the way.

This is how we will be worthy of the sheep's trust. Rory Noland writes:

> My challenge is this: [whatever it is you want your church to get better at, make sure **you** are getting better at the same thing.] In other words, be an example of what you want your church to become. Paul wrote, "We put no stumbling block in anyone's path, so that our ministry will not be discredited" (2 Corinthians 6:3).[35]

As undershepherds of God's precious sheep, we owe it to them to first examine ourselves. As we look through the lens of the Holy Spirit at all the **W**'s we've written for ourselves, we must ask continually: In what ways can I be a better leader?

A Worship Undershepherd's Need For Vision

One of the first things the Holy Spirit showed me as a new director of our church's worship ministry was that I needed a vision for where we were headed. As I sought His counsel, praying about it with my husband and our worship leadership team, He showed me some of the things He was calling us to be as a worshiping church:

- A church of all ages, worshiping together
- A church showing grace to one another as we worship

- A church whose worship is anchored in the Word
- A church growing in our understanding of wholehearted worship
- A church recognizing the value of worship, past and present
- A church led in worship by people who are sincere, humble, and invitational
- A church raising up new generations of worship ministry servants

This vision proved to be an indispensable filter for me as I worked toward goals and made decisions. It also helped me to know what were the important things to communicate to my congregation and my teams.

Much as I would have liked my worship leadership team to live and breathe worship ministry as I did, bubbling over with inspired dreams and working toward them with inexhaustible fervor, I learned that, ultimately, God held *me* responsible for casting and carrying the vision. Not that the others weren't involved in the process. But, as the undershepherd of this ministry, I was called to keep the vision in front of us even when others lost sight of it. This is what I had signed up for.

However, I had far to go in learning how to effectively direct us toward the vision. As my passion for the vision grew, so did my impatience toward people who did not share it. Along with impatience came bouts of discouragement and cynicism. On top of this, my inability to help move us toward the ideal as quickly as I had hoped caused me to doubt myself.

It is easy to be deceived by Satan's lies when we are in such a vulnerable state of mind. He would have us believe that we will never become the leaders we should be. He would be delighted to see us stop trying. He would consider it a coup to get us to focus more on the slowness of our journey than on the good things God is doing in us along the way.

Fortunately, our Shepherd has better plans for us.

A Worship Undershepherd's Need For Tools

Our brothers and sisters are counting on us to move the worship ministry forward; our Shepherd is too. This is why He has put good tools at our disposal—tools that will encourage, energize, and inspire us; tools that will hone and grow us; tools that will contribute to the arsenal of skills required for this eternally significant ministry we are called to.

Our Shepherd has promised to provide every single thing we need for the ministry He's called us to:

Seeing that His divine power has granted to us everything pertaining to life and godliness, through the true knowledge of Him who called us by His own glory and excellence. (2 Peter 1:3)

He longs to equip us for this work. If we ask Him, He will lead us to the tools that will equip us best in our individual ministries. Some of the tools that have been most valuable for me (besides prayer and the Word) are:

- *People whose wisdom and heart I trust:* God is faithful to bring people into our lives who can come alongside us with counsel, prayer and support.
- *Good books:* I find my motivation sparked and my vision expanded when I read books about worship, ministry, theology, art, history, leadership, and the lives of fellow believers.
- *Good magazines:* The articles in *Worship Leader Magazine* have been especially helpful to me, in both their philosophical and practical discussions of worship ministry.
- *Worship conferences (corporate worship):* There is something soul-filling about worshiping with hundreds of people of like mind and being led by musicians who possess different giftings than I.
- *Worship conferences (workshops):* I've come away from these workshops with boatloads of information and encouragement that I can take home and apply to both my ministry and my music.

- *Worshiping at other churches:* Not only do I find ideas I can use in my own ministry, but my appreciation for the family of God as a whole broadens.
- *Listening to music of various genres:* This expands my understanding of different types of music, and it inspires me to try new things musically with my teams.
- *Music lessons:* Taking guitar and drum lessons has helped me to expand my musical abilities and communicate better musically with those who play these instruments on the team.

As we commit ourselves to being the best undershepherds we can be, it will take hard work; it will take time; and it will take patience. Perhaps it is through being patient with the work our Shepherd is doing in us that we will learn to be patient with the work He is doing in the lives of *those around us.* On Day 5, we will discuss patience toward our teams and our congregations.

A Conversation With My Shepherd

My life

Out of all the **W**'s I wrote on the chart for myself, are there one or two that You are leading me toward first?

What are some aspects of the vision You are giving me for my ministry? (If I don't have a vision, can You help me start thinking of one?)

What is one tool I can make better use of as I patiently work toward improving as a worship leader (either from the list in today's reading or some other tool not listed)?

Your Word

According to 2 Corinthians 6:3, why is it worth the effort to make sure I myself am becoming the undershepherd You want me to be?

What beautiful promises do You give me in 2 Peter 1:2-3?

Your Word (continued)

What are some of the things You are working to build in me, according to 2 Peter 1:4-7?

As You patiently build these qualities in me, what will be the result in my ministry and in my life (2 Peter 1:8)?

Your thought for me

What is one thing You want me to remember from today's lesson?

My heart before You

(Talk to your Shepherd about all or part of the following.) Here's what I need to confess to You; how I want to praise You; what I hope to do with what You've shown me; what I need You to help me with:

DAY 5: PATIENTLY LOOKING TO MY SHEPHERD TO BRING *OTHERS* TO WHERE THEY NEED TO BE

Our Worship Teams

Thursday night—worship team rehearsal. I arrive early on this particular Thursday night, a cup of caffeine firmly in hand. I have prepared well ahead of time: transitions and tempos—check! Corrections to visuals—check! Music handed out earlier—check! Prayed-up—check!

Everyone arrives on time and in good spirits. I feel confident we will finish early.

After sound checks, we start right in on a song that will be accompanied by a video of images and lyrics. Though we have never done this before, and we have no in-ear monitors or click tracks, I feel confident. We have a capable and willing drummer, and I have worked it out ahead of time:

1) The drummer starts with 6 cymbal taps
2) The visual tech hits "play" on tap #5
3) The keyboardist begins on measure 2
4) The pianist (me) begins on pickup to measure 6
5) The drummer keeps us religiously to a tempo of MM 62
6) We all remember how many beats between each verse, chorus, and interlude.

Nothing to it. We begin what I assume will be a single run-through.

Forty-five minutes later we finally get in synch with the video. The practice has gone something like this:

Me: "Okay, we all know what to do. Drums begin."

(Musical intro, vocals start singing. Four lines in:)

Lead vocalist: "The words are coming up too late."

Me: "Hmm. Let's try again."

(Same thing)

Visual tech: "Maybe the computer video speed is set too fast. I'll change it."

*(I'm thinking, "Why can't there just be a normal default speed?" But
    then I am technologically challenged, so what do I know?)*
Me: "Let's try another time."
(We get to verse 2. The drummer stops.)
Me: "What's going on?"
Drummer: "It seems to be speeding up and slowing down. I'm
    trying to stay with it."
Me: "Well, I know it works perfectly at MM 62 if we can just
    stay at that tempo. Let's try again."
(We get to verse 3 this time. All the vocalists look very confused.)
Vocalist: "It's not working. Have the video tech push 'start' on
    cymbal tap #4 instead."
(We try this. Nope.)
Another vocalist: "How about cymbal tap #6?"
(We try this. Nope again.)
Third vocalist: "Can we try #5.75?"
(I think she's being facetious, but I'm not sure.)

After several more false starts, we finally get it figured out. My
hopes of finishing early have vanished. We stumble through the rest of
rehearsal, every one of us trying valiantly to maintain a gracious spirit
toward one another.

We worship leaders need patience with our teams, just as they need
patience with us. Some rehearsals progress flawlessly; others, like this
one, flounder comically. Some seasons see the teams improving by leaps
and bounds, while other seasons find us limping along.

There are principles to be gleaned from this fiasco that apply to
everything we do as worship leaders trying to lead our teams along:
- We need to know where we are headed.
- We need to be able to communicate the plan.
- We need to be able to communicate the reason for the plan.
- We need to be patient when others are slow to understand
  and follow the plan.
- We need to be open and vulnerable when we are struggling
  so that the team knows we are with them, not above them.
- We need to trust God to get us there so that we don't give
  up in frustration.

That Sunday morning, as the team gathered before the first service, I confessed to them how inept I had felt at rehearsal. I told them how I had regretted keeping them so late. I shared with them how the Lord had spoken to me in the days since, reminding me that He was in control and that He would get us to where we needed to be as we worshiped with the congregation.

In my years as a worship leader, I've had some successes, and I've had many failures. Along the way I've learned much about how to patiently help my teams get to where they need to be. Here are some of the things my Shepherd has taught me:

- *Pray for the teams, and pray with them:* Pray for them to trust in the Lord's plan even when things feel discouraging. Pray for wisdom in helping them work toward all those **W's** on the chart.

- *Teach them, and learn along with them:* One way to do this is to dedicate some rehearsal time to discussing books the team is reading together.

- *Model a life of worship:* Just as a parent cannot expect his child to follow Jesus if he himself is not following Jesus, neither can we expect our teams to have pure hearts of worship if we are not cultivating our own.

- *Communicate the vision, and communicate it often:* Remember all those things God showed me early on about who we were to be as a worshiping church (see Day 4)? I needed to speak frequently of these to the worship teams so that they would remember what we were about.

- *Applaud and encourage them:* Not just for how well they play or sing, though a well-timed sincere compliment can spur someone on for a very long time. Commend them for other things: faithfulness, servant-heartedness, timeliness, diligence, sacrifice, and kindness.

- *Help team members find their niche:* I love helping team members find their place on the team and seeing them prosper in that place. But sometimes I have to tell someone that they do not belong in the place they think they belong. It tears me apart to do this, but I know they will find more joy in fulfilling the call God gives them than in trying to fit into another one.

- *Evaluate with them:* Talk with the team members following the service. Ask them: Could the team have done anything better? Did team members receive any comments, positive or negative, about the service? What blessed the team members during the service?

- *Inspire them and train them:* Take the worship teams to conferences. Plan special gathering times and retreats. Use these times to brainstorm, discuss the future of the ministry, divide into workshops, pray, and worship together.

- *Mentor them:* Mentoring is not only for current team members but for potential ones as well. Take a whole summer to meet weekly with kids in the youth group who want to learn more about worship ministry. Work with a worship intern. Spend time with specific individuals on the team that God has placed on your heart (men with men, women with women).

Does all this take work? Absolutely. But the reward of seeing our teams grow in their ability to serve the Lord with gladness and skill, learning how to love their church family and each other along the way, far outweighs the sacrifice of time and effort we put into it. It will be worth it.

Our Congregation

Having patience with our congregation is different from having patience with our teams. The people sitting in the pews on Sunday morning have not been preparing worship music throughout the week. They haven't seen the songs ahead of time. They haven't arrived at the crack of dawn to prepare for worship. They are not all musical. Many of them consider other ministries in the church more important. They have not read the worship books we have read or gone to the conferences we've gone to. Not all of them place worship as a high priority in their lives. Not all of them are even Christians.

As we consider this, the *first* thing it should prompt us to do is *regard them with compassion*. I think of how Jesus viewed the people around Him. Mark tells us:

> When Jesus went ashore, He saw a large crowd, and He felt compassion
> for them because they were like sheep without a shepherd...
> (Mark 6:34a)

Our brothers and sisters have much to learn from the Shepherd, as do we. We must serve them with compassion, never looking down on them when they are slow to come along in their understanding of worship. They may be light years ahead of us in other areas of spirituality.

The *second* thing it should prompt us to do is *pray for them*. All the good undershepherds of Scripture prayed for the sheep in their care. Moses did (Exodus 32:11-13). Elijah did (1 Kings 18:36-37). Daniel did (Daniel 9:15-19). Paul did (Philippians 1:9-11).

As we view our fellow sheep with compassion, praying for them will be a delight and a privilege. On many Saturday mornings I have entered the dark sanctuary and brought my church family before the Lord. On Sunday mornings, the worship teams and I do the same thing. After sound checks and before practice, we take a few minutes to disperse throughout the sanctuary, praying for our beloved brothers and sisters who will soon be joining us in worship.

The *third* thing it should prompt us to do is *teach them*. Just as Jesus, when He saw the crowds and had compassion on them, "began to teach them many things" (Mark 6:34), so too must we show the same intentionality with the crowds He places in our care. As the undershepherds of His sheep, we must communicate with them what God expects of all worshipers. We must communicate with them the vision for our church. We must communicate with them why we do what we do as a church family in worship. We must communicate clearly, and we must communicate tirelessly. It is the only way we will move ahead with all those **W**'s. Here are a few ways we can communicate with our congregation:

- *Communicate during the worship service:* Draw their attention to lyrics and Scriptures; share something the teams have read together recently; pray prayers that reflect a true heart of worship; tell them the purpose of various elements of the service.

- *Communicate through media:* Print out lyrics for the congregation to take home; put thoughts about worship on the overhead screen; use the church website or newsletter to communicate things you believe are important for the congregation to understand; direct your congregation to worship websites such as worshipminute.com.

- *Communicate through classes:* In the new members' class, talk about the scriptural view of worship; offer a Sunday School class on the subject of worship.

- *Communicate through conferences and special speakers:* Sometimes someone else can say the same thing we've been saying to our congregation, but because it's said by someone different, people hear it with fresh ears.

- *Communicate in conversation:* Even the most casual of conversations can impact people. As we spend time with our brothers and sisters in the hallways, at gatherings, or in homes, it is important to be attentive to opportunities to choose gracious words that display a heart of worship.

The Sure Result Of Patience

Have you ever heard someone say, "Be careful when you pray for patience"? They mean that God might answer by putting us in difficult situations where our patience is tried. Friends, He *will* put us in situations that require patience, whether we ask for it or not. As worship undershepherds, we are daily given occasions to grow in patience as we lead His sheep on this journey of worship. Rather than seeing these as impediments to our ministry, how much better to view them as opportunities to grow in faithfulness and to give praise to our God who will finish His good work in all of us.

There's much work to be done: in our teams, in our congregations, and in us. It will take time, and it won't be easy. The good news is that we follow a Shepherd of infinite patience who promises that our efforts won't be in vain.

> *Therefore, my beloved brethren, be steadfast, immovable, always abounding in the work of the Lord, knowing that your toil is not in vain in the Lord.* (I Corinthians 15:58)

A Conversation With My Shepherd

My life

Out of all the **W**'s I wrote on the chart for my *teams*, are there one or two that You are leading me toward first?

Out of all the **W**'s I wrote on the chart for my *congregation*, are there one or two that You are leading me toward first?

What do I need to learn from You about showing patience to my *teams*?

What do I need to learn from You about showing patience to my *congregation*?

My life (continued)

Do I see occasions for patience as impediments to my ministry or as opportunities to trust You to finish Your good work?

Your Word

As Your worship undershepherd, what can I learn from the heart You showed toward Your sheep (Mark 6:34)?

What can You teach me from Philippians 1:9-11 about how to pray for my brothers and sisters as I patiently look to You to work in their lives?

According to 1 Corinthians 15:58, what is it that You ask of me as I consider the work You've given me to do?

Your thought for me

What is one thing You want me to remember from today's lesson?

My heart before You

(Talk to your Shepherd about all or part of the following.) Here's what I need to confess to You; how I want to praise You; what I hope to do with what You've shown me; what I need You to help me with:

A PRAYER TO PRAY

Patient Shepherd, thank You for never giving up on me or my church family. Thank You for leading us down sure paths toward worthy goals of Your design. Thank You for taking us from one degree of Christlikeness to the next. Thank You for promising that there will be a good result if we carry on.

There is so much work to be done, and sometimes I question whether You will get us where we need to be. Please forgive me when my faith fails. Please strengthen me when my faithfulness falters.

Will You replace my doubt with trust, my lethargy with devotion?

As Your undershepherd, I long to see Your sheep arrive at good pastures of worship. I have far to go, and so do they. Will You help me to patiently lead them, as You bring us all there?

CHAPTER 9

OUR SHEPHERD SPEAKS SUBMISSION

DAY 1: IT STARTS WITH THE HEART

When my husband walked in the door one night a few years ago, I could see it on his face: battle-weariness. This gentle man with a tender shepherd's heart, a peacemaker by nature, had just come from an elders meeting. He loved these men who carried the weight of the flock with him. They were his friends: godly men of integrity. Men of prayer. Men who cared deeply about the well-being of our congregation.

Men, he had assumed, who were at peace with the trajectory of worship our church was on. True, some of the men were more traditional and reticent to embrace the newer songs, but vehement discussions of substance and style had been put to rest long ago. Now, it had seemed, they were in agreement that God had brought us to a good place in worship; a place where He was being glorified, and we were being edified.

When I greeted Greg that night, I immediately knew his assumption had been challenged, in a heart-rending way. An intense discussion during the meeting had revealed foundational philosophical differences over worship. These differences went deeper than music choices and service flow; they went to the heart of what it means to be a congregation that worships together.

There was strong disagreement between the men over the answers to very basic questions: What priority does God place on corporate worship? Are scriptural examples of corporate worship intended to be taken as rules of practice? Is the sole purpose of corporate worship to lift up the name of the Lord, or does it also include drawing near to the Lord, hearing from His Spirit, and encouraging one another? Does it matter if we sing or not? Is worship music primarily a prelude to the sermon?

As Greg sat on the couch with me and shared about the meeting, our hearts were heavy. God had brought our church a long distance in worship, teaching us patiently and protecting us from division. It seemed clear that He had been forming us into a congregation that increasingly understood what it meant to worship in spirit and in truth; furthermore, we had been learning how to love one another as we worshiped together. Was this growth to be undone?

That night we felt, like few times before, that there was a battle going on for the soul of our church. Not a human battle, where one side was right and the other side wrong. No, this was a spiritual battle, in spiritual places. Angels and demons, forces of darkness and light, locked in conflict.

This conflict was on three fronts. The first front was a contest over whether we would be a church whose worship was pleasing to God as He intended it to be for this body of believers. The second front was a clash over whether we would be a church that loves one another and preserves the unity of the Spirit no matter what our differences are. The third front was a war within our own souls over whether, as undershepherds of Christ's precious sheep, we would be willing to lay aside some of our deeply-treasured values so that we could serve them better.

We were confused as to how to proceed.

Was God asking Greg, as senior pastor, to pick up his sword and lead the charge toward what he believed with all his heart was the right vision for our church? Or was God asking him to lay down his sword and wait to see what would happen, opening up the very real possibility that we would become a church whose worship was far different from what he had envisioned?

Was God asking me, as director of worship ministry, to hold fast, continuing to design worship sets in the way I felt He had been leading me? Was I to keep communicating to my co-laborers and my congregation what I believed to be the scriptural view of worship, or was He asking me to be quiet for a while and take a couple of steps back?

We prayed fervently: "Lord, do NOT let us divide this church; that would be Satan's victory. Though we feel afraid right now, we trust You to preserve this body of believers as You always have. If You ask us to continue on our present course, we will do it (though there might be painful fallout). If You ask us to give up our ideals and let others determine the course, we will do it (though it would mean releasing our vision and perhaps finding that our vision has been wrong). If You ask us to leave our church family, we will do it (though our hearts would break)."

Our Shepherd's Voice: "Submit to Me first."

Rarely had we been so aware of the need to respond well to a situation, and rarely had we been so confused about what "responding well" meant. As we leaned in close to hear what our Shepherd was saying to us, we heard one directive, unmistakable and unambiguous: Submit. To Me.

We won't hear Him without a submissive heart

As we sat on our couch that evening, desperate for a word of encouragement, a word of direction—*any* word at all—He made clear that we would never be able to hear Him if we did not first submit our will completely to His. If we gave credence to our own desires at the expense of His desires, our ears would become too clogged to catch what He was saying to us.

It's like conversations I sometimes have with my daughter. She works in downtown Chicago, and we often talk while she takes a walk during her lunch break. I have purchased a good set of ear buds so that I can hear her well. Yet, even with the ear buds shoved deep into my ears, her words can be obscured amidst the honking horns, racing trains, animated conversations, street musicians, and blustery winds of those Chicago streets.

The same thing can happen when we try to listen to our Shepherd. Our ideals, goals, and presumptions can provide such cacophonous sound interference that we cannot hear His voice above the clatter.

Hearing our Shepherd's heart for the Church

As undershepherds given the charge of bringing Christ's sheep together in worship, there is too much at stake *not* to hear Him well. Listen to what was on His heart as He prayed for the church the night before He died:

> *"I do not ask on behalf of these alone, but for those also who believe in Me through their word; that they may all be one; even as You, Father, are in Me and I in You, that they also may be in Us, so that the world may believe that You sent Me."* (John 17:20-21)

Christ's ardent prayer for us was that we would be one so that He would be known. If this was the one thing near and dear to Jesus' heart, it is the one thing Satan will thrash furiously to prevent. Though Jesus assured us that He would build His church and the gates of hell would not overpower it (Matthew 16:18), Satan is committed to trying anyway.

This is why Paul, in his parting words to the elders of the Ephesian church, said:

> *Be on guard for yourselves and for all the flock, among which the Holy Spirit has made you overseers, to shepherd the church of God which He purchased with His own blood.* (Acts 20:28)

How do we guard ourselves against such a formidable enemy? James 4:7 gives an answer: *"Submit* therefore to *God.* Resist the devil and he will flee from you"* (emphasis added). We undershepherds cannot hope to resist this hostile adversary if we are not first wholly submitted to our Shepherd.

Why? Because if we are not listening to our Shepherd with a heart ready to receive everything He tells us, no matter how difficult, then we leave ourselves vulnerable to the lies of the enemy. Satan is subtle, and he is clever. He will employ every scheme in his attempt to fill our ears with fiction and deafen us to the truth.

One way he will try to clog our ears is by convincing us to fight the wrong battles. As worship leaders, the irony is not lost on us that music, a primary means God has given to unite His people in worship, can also be the most divisive thing. Leave it up to Satan to turn a fragrant offering into an odious one. Our Shepherd may be saying to us, "There is murmuring among My sheep right now, and they are in danger of being divided. I need you to step up and show them how to love each other." But the only thing our ears may be able to hear is the call of our own prized worship ideal drawing us to secure it at any price. Wouldn't it be an ingenious trick of Satan to use our vision of worship as a decoy?

Another way he will try to impair our hearing is by duping us into believing that the fight is against each other. While it's true that people may stand in the way of God's plan for a church, the ultimate battle is not against our brothers and sisters:

> *For our struggle is not against flesh and blood, but against the rulers, against the powers, against the world forces of this darkness, against the spiritual forces of wickedness in the heavenly places.* (Ephesians 6:12)

If we believe that our fellow sheep are the enemy, we will be tempted to wage a holy war on them in an ill-advised attempt at achieving better worship. Rather than girding ourselves with truth and peace, we will come out fighting with our bare fists against a phantom enemy of our own making.

Satan will also try to stop up our ears by luring us into making worship itself an idol. Anything can become an idol, even very good things. Having a strong vision of worship for our churches is an excellent thing. (We discussed this in Chapter 8.) But if we try to preserve this vision at any cost, we will come up empty-handed: both our vision and our church will suffer. After all, how can our vision of God-honoring worship be realized if we love the vision more than we love God Himself? And how can our church thrive if we love the vision more than we love Christ's precious sheep? By idolizing worship itself, we will have put a worthy goal in front of the one goal that trumps all others: Love. Love for God and love for one another.

Are we submitted enough to our Shepherd to pray the following words, even about the worthy goals we have for our church?

The dearest idol I have known,
Whate'er that idol be;
Help me to tear it from thy throne,
And worship only thee [36]

A Conversation With My Shepherd

My life

Is there any area of my ministry where You are asking me to either "lead a charge" or "hold fast and just be quiet"? Whose voice am I listening to about this—Yours or the enemy's?

Is there anything You are asking me to submit to in my church that has the potential to cause division?

Will You show me if there is any way I am making my worship ministry an idol?

Your Word

What would You like to show me about Your heart for Your church from the prayer You prayed in John 17?

Your Word (continued)

What do the following Scriptures teach me about how to carry out my role as undershepherd of the sheep You've purchased with Your own blood?

Acts 20:28

James 4:7

Ephesians 6:12

Your thought for me

What is one thing You want me to remember from today's lesson?

My heart before You

(Talk to your Shepherd about all or part of the following.) Here's what I need to confess to You; how I want to praise You; what I hope to do with what You've shown me; what I need You to help me with:

DAY 2: SUBMITTING TO OUR FELLOW SHEEP

God has given us the sacred trust of guiding our churches into worship that honors Him. He is pleased when our hearts pulsate with joy over the vision He has given us for worship in our church body. It is imperative that we keep this vision clearly in view so that we don't desert it at the first sign of resistance.

However, this is *His* vision. It belongs in *His* hands, not ours. We don't want Him to have to pry it loose from our tight fists, do we? This was the very question Greg and I wrestled with that night after the elders' meeting.

Holding Our Vision Loosely For The Sake Of The Sheep

It is a tough responsibility, this open-handed holding of the vision. When people oppose our vision, how easy it might seem to either toss it out in defeated resignation or hang onto it in bulldog defiance. But to carry it with both hopefulness and a willingness to let it go—now that takes courage.

If we are to hold onto *anything* with utter tenacity, it is this admonition from the apostle Paul:

> *Therefore I, the prisoner of the Lord, implore you to walk in a manner worthy of the calling with which you have been called, with all humility and gentleness, with patience, showing tolerance for one another in love,* **being diligent to preserve the unity of the Spirit in the bond of peace.** (Ephesians 4:1-3, emphasis added)

As worship undershepherds, we are to guard the unity of the Spirit with our lives. We are to submit every one of our ideals, every single goal, and everything that brings us joy to the *greater* joy of seeing God's people loving one another well as they worship Him in spirit and in truth. This is the only way Jesus' prayer for us will be fulfilled.

How I would love a clear-cut formula for knowing when to hold onto a vision and when to release it. How much comfort I would find in a definitive set of instructions for knowing when to let the objections of my fellow sheep persuade me to change and when to set those objections aside in favor of plowing through with the vision. There are no such well-defined directives; only our Shepherd knows whether it is time to release or time to hold fast. This is why we must have unobstructed ears to hear and receive what He is telling us.

I wonder if the leaders of the Ephesian church had to grapple with this issue of deciding when to promote their vision of worship and when to sacrifice some of it for the unity of the body? I wonder if that's why Paul juxtaposes worship with submitting to one another in his letter to that church:

> ... but be filled with the Spirit, speaking to one another in psalms and hymns and spiritual songs, singing and making melody with your heart to the Lord; always giving thanks for all things in the name of our Lord Jesus Christ to God, even the Father; **and be subject to one another in the fear of Christ.** (Ephesians 5:18b–21, emphasis added)

Sometimes when I've read this passage, I've carelessly passed over the connection of corporate worship to submission. Submitting to one another in love is an indispensable component of God-pleasing worship. Whether or not our Shepherd asks us to relinquish the vision He's given us, He most certainly asks us to show His sheep the same humble spirit of submissive love He has shown us.

Submitting In Word *And* Deed

When our kids were young, we owned a dog named Koot, an Australian shepherd/blue heeler mix. We had no business bringing him home from the animal shelter and confining him to our tiny suburban back yard. We would often drive up to our house just in time to catch a flash of fur catapulting off our front steps, streaking across the side lawn, and flying over the back porch rail and onto the porch. We would quickly park the car and run to the back porch, only to find Koot resting at the opposite end, an expression of studied innocence plastered on his face.

"Koot. Koooooooooooooot. Where have you been?"

Face now buried in paws.

"Kooooooooooooot. Koot! Come here."

With the slow deliberation of a tortoise, Koot would slink across the porch, paw over paw, hind legs dragging as if useless, until he appeared before us. There he would crouch, the very picture of submission. There he would remain, eyes utterly free of guile, through the entire scolding. (He could probably recite it from memory.)

Koot would stay in this remorseful posture until we walked into the house. Moments later, we would catch a flash of fur out the kitchen window as Koot leapt off the porch in unabashed response to the call of the wild once again.

Koot knew the benefits of confession, but he had no appreciation for the value of repentance. Koot knew how to adopt a persona of docility, but he had no use for a heart of submission.

Aren't we the same way sometimes? We worship leaders can be quite adept at speaking about submitting to the Lord and to each other. We may have learned all the pertinent Scriptures. We may even know how to adopt the most persuasive vocal inflection and facial expression when we speak of it. But in the day-to-day interactions with our brothers and sisters, we reveal what's truly in our hearts. It's not always pretty.

At a family gathering a few years ago, I was talking with my sister about the challenges of worship ministry (she had just accepted a worship leadership role at her own church). I was sharing how it's hard when everyone has a different opinion of what "good" worship is. I gave an example of a visitor who had initiated a discussion with me about music and how he had used some illogical reasoning to try to prove his point of view. I then related to my sister how I had deftly refuted his arguments.

Later that day, my mom took me aside and gently pointed out that my words had sounded judgmental. My immediate internal response was, *But you don't get it. I was just talking, one worship leader to another, about some of the challenging people we have to deal with. And besides, you shouldn't have been listening in anyway.*

But she *had* been listening, as had some of my nieces and nephews. The next day I called her to thank her for pointing out what was obvious to probably everyone in the room but myself: My words had revealed a heart unwilling to submit in love to a fellow believer. They had exposed a heart antithetical to the heart described in these verses:

> *Therefore be imitators of God, as beloved children; and walk in love, just as Christ also loved you and gave Himself up for us, an offering and a sacrifice to God as a fragrant aroma.* (Ephesians 5:1-2)

I had been giving myself up for no one. I had not been loving this man as Christ loved me. My aroma definitely had not been fragrant.

Have you ever noticed how much easier it is to be submissive to the Lord than to other people? How much simpler it is to confess our selfishness to our Father than to live selflessly with our brothers and sisters? Here's the thing about our Shepherd: He is not fooled. Though *we* may believe our hearts are in the right place before Him, *He* knows the truth. And He is wise enough to place us within a local body of believers where we will have plenty of opportunities to see the truth for ourselves.

A Conversation With My Shepherd

My life

Does my heart "pulsate with joy" when I think of what You might be planning to do in the area of worship in my church family?

When people in my church family are opposed to the vision I think You have for us, am I more inclined to give up in defeat, hang on in defiance, or submit to You with hopefulness?

Will You show me some ways I can intentionally pursue "unity of the Spirit in the bond of peace" with the brothers and sisters I worship with?

Will You show me if I have done anything this week to demonstrate a less-than-submissive spirit?

Your Word

According to Ephesians 4:1–3, what things will show that I am walking in a manner worthy of the calling You've given me?

Your Word (continued)

In Ephesians 5:18-21, what is the connection between worshiping You and being submissive to one another?

According to Ephesians 5:1-2, how will I know if I have a heart like Yours in caring for Your sheep?

Your thought for me

What is one thing You want me to remember from today's lesson?

My heart before You

(Talk to your Shepherd about all or part of the following.) Here's what I need to confess to You; how I want to praise You; what I hope to do with what You've shown me; what I need You to help me with:

DAY 3: SUBMISSION TO AUTHORITY—WHY MUST WE DO IT?

Two Kinds Of Submission

That evening after the elders meeting, there were two considerations for my husband and me as we wrestled with what it would mean to respond with a heart of submission. Let me explain.

In the family of Christ we are called to two kinds of submission. In the *first* kind, we will subjugate our desires to someone else's *if this is the best way to love them*. It's the kind of attitude Jesus told His disciples, and us, to have toward everyone:

> ... but whoever wishes to become great among you shall be your servant; and whoever wishes to be first among you shall be slave of all. For even the Son of Man did not come to be served, but to serve, and to give His life a ransom for many. (Mark 10:43–45)

It's a submission that emanates, purely and simply, from a heart of love. It's this willingness to submit that we are called to have toward *all* people, *all* the time.

In the *second* kind of submission, we will subjugate our desires to someone else's *if they ask us to* (unless what they ask of us is contrary to the principles of the Word). It's the kind of submission we are to have toward those whom God has placed over us as spiritual guardians in the body of Christ:

> Obey your leaders and submit to them, for they keep watch over your souls as those who will give an account. Let them do this with joy and not with grief, for this would be unprofitable for you. (Hebrews 13:17)

This is a submission that emanates from a heart of love (*always* love), but *also* from a resolve to follow the order God has set up for His church.

It was this second kind of submission that stared us hard in the face that evening.

Church Structures Vary; Submission Remains A Constant

The hierarchy of authority in my church may look different from yours, because polity varies from church to church. In some churches, all major decisions are decided by a congregational vote; in others, decisions are under the sole authority of the elders. In some churches, the senior pastor has the final say; in others, he is just one voice among several in authority. In some churches, the pastoral staff is considered elders; in other churches, they are separate from and subject to the elders. Some churches have a denominational hierarchy they must answer to; other churches are completely autonomous.

Whatever model each church follows, there will always be a person or a group of people to whom we are accountable.

Obedience: Good For Our Leaders, Good For Us

We worship leaders may find it fairly easy to follow God's order of authority when those He places over us share the same view of worship that we do, but there may be those over us who hold a different view of worship. They may not have come to accept the vision we believe Christ has given us for our church's worship. How easy is it to submit to *these* people? Can we trust our Shepherd enough to obey them as He commands?

Even as I write this word "obey," it feels strange to me. Archaic, old-school. Stark and cold. Oddly out of place in a church family where all of us sheep are learning together what it means to follow our Shepherd. As an undershepherd myself, I have never been comfortable with the idea that others are called to "obey" me. I much prefer to think of myself as one who comes alongside others to encourage them in their service to our Shepherd.

Yet I do know, from my experience in this role, how helpful it is to me when those I lead have a willing heart of submission. I am most able to serve with confidence and freedom when those under me show their support by following my lead without digging in their heels.

Isn't this the gift I want to give those who are over *me*? I *want* them to lead "with joy and not with grief" so that their service is unhindered by any concern that I will prove to be a stumbling block. It would sadden me if I got in the way of their ability to hear and follow their Shepherd's voice.

Obeying my leaders with a heart of submission is a gift to myself as well. What kind of working relationship would I have with those over me if I followed their lead with a reluctant spirit? What respect would I receive from them? How much freedom would they feel comfortable giving me in my leadership role? Would God honor my efforts for Him if I offered them in direct disregard for His express directive to submit?

I have had the privilege of working under leaders who love the Lord and love His church; leaders who seek with all their hearts to lead with integrity and humility. I hope these are the kind of leaders you serve under. But even the best-intentioned leaders can get it wrong sometimes. They can say no to plans the Lord has given us to carry out. They can ask us to do things that will be a genuine setback to what God has been doing in our midst.

In such situations, we are not held accountable for the final decision. The Scripture from Hebrews quoted earlier tells us that it is those over us who "will give an account."

So, what *does* the Lord hold us accountable for in these circumstances? Faithfulness. Love. Humility. Obedience. We are to seek His direction in all things and to communicate well the vision He gives us, working toward it with all our heart. At the same time, if those over us do not give us the go-ahead, we must submit our will to theirs. Scripture tells us we are to do this "as to the Lord, and not to men" (Ephesians 6:7; also see Colossians 3:23). Ultimately, we are submitting our will to the Father's, because He has asked us to follow them.

If we really believe that Jesus Christ is the ultimate guardian over His church, and that He can take any wrong decision and work it to His glory, we will be able not only to *obey* our leaders but to serve them with *gladness*. There is much joy implied in the mutually respectful relationship described in 1 Thessalonians 5:12-13:

But we request of you, brethren, that you appreciate those who diligently labor among you, and have charge over you in the Lord and give you instruction, and that you esteem them very highly in love because of their work. Live in peace with one another.

If we worship leaders have this heart toward those in authority over us, then the words we speak about them in hallways, in meetings, and over coffee will exude affection. Whether we agree with their decisions or not, the sheep we shepherd will not hear ridicule from our lips, nor will they see us rolling our eyes in exasperation. Our figures of speech will be free of exaggeration and unfair characterization. The stories we relate about our leaders will be full of grace and will only include details they themselves would be willing to share. Any answers we give to questions about their ability to lead will give them the benefit of the doubt. Where there are genuine concerns that need to be acknowledged, these concerns will always be discussed with a spirit of charity.

Paul's words to the Thessalonians are happy words: Appreciate. Diligently. Esteem. Love. Peace. Can you see God just smiling when our working relationships are characterized by such words?

A Conversation With My Shepherd

My life

Who are the spiritual authorities You are asking me to submit to in my church?

Here are some things I'm thankful for about the people You've placed over me:

Will You show me how I can be someone who brings them joy, not grief, as they do their job?

Your Word

What do You tell me in Mark 10:42–45 about the attitude I am to have toward everyone?

Your Word (continued)

From Hebrews 13:17-21, what can You teach me about:

The reasons for submitting to those You've placed over me (verse 17)?

How to pray for those You've placed over me (verse 18)?

According to 1 Thessalonians 5:12-13, what is the attitude You want me to have toward those You've placed over me?

Your thought for me

What is one thing You want me to remember from today's lesson?

My heart before You

(Talk to your Shepherd about all or part of the following.) Here's what I need to confess to You; how I want to praise You; what I hope to do with what You've shown me; what I need You to help me with:

DAY 4: SUBMISSION TO AUTHORITY—WHAT DOES IT LOOK LIKE?

Today, we will look more specifically at what it means to submit to those who have spiritual authority over us in the church. We'll begin with the senior pastor.

Submitting To The Pastor

Most worship leaders answer to their senior pastor. Most churches recognize that God has given their senior pastor oversight over the church as a whole. Most pastors take this responsibility very seriously.

Greg and I have spent a lot of time with pastors and pastors' wives. Every one of them cares deeply about the welfare of their church. When their church is thriving and united in spirit and bearing fruit, they are overjoyed and thankful. When their church is limping along and full of division and exhibiting little fruit, their hearts are heavy. It can't be helped.

In Chapter 2, I referred to 2 Corinthians 11:28-29 as a good description of how worship leaders care about their congregations. It's worth quoting again here, because senior pastors, of all people, carry the whole congregation continually in their hearts:

> *Apart from such external things, there is the daily pressure on me of concern for all the churches. Who is weak without my being weak? Who is led into sin without my intense concern?*

As the wife of a senior pastor, I've come to understand that how I respond to his concerns can either buoy him or deflate him. It does not help to point out weaknesses in our church (or in him) that he is already aware of. It is discouraging to bring concerns to his attention that he can do nothing about. If I do not agree with a decision he's made about something we've discussed, it does him no good for me to take potshots at it when things go awry. Greg needs me to carry the weight of responsibility *with* him, not wield it *against* him.

Your pastor needs this from you as well. Worship leaders are called to submit to their pastor as one who "keeps watch over your soul." As we support and follow this leader whom the Lord holds accountable for us, there are ways we can foster a relationship that is an encouragement to him.

First, we can pray for him. We give our pastor a gift he will treasure when we tell him we are praying for him. It means all the more when we ask *how* we can pray and then follow up later to see how things are going.

Besides praying, we can ask our pastor questions that reflect our heart to serve him. Worship leader Tommy Walker suggests three such questions:

- "How can I serve you?"
- "What does great worship look like to you?"
- "What traits are the most important for a worship leader to cultivate in order to be successful at their position?"[37]

If we ask such questions and listen unguardedly to the answers, we give our pastor the blessing of knowing we are willing to submit to him as the Lord tells us to.

Finally, we can communicate to our pastor that we stand with him by treating him with the same respect we hope to receive from him. Are we affirming him as a person? When we disagree, are we being careful not to second-guess his motives? Do we empathize with the unique position he holds as guardian over the whole church? Do we speak words that show respect for his musical preferences and understanding (or lack of understanding) of music itself? In short, are we committed to showing him the kind of honor he deserves as the undershepherd God has placed over us?

Submitting To Other Spiritual Authorities Over Us

In my church, the worship leader is under the authority of both the pastor and the elders. Our elders are all men who have jobs outside of the church (with the exception of Greg, who is the only pastoral staff included in the elders). They also serve in other capacities within the church.

Church ministry is not their day job, and none of them are involved in the worship ministry. So, when their discussion of worship ministry issues seems to miss the pulse beat of what we do, it can be tempting for me to respond in a passive-aggressive manner or to be dismissive of them, thinking, "What do they know? How much time have they spent thinking and praying about this?"

As I write this chapter, I am intensely mindful of the difficult situations many worship leaders are in. Some of you may serve in churches where those to whom you answer have no understanding of the heart of worship. They may question everything you do. They may stand in the congregation with scowls on their faces. They may talk behind your back.

It has not always been easy for me to lightheartedly and graciously submit to the decisions of our elders, good men though they are. I do not write a single word of this chapter cavalierly. I write with painstaking awareness of the spiritual battle that may have to take place within your heart to submit to your leaders. I write with a firsthand understanding of the faith you may have to muster as you trust the Lord with this ministry you hold so close to your heart.

However, if God is calling us to serve in our present ministries, He is calling us to do it within the parameters He has clearly set forth in His Word: He is calling us to do it with a spirit of loving submission.

Romans 14:19 tells us to "pursue the things which make for peace and the building up of one another." When Greg and I talked that night after the elders' meeting, our thoughts ran all over the place. God, in His kindness, cut through our emotional racket and impressed on us that, no matter what course we took, we must pursue peace. We repeated to each other Paul's admonition: "If possible, so far as it depends on you, be at peace with all men" (Romans 12:18).

We knew this would mean, first and foremost, to love these brothers in Christ, showing them respect with the submissive spirit Christ requires of us. And we knew that one of the best ways to show care for these leaders was to pray for them. Those whom Christ has called to be our undershepherds need our prayers; they count on them.

As Paul asked, with humble simplicity: "Brethren, pray for us" (1 Thessalonians 5:25).

Because worship ministry is my passion, it is natural for me to carry it in my heart and in my mind, praying for it often. Because Greg is my husband, my thoughts and prayers easily and quickly focus on him. But praying for the elders? That is something that takes a little more intentionality. So I try to remember one morning a week to pray for them as I pray for the whole church. I pray that they will be personally encouraged as they serve us. I pray for their families, many of whom are struggling in various ways. I pray for their wisdom and courage. When I pray like this, I see the elders not as a monolithic block that can make or break the worship ministry and the church; rather, I see them as brothers in Christ who care for the sheep as I do.

It blesses our leaders to know that individuals in their church family are lifting them up. But it also blesses them to be able to pray for *us*. When we share with them our own prayer needs, it shows them honor and trust. Depending on how comfortable we are in our relationship with them, we can share specific ministry challenges, personal struggles, or family concerns. It will help them see us not only as worship leaders but also as fellow sheep who are following the Shepherd along with them.

Building this mutual trust paves the way for one more thing that is absolutely necessary for a good working relationship with our leaders: a two-way conversation. They need to hear our heart about our church's worship; we need to hear theirs. They need to know what it takes for us to lead this ministry; we need to know what it takes for them to guide all the ministries of the church and where worship fits into that. The lines of communication vary from church to church, but it's vital that we use whatever lines we have to be sure there is mutual understanding between us and the leaders over us.

This brings us back to submission. After all the prayer, after all the expressions of friendship, after all the communication, we are still called to submit to our spiritual authorities. We may genuinely be doing all we can to "pursue the things that make for peace," but there may still remain an impasse. This is where the spiritual battle in our hearts will be won or lost: Will we submit willingly, or will we not?

Stay Or Leave?

If we cannot submit willingly, there is one of two things going on inside of us: Either we have a stubborn heart in need of the Spirit's refinement, or we are being spurred on by the Spirit to move out of our present position. It is not a scriptural option to push our way forward in spite of what our leaders are telling us to do, nor is it scripturally justified to obey our leaders while retaining an attitude of rebellion. On the other hand, we obey a higher authority than the church authorities over us, and that is the Chief Shepherd Himself. If, after much prayer and wise counsel, we believe we cannot, in good conscience, continue on the course that our leaders are asking us to take, then He is probably asking us to leave our present position.

We examine our heart, always. If we have confessed any sinful attitudes and been reassured by the Holy Spirit that we are right before Him, then we must decide whether to stay in our present position or move on from it. Here is the spiritual litmus test that will help us decide: *Can we joyfully serve here, free from embitterment and with a clear conscience?*

Joyfully serve here: In our present ministry calling, can we find joy in using our gifts, in entering into relationships with our brothers and sisters, and in worshiping wholeheartedly and without reservation?

Free from embitterment: In our present ministry calling, can we choose grace toward those in authority over us, submitting to them with a heart of love?

With a clear conscience: In our present ministry calling, can we follow the ministry requirements of our church leadership with a clear conscience before the Lord?

If the answer to all these questions is yes, there may be very good reason to stay. If the answer to the first two questions is no, then we must consider carefully whether we need an attitude adjustment. It may also be possible that our Shepherd is leading us out of our present ministry. If the answer to the third question is no, then He very likely is leading us to serve in another place or capacity.

A Conversation With My Shepherd

My life

Will You bring to mind some ways that my pastor shows concern for Your sheep?

Is there anyone in authority over me with whom I need to have a more peaceful relationship? If so, will You show me how?

What are some things You would like me to pray for those in authority over me?

Will You show me: Am I serving my church joyfully, without bitterness, and with a clear conscience?

Your Word

Will You remind me from 2 Corinthians 11:28-29 why I need to be praying for my pastor?

Your Word (continued)

As I read Romans 14:15–20a, substituting the word "your worship vision" for phrases related to food or eating, what message do I need to hear from You about submitting to those in authority over me?

What does Your Word tell me about where my responsibility to pursue peace begins and ends (Romans 12:18)?

Your thought for me

What is one thing You want me to remember from today's lesson?

My heart before You

(Talk to your Shepherd about all or part of the following.) Here's what I need to confess to You; how I want to praise You; what I hope to do with what You've shown me; what I need You to help me with:

DAY 5: A BEAUTIFUL SYMBIOSIS

"Symbiosis": A mutually beneficial relationship between different people or groups.[38] When the body of Christ is working as it should—when sheep are submitting out of love and obedience to their undershepherds; when undershepherds are submitting in the same way to the undershepherds over *them*; and when everyone is submitting to the Chief Shepherd—we will see Christ's prayer for His church answered. We will all be one, and the world around us will see that we belong to Jesus. Many who see will believe in Him as a result.

We cannot make this happen in our churches, because we cannot control the heart of anyone else. When those in authority over us do not embrace the vision we believe God has given our church for worship, we cannot know how it will all end. It could be that our leaders will have a change of heart and come to accept our view. It could also be that they may disagree with us so strongly that they will ask us to step down. Or, it could happen that, though they continue to believe we are wrong, *they* may decide to step down rather than to divide the sheep they care for. God may move some of them out, and He may bring others in. We simply cannot know the future.

For Greg and me, the future that night after the elders' meeting seemed murky. This was unsettling to us, even anguishing. Yet, we renewed our commitment to seek the Lord and submit to Him for the good of the church, no matter what He asked of us. The elders, for their part, proved over time that they were committed to the same thing.

Some conversations were tabled; others were hashed out. Sometimes an uneasy truce was the only way to keep the peace; other times we were surprised to find that there was more common ground than we had realized. Through it all, as we each set our heart to submit to the Lord and to each other for the sake of our church family, He graciously preserved our unity and helped us to grow as a worshiping church.

It doesn't always end this way, I know. Even now, there is no guarantee for my own church that the road won't get bumpy again. Whatever happens, my goal—and I trust it's yours as well—is to show my leaders a heart of loving submission so that the following benediction will be realized in our midst:

> *Now the God of peace, who brought up from the dead the great Shepherd of the sheep through the blood of the eternal covenant, even Jesus our Lord, equip you in every good thing to do His will, working in us that which is pleasing in His sight, through Jesus Christ, to whom be the glory forever and ever. Amen.* (Hebrews 13:20-21)

As our Shepherd brings this prayer to fruition, we *worship leaders* will see ourselves equipped to do His will in our callings. Our *leaders* will see Him working things through them that are pleasing in His sight. And *our churches* will fulfill the purpose for which they were designed: to bring God glory forever.

Now *that* is a beautiful symbiosis.

A Conversation With My Shepherd

My life

If someone who didn't know my church was observing it, would they see that we are submitting to one another out of love for You?

Will You show me if I have had a loving heart of submission lately?

Will You show me some of the ways I could submit to You *better* in my ministry, so that You receive the glory You deserve?

Your Word

As I consider what You've been showing me about having a heart of submission, how can the following things encourage me to trust You with my church (Hebrews 13:20-21)?

Your power on our behalf

Your heart toward us

Your Word (continued)

Your commitment to us

Your purpose for us

Your thought for me

What is one thing You want me to remember from today's lesson?

My heart before You

(Talk to your Shepherd about all or part of the following.) Here's what I need to confess to You; how I want to praise You; what I hope to do with what You've shown me; what I need You to help me with:

A PRAYER TO PRAY

Praying Shepherd, how closely You carried Your sheep to Your heart even as You faced an unimaginably cruel death, asking fervently for the Father to make us one. How tenaciously You carry us still, as with nail-scarred hands You intercede for us before the throne.

How could I ever be so ungrateful as to place my will above Yours? How could I ever grieve You by jeopardizing the unity of the flock You hold so dear? How could I allow myself to break Your heart by refusing to honor and submit to those You have wisely placed over me?

Yet I do break Your heart sometimes. It makes me sad to say this, because I know You have purchased Your church at great cost. I do say it, though, because it's true.

Please forgive me:

> *For the times when I've focused my energies on winning an argument rather than battling the spiritual forces whose pleasure it is to divide us.*

> *For those occasions when I've looked at a spiritual overseer as a roadblock instead of as a co-laborer through whom You can accomplish Your will for our church.*

> *For the countless instances when I've elevated my own vision for worship above Your ardent prayer for our unity.*

Bring me to my knees. Give me again a heart wholly submitted to You. Shape my will so that I submit out of love and obedience to those You've placed over me, knowing I submit ultimately to You in all things.

You love Your church. I love it too. Help me to love it better still.

CHAPTER 10

OUR SHEPHERD SPEAKS COMMUNITY

DAY 1: OUR FIRST CALLING—LOVE

Sunday morning in my church:
- The elderly woman leaning on her cane, precarious health tempered by prolific humor
- The preschooler rolling down the aisle during worship
- The man waving vigorously all through the opening song until one of our worship team members waves back
- The lady with the whimsical hats and the heart of gold
- The man who punctuates our services with an energetic "Hooah!" whenever the moment strikes him
- The woman who laughs boisterously at my husband's jokes
- The front-row youths huddled head-to-head in animated conversation
- The back-row saints freely sharing their observations

These are the people I am called to be family with: the courageous and the quirky, the puzzling and the off-putting, the endearing and the enduring. From my place on the platform I watch them gather in the pews, and I am ever in awe that our Shepherd calls us to knit our hearts, nullify our disparities, and become one flock together.

As I consider my church family, do I imagine that my first calling is to lead them in worship? Do I think it's more important for me to prepare music for them than to prune my heart to love them? 1 Corinthians 13:1 tells us that without love, the only sound our efforts will produce is a noisy gong or a clanging cymbal. No amount of rehearsing (or prayer for that matter) will make this music sound beautiful.

The music we are called to sound out is the sweet melody of persistent love. This is no elevator music, filling up a few empty moments with distraction. This is no iTunes playlist we can pause or stop at will. This is no naive love song that glosses over the painful process of learning to live in harmony with each other. The love in this song is no blind love, stumbling blithely along until some briar patch catches it off guard and trips it up.

No. The love we are called to sing has eyes opened wide to the shortcomings of our fellow sheep (and of ourselves) yet opened wider still to the face of our Shepherd. It is a love that keeps its eyes on the Savior and comes to view ourselves as He does.

How Our Shepherd Views Us

So what does our Shepherd want us to know about His view of us? If we regard ourselves through His eyes, what will we see?

Our Shepherd's Voice: "I see you as both flawed and forgiven."

If we look through His eyes, we will see ourselves and our brothers and sisters, first, as the shockingly flawed and astonishingly forgiven sheep that we are. We must see this clearly, if we are to lead with the love Christ asks of us.

Author and teacher Gordon MacDonald tells of a pivotal moment in his life when he was preparing to go into pastoral ministry. A seminary professor was talking to him and a small group of students about Acts 20:28 ("…Shepherd the church of God which He purchased with His own blood"). The conversation ended like this:

Then he asked me, "How do you think God feels about the Church?"
I looked down at the verse stalling for time and then I said,
"Apparently God thinks the Church is precious."
"Why do you think that?"
"Because He purchased it with His own blood."
Then the professor stepped back and he said, "Gentlemen (there were
no women at the table), I trust that you will treat the Church in the same
way." And he walked away.
That conversation made me a pastor. [39]

When we are able to view Christ's imperfect sheep as tenderly as He does, we will be ready to grow into the loving worship leaders He is calling us to be.

Our Shepherd's Voice: "I see you as tied to My heart."

When we view ourselves and our churches through our Shepherd's eyes, we also see how closely to His heart we are held. We are the bride of Christ (Revelation 19:7). We are His own body (Ephesians 4:12). Scripture tells us:

...for no one ever hated his own flesh, but nourishes and cherishes it, just as Christ also does the church, because we are members of His body.
(Ephesians 5:29-30)

I recently spent some time looking at the seven churches in Revelation 1-3. Though I had read these chapters many times before, this time I was moved by the way Jesus relates to each church. Whether the words are gentle or strong, Christ makes it known that He is intimately acquainted with each family of believers. He is mindful of them. He sees them. He is actively at work in them to refine them. He does not give up on any of them.

If our Shepherd is this tender and attentive toward His sheep, in whatever groupings He has called them together, what does this say to worship undershepherds about the heart with which we should care for our brothers and sisters in community with us?

Our Shepherd's Voice: "I see you as tied to one another."

The third thing we see through the eyes of Jesus is that He has linked us inextricably to one another. We are individual stones being built up into one building (1 Corinthians 3:9). Beyond this, we are one *temple* where the Spirit of God dwells (1 Corinthians 3:16). We are loved individually as His children, but we are *also* in some wondrous way loved *together* as He makes His presence known in and through us.

There is only one corner stone to this sacred building, and it's Jesus (Ephesians 2:20). As for the rest of us, we find our significance fully realized only as we identify ourselves as part of the magnificent whole, built upon our Savior. We worship leaders are merely one stone in this temple, no greater than any other, living and loving among them for the glory of God.

Why Does He Love Us So?

Why does our Shepherd love all of us helpless sheep so much that He takes us and shows us mercy, holding us close to His heart and building us up for His glory? Does anyone know the answer to this question? Many before us have asked it:

Moses asked it: "Who am I, that I should go to Pharaoh, and that I should bring the sons of Israel out of Egypt?" (Exodus 3:11).

David asked it: "Who am I, O Lord God and what is my house that You have brought me this far?" (1 Chronicles 17:16).

Solomon asked it: "Who am I, that I should build a house for Him, except to burn incense before Him?" (2 Chronicles 2:6).

What is God's answer to His children who ask such a question? The only answer that can be given: God *is* love. There can be no rationale for it other than that He *lives* to love. As Moses told the children of Israel:

> *The Lord did not set His love on you nor choose you because you were more in number than any of the peoples, for you were the fewest of all peoples, but because the Lord loved you and kept the oath which He swore to your forefathers, the Lord brought you out by a mighty hand and redeemed you...*" (Deuteronomy 7:7-8a)

God has always been love, long before we existed. The Father, Son, and Spirit have had a loving relationship from eternity (John 17:24). Because God is love personified, He delights to pour that love into the hearts of His children through the Holy Spirit (Romans 5:5). As His children, we stand under a shimmering shower of grace that has forever emanated from His loving heart:

> *just as He chose us in Him before the foundation of the world, that we would be holy and blameless before Him. In love He predestined us to adoption as sons through Jesus Christ to Himself, according to the kind intention of His will.* (Ephesians 1: 4-5)

His Love, Our Bond

Love is the one element that has always been present, from that moment in eternity when our Father called us by name all the way through this moment now when He continues to permeate our hearts with His Spirit. God's love among us is what sets the community of Christ apart from all other communities on earth. It is the festive ribbon with which He ties our hearts together and gives us the reason and the means to celebrate this family of believers called the church.

A Conversation With My Shepherd

My life

Who are some of the people You have endeared me to in my congregation (including those with quirks and idiosyncrasies)?

Is there anyone in my church family that I am not viewing through Your eyes of love?

As I imagine Your eyes looking at me and my church from the cross, here is how it impacts me:

Your Word

What do the following Scriptures show me about how You view the church?

Acts 20:28

Ephesians 5:25-30

1 Corinthians 3:16

Your Word (continued)

What can I learn about Your love for me and my church from the following Scriptures?

Deuteronomy 7:7–9

Romans 5:5

Ephesians 1:3–7

Your thought for me

What is one thing You want me to remember from today's lesson?

My heart before You

(Talk to your Shepherd about all or part of the following.) Here's what I need to confess to You; how I want to praise You; what I hope to do with what You've shown me; what I need You to help me with:

DAY 2: WHY DO WE GATHER *TOGETHER* TO WORSHIP?

I am a person who covets time by myself—time to read, write, reflect, plan, gain perspective, worship, study the Word, go for a stroll, or play a musical instrument. All of these things, when done for Christ's glory, are acts of worship. However, as much as I enjoy these "alone" activities, there is nothing that can ever take the place of gathering *together* with my church family to worship our Lord. Nothing. Not a prayer walk in the woods, not a tears-flowing worship moment in my kitchen, not a rousingly inspirational podcast.

There is no thought in Scripture of a Christian living life alone, disconnected from other Christians, independent and self-sufficient. There is no room for the idea that a sheep can reside in a field alone, merrily cordoning itself off with its Shepherd in some distant acre, amassing the blessings of fellowship and keeping them all to itself.

Not to say that this idea won't enter our minds from time to time, even we worship leaders. God knows this, which is why I imagine He inspired the writer of Hebrews to encourage the church with these words:

> *And let us consider how to stimulate one another to love and good deeds, not forsaking our own assembling together, as is the habit of some, but encouraging one another; and all the more as you see the day drawing near.* (Hebrews 10:24-25)

The practice of corporate worship was not invented by some lonely believer looking for a coping mechanism. It was given to us as an indispensable and invaluable gift from our very wise Shepherd. We worship leaders surely know this; why else would we pour ourselves into preparing for this gathering, week after week? But *because* we do it week after week, we can sometimes forget the import of what we do. Especially in those no-margin seasons when it feels like we are churning out service after service with no tangible reward to show for it.

Yet there is great reward; some very important things happen when the church gathers together to worship.

Worship In Community Fortifies Us

First, the sheer act of gathering together in worship causes us to garner courage and gain strength for living out our lives as Christians in the world. God's Word tells us that when we come together for worship, we are to "speak to one another" and "teach and admonish one another" (Ephesians 5:19; Colossians 3:16). Worship is vertical (directed toward God), but its effects are both vertical and horizontal (God is honored, and we are built up). As we listen to the Word and sing its truths, we are reminded that this is not simply a philosophy we've adopted; it is the very living and active Word of God alive and at work in us. As we immerse ourselves in the company of fellow believers, shoulder to shoulder and voice to voice, we *know* and we *feel* that we are part of a great army called together to meet our world head-on with grace and hope. As we catch the eye and grasp the hand of those who share our struggles and fears, we know that we are not alone.

One spring a few years ago, I received a phone call while we were visiting our son in California. It was one of those phone calls that rocks your world, tsunami-like. Its ramifications were far-reaching and devastating. I was shaken. I sat in our son's church that Sunday morning unable to sing a single word. What I remember most vividly about that worship service is that I was surrounded by Christians who were singing lyrics of truth and grace with all their hearts, and it soothed me like the sweetest balm.

Worship In Community Focuses Us Outward

Second, worshiping with our brothers and sisters lifts us out of our self-absorption. The first century believers understood that the church was not comprised of separate individuals out to please themselves. Acts 2:44-47 describes this fledgling community as generous and sincere, thoughtful and other-minded as they worshiped together.

Worshiping in community speaks to our selfishness and notifies our narcissism, driving home the reality that we do not live for ourselves;

we live for one another. As C.S. Lewis relates, beautiful things can happen in our hearts when we worship shoulder-to-shoulder with our brothers and sisters:

> *I realized that the hymns (which were just sixth-rate music) were, nevertheless, being sung with devotion and benefit by an old saint in elastic-side boots in the opposite pew, and then you realize that you aren't fit to clean those boots. It gets you out of your solitary conceit.* [40]

Worship In Community Foreshadows Future Worship

Third, coming together in worship gives us a glimpse of the future day when together we will assemble around the throne of God. As the apostle John labors to capture the inconceivable scope of this future gathering, his words tumble out in awestruck wonder:

> *Then I looked, and I heard the voice of many angels around the throne and the living creatures and the elders; and the number of them was myriads of myriads, and thousands of thousands, saying with a loud voice, "Worthy is the Lamb that was slain to receive power and riches and wisdom and might and honor and glory and blessing." And every created thing which is in heaven and on the earth and under the earth and on the sea, and all things in them, I heard saying, "To Him who sits on the throne, and to the Lamb, be blessing and honor and glory and dominion forever and ever."* (Revelation 5:11-13)

How many worshipers are in this vision? Just you? Just me? Why would we wait until some future day to join with others in worship? When the time comes to join with *all* worshipers from *all* times, our hearts will be all the more primed to do so for having begun *now*.

Worship In Community Reminds Us Of Christ's Uniting Presence

Finally, gathering together in worship serves as a powerful reminder that Jesus is among us, uniting us as one body. According to Hebrews 2:11-12, our Savior Himself stands in our midst, calling us brethren and singing His Father's praises right along with us. Oh, may the Spirit open our eyes and ears to this breathtaking reality whenever we gather to worship Him! And, with this reality firmly in mind, may our hearts and voices join as one, to His glory:

Now may the God who gives perseverance and encouragement grant you to be of the same mind with one another according to Christ Jesus, so that with one accord you may with one voice glorify the God and Father of our Lord Jesus Christ. (Romans 15:5-6)

A Conversation With My Shepherd

My life

What is one way I need You to strengthen me this week when I gather to worship with my brothers and sisters?

Is there someone You would like me to look for to encourage next time I worship with my church family?

Here is one of the things I'm looking most forward to about worshiping You in heaven:

Your Word

Remind me again why it's important to gather regularly with my church family in worship (Hebrews 10:24-25):

Your Word (continued)

What does Your Word tell me about worship as both "vertical" and "horizontal" (Ephesians 5:19-20; Colossians 3:16)?

What beautiful picture of You as our Savior is described in Hebrews 2:9-12?

Will You show me from Revelation 5:6-14 what aspects of future worship Your church can engage in now?

Your thought for me

What is one thing You want me to remember from today's lesson?

My heart before You

(Talk to your Shepherd about all or part of the following.) Here's what I need to confess to You; how I want to praise You; what I hope to do with what You've shown me; what I need You to help me with:

DAY 3: WORSHIPERS IN COMMUNITY

There is a gentleman in our church who used to make a habit of approaching me after each service and giving me an evaluation of the music. A quantifiable evaluation. Based on a scale of one to ten. The specific criteria weren't clear, but they seemed to include (1) the number of older hymns we sang, (2) the number of times a chorus was repeated in a song, and (3) the theological depth of the lyrics. Most often the grade hovered around a 5, though once or twice the music was awarded a 7.5 or an 8.

When I first began to receive these scores, my response vacillated from defensiveness to amusement to flippancy to receptivity (well, not completely receptive). I tried to maintain an easy demeanor, attempting to infuse a little lighthearted humor into the conversation. The problem was that what I intended to sound humorous often came across to this man as defensive and sarcastic. (Perhaps he was more perceptive than I had hoped he would be?)

One Sunday after one of these exchanges, I left church feeling troubled. A few minutes after I got home, the phone rang. It was this man. "Hello, this is _____. I'd like to apologize for how I came across this morning…" As I heard his words, I wondered, "Is this what it means to have burning coals heaped on my head?" I felt embarrassed, and I felt humbled. I felt that he was by far the bigger Christian.

Community Is Not For The Faint Of Heart

Relationships can be tricky. Complicated. This brother of mine was trying to feel his way around this friendship just as I was, both of us getting it wrong sometimes. But over time he and I have had the opportunity to engage in more conversations. Conversations about life in general, about family, about mutual preferences. He has trusted me enough to share some significant events in his life that have brought him to his present view of worship music, and I have come to filter his comments through a more generous lens.

I recently read a compelling article about community by author and musician Carolyn Arends.[41] She argues that, in spite of the challenges of living and loving within the context of community, God's intention has always been for us to be in fellowship with one another:

> *The triune God has always been into community. And community, I am forced to admit, ultimately requires meeting together with flesh and blood folks I cannot "block" or "unfriend" should they become annoying. It means getting close enough to hug and to arm wrestle, to build (and sometimes hold) each other up, even as we risk letting each other down.*

Living in community is not for the faint of heart. The sooner we accept this, the sooner we can get down to the business of embracing it for all it's worth.

We Are Family

Scripture makes it clear that in the church we are to consider each other as family (1 Timothy 5:1-2). We are not family simply because we worship together on Sunday mornings; we are family because our Father has called us to engage one another in relationship as His children. He has woven our lives with other believers in a local fellowship to give and receive love.

Picture a multitude of worshipers walking together, singing the following words:

> *Behold, how good and how pleasant it is*
> *For brothers to dwell together in unity*
> *It is like the precious oil upon the head,*
> *Coming down upon the beard,*
> *Even Aaron's beard,*
> *Coming down upon the edge of his robes.*
> *It is like the dew of Hermon*
> *Coming down upon the mountains of Zion;*
> *For there the Lord commanded the blessing—life forever.*
> (Psalm 133)

Psalm 133 is one of 15 Songs of Ascents which three times a year the people of Israel would sing together as they came to Jerusalem and made their way to the top of Mount Zion. The brotherly and sisterly fellowship described in this song and demonstrated by those singing it was like sacred oil glistening on their heads and running over priestly garments, beautifying them and setting them apart as belonging to their God. In the same way, when the church today is overflowing with love and clothed in the holy robe of kinship as God's beloved children, we will proclaim indeed that we are "a chosen race, a royal priesthood, a holy nation, a people for God's own possession" gathered to proclaim His excellencies (1 Peter 2:9).

Our lives are knit together in the fabric of this holy robe. Under its covering we grapple and we give grace, but never at a distance. We are family.

Community: An Ideal Or An Investment?

If our Father has such beautiful intent in calling His children to be family, why is it that people can drift so easily away from the body of Christ? There are countless reasons, but over the years one recurring reason has been especially unsettling to my husband and me: they simply see no use for it.

A few weeks ago I had a conversation with a good friend of mine. My friend loves Jesus. She reads the Word, she prays, and she talks about Him with her husband and children. Yet, somehow she does not see His directive to live in community as something that is important for her to do. As we talked, she explained to me that, because of some hurtful things she has experienced within the church, it has seemed easier to live as a Christian outside of church life than inside.

On some levels, I have no argument. Living as family with our brothers and sisters can be disillusioning. Especially if we assume that Christians will always act—well, like Christians.

In his book *Life Together,* Dietrich Bonhoeffer builds a beautifully persuasive argument for community. He also warns about the dangers of making the _ideal_ of community more important than the _people_ in the community:

> *Those who love their dream of a Christian community more than the Christian community itself become destroyers of that Christian community even though their personal intentions may be ever so honest, earnest, and sacrificial.*

> *...If we do not give thanks daily for the Christian community in which we have been placed, even when there are no great experiences, no noticeable riches, but much weakness, difficulty, and little faith—and if, on the contrary, we only keep complaining to God that everything is so miserable and so insignificant and does not at all live up to our expectations—then we hinder God from letting our community grow according to the measure and riches that are there for us all in Jesus Christ. [42]*

As worship undershepherds, we must carry this call to community firmly in our hearts. When we are tempted to exchange interaction with tussling sheep for isolation on some far-off tuft of grass, we must remember that our Shepherd knows each of these sheep by name. He is deeply invested in them, and He expects no less from us.

A Conversation With My Shepherd

My life

What is one of the most difficult things for me about being part of this church family You've placed me in?

How can I learn from You in this difficult area?

What are some of the biggest blessings You've given me in my church family?

Your Word

What does 1 Timothy 5:1-2 show me about how I should treat my fellow sheep as family?

According to Psalm 133, what is one quality of Your people that You look upon with pleasure?

What do You teach me from 1 Peter 2:5, 9-10 about who the church is and why it exists?

Your thought for me

What is one thing You want me to remember from today's lesson?

My heart before You

(Talk to your Shepherd about all or part of the following.) Here's what I need to confess to You; how I want to praise You; what I hope to do with what You've shown me; what I need You to help me with:

DAY 4: LIVING PASTORALLY WITHIN OUR CHURCH COMMUNITY (PART 1)

Job Description Or Heart Condition?

What does your job description look like? If your church is anything like mine, the worship leader's job description includes planning services, rehearsing musicians, leading or finding someone to lead Sunday morning worship, going to meetings, staying within a budget, and numerous other responsibilities.

What is the title your church has given you? Minister? Coordinator? Leader? Pastor? My church gave me the title "Director of Worship Ministry." It was an apt title; but it was only a title.

The title and the job description we are given may provide a summary of the role we play in our church, but they neither define our heart nor determine our fruit. Whatever our title or job description, it is the Christ-like attitude of our heart that will provide soft soil for the Holy Spirit to till and water and cause a harvest to spring up for His kingdom.

What is the condition of our heart as we carry out our ministry? Do we see ourselves first as a musician or as a pastor? The term "pastor" comes from the Latin noun "herdsman" and the Latin verb "to feed." In other words, a pastor is simply a shepherd who cares for the sheep. Do we see ourselves as a shepherd? Do we take seriously Peter's admonition to shepherd the flock of God among us with eagerness (1 Peter 5:2)? The Lord will shepherd His flock without fail (Ezekiel 34:11-16), but He also expects us to be His undershepherds, caring for them as He does.

Have we come to understand, as Matt Redman puts it, that "the musician in me must learn to submit to the pastor in me"?[43] Since our first calling is to love, and the framework in which we worship leaders are called to love is our local community of believers, the quality of a pastoral heart is a nonnegotiable for us.

Having A Pastoral Heart Toward Our *Congregation*

Because of the nature of worship ministry, the worship leader and teams can easily be perceived as exclusive. Think about it from the perspective of our congregations: they gather side by side to worship in the pews, and as they turn their faces toward the platform, what do they see? A group of musicians and singers looking back at them. It's them and us—we are "other," at least in proximity.

As I've talked with my brothers and sisters in the congregation over the years, I've learned that many of them view worship ministry as the "fun" ministry in the church. Many people who are musical would love very much to be part of this group. Many others who are not musical wish very much that they were.

Throw into this mix of "otherness" the ingredient of musical choices. Who gets to make the decisions about what music the congregation sings? Isn't it primarily the worship leader, with perhaps some input from the worship teams? It can be frustrating for our brothers and sisters who are not part of this ministry. For most of them, worship is a very important component of their Christianity. How must it feel to them when they come to worship but have little say about the music we sing?

How can we as worship leaders help our congregations know that we are with them, not set apart from them? Following are two suggestions.

Give a gentle answer

One morning I opened an email and found this terse note from a couple in our church: "We are heartbroken over what you've done to 'Amazing Grace.'" (We had sung Todd Agnew's "Grace Like Rain" the previous Sunday.)

Another time a man in our church approached me about a series of newsletter articles I was writing called "Worship Music: Uniting or Dividing Us?". He said to me, "I'm looking forward to your next article. But I have to tell you I'm a 'hymner.'" Fine so far, but then he added, "I just sit and don't sing on all those other songs."

As a worship leader whose daily prayer has been for our congregation to enter into worship with their whole hearts, comments like these sadden me. Actually, I am being a little generous when I write it like that; comments like these can also anger me and put me on the defensive. My first instinct in such situations has often been to fire back a strongly-worded, scripturally-informed, impeccably-argued defense of my position.

But is this what would serve my fellow sheep best? Is this the right heart for an undershepherd called to be in community? Would such an answer be helpful to my brother in his desire to worship our Shepherd, or would it, rather, provide yet one more obstacle for him to have to overcome as he worships—namely, my obstinate spirit?

If our goal is to demonstrate to our brothers and sisters that we are *with* them in this family, caring for them and learning along with them, we will not aim to shoot them down or overpower them with persuasive arguments. Rather, we will aim to let them know they are heard and that we care about their heart. God's Word tells us that "a gentle answer turns away wrath, but a harsh word stirs up anger" (Proverbs 15:1). Colossians 4:6 admonishes: "Let your speech always be with grace, as though seasoned with salt, so that you will know how you should respond to each person." This is what it means to enter into community with our brothers and sisters with the heart of a shepherd.

Spend time with them

The second suggestion for helping our congregation know we are with them and not set apart from them is to spend time with them. I love my church family, but on some days it seems that it would be so much easier to hang out exclusively with those who "get" worship like I do (how presumptuous is that?). How harmful would it be to the fellowship of our body if I approached church life like a group of little clubs, picking and choosing the clubs I want to be part of and ignoring the others? Furthermore, how impoverished would I be if I based my sphere of fellowship on such narrow-minded criteria?

We are told in 1 John 1:7 that "if we walk in the Light as He Himself is in the Light, we have fellowship with one another." It does not say, "If we are more passionate about corporate worship than children's ministry, then we can have fellowship with one another." Nor does it say, "If we would rather attend a worship conference than go on a missions trip, then we can have fellowship with one another." Scripture assumes that we will have fellowship based solely on the fact that we love Jesus and live to honor Him.

As worship leaders who care about our entire congregation, it is important that we spend time with those outside of our ministry: we attend their Sunday school classes; we belong to their home Bible study groups; we invite them into our homes; we go to concerts and sporting events with them; we seek them out in the hallways and in the parking lot. In short, we do everything we can to let them know that we value them and that without them our lives would be diminished.

On Day 5, we will discuss how to live pastorally with another part of our church community: our worship ministry co-laborers. But first, I encourage you to spend some time with your Shepherd and ask Him to speak to you about what we've discussed today.

A Conversation With My Shepherd

My life

Do You see my heart as soft soil for Your Spirit to till and water? What areas need Your Spirit's work as I tend Your sheep?

As I've communicated with my brothers and sisters this week, has my speech been gentle and seasoned with grace?

Is there a particular group of people in my congregation that You'd like me to intentionally spend time with in the weeks ahead?

Your Word

According to Ezekiel 34:1-6, what do You expect of Your undershepherds?

What can You teach me from the following verses about showing the sheep in my care that I'm with them, not set apart from them?

Proverbs 15:1

Your Word (continued)

    Colossians 4:6

    1 John 1:7

Your thought for me

    What is one thing You want me to remember from today's lesson?

My heart before You

    (Talk to your Shepherd about all or part of the following.) Here's what I need to confess to You; how I want to praise You; what I hope to do with what You've shown me; what I need You to help me with:

DAY 5: LIVING PASTORALLY WITHIN OUR CHURCH COMMUNITY (PART 2)

In Day 4 we looked at what it means to have a pastoral heart toward our congregation. Today, we will look at what it means to have a pastoral heart toward our fellow servants in the worship ministry.

A Community Of Co-Laborers

I left church one night happily thanking God for my brothers and sisters in worship ministry with me. The events of the previous two hours had been the very picture of what it means to be in partnership together. It had been the kickoff of Worship 101, the summer-long training program for youth who wanted to know more about serving in worship ministry. Some of the worship team members had prepared a meal for the youth and volunteers. Another worship team member had led the discussion as we delved into the topic of worship as a way of life. A team of audiovisual volunteers in the sanctuary had demonstrated how a soundboard functions. A group of students and worship volunteers huddling over a table in the fireside room had brainstormed artistic ideas. Trumpets, flutes, keyboards, pianos, drums, congas, guitars, violas, basses, and voices had sounded out from various corners of the building as worship team instrumentalists and vocalists had prepared music for a church worship service later that summer.

We had left elated and exhausted. As I walked to my car, I thought to myself, "I love serving with these co-laborers!"

Have you ever had moments when you felt like this? Not all my moments with my worship teams have felt this way. There have been other moments when I have peevishly chosen to believe I was the only one who cared about the success of the ministry; moments when my co-workers have let me down, irritated me, shown up with bad attitudes, or failed to take their role seriously. Still, I cannot imagine doing this ministry without them.

Having A Pastoral Heart Toward Our *Co-Laborers*

It is a profound privilege to shepherd a worship ministry team. We will not shepherd them perfectly, nor will they function perfectly as a team, but we are given the beautiful mandate to come alongside them with a pastoral heart. Paul understood what it meant to come alongside his fellow workers with such a heart. Time and time again he filled his letters with words of affirmation and respect for those who served alongside him. Take a look at some of those he commends in his letter to the Philippians:

- "women who have shared my struggle in the cause of the gospel" (4:2)
- "my fellow workers, whose names are in the book of life" (4:2)
- "Epaphroditus, my brother and fellow worker and fellow soldier, who is also your messenger and minister to my need" (2:25)
- "Timothy… I have no one else of kindred spirit who will genuinely be concerned for your welfare" (2:19)

We worship leaders are not here merely to help our teams learn to play music well together. We are called to give them encouragement and affirmation at a much deeper level.

Who are these friends of ours? What roles are they being asked to play? How do these roles affect them emotionally and spiritually? Do we know if they feel discouraged? Encouraged? Let's consider how we can come alongside some of these co-laborers with a pastoral heart:

Our fellow artists

What about the singers and musicians who pour out creativity, eagerly offering their musical talents to the Lord and putting themselves on the line each week in front of a congregation of peers? It may look like fun to the congregation, and indeed it may even feel fun some of the time to these fellow artists, but what kind of emotional toll can it take to be so out-there? What kind of spiritual toll can it take to fight against the enemy in a valiant effort to maintain a pure heart of worship week in and week out?

As the undershepherd whom God has called to serve them, we must study them so that we know what type of encouragement builds them up the most. We can show special appreciation for the mom who brings her two young daughters early to church each Sunday morning though her husband doesn't attend. We can affirm the novice vocalist for the strides she is making in her level of comfort singing up front. We can ask the chronically tardy bass player if there are things in his life that are weighing him down lately. We can sit with the young keyboardist and help him become more confident with chord charts. We can speak carefully and kindly to the guitar player whose past life experiences have caused her to be overly-sensitive.

The audiovisual techs

Our brothers and sisters who serve in the audiovisual ministry open themselves up to the possibility of criticism every week. Drums too loud? Lighting too dim? Words not coming up on the screen quickly enough? Violin too soft? Pastor's mic has feedback? They sit at the sound booth twisting knobs and tracking with musicians, all the while trying to maintain their own heart of worship, and the odds are that something will go wrong and that someone will point it out to them.

How can we come alongside these invaluable fellow servants with a pastoral heart? We can acknowledge their indispensability. We can affirm the difficulty of their job. We can speak our appreciation of them to anyone who will listen. We can include them in worship team discussions and prayer times. We can ask them what they need from us to make their job easier. And we can be careful of our terminology: when speaking of "worship teams" or "worship ministry," we can make it clear that these terms include not only the musicians but also the technicians.

Other worship ministry co-laborers

On any given Sunday there may be others who join with us in the worship ministry: creative arts teams, Scripture readers, people who bring "special music." As an undershepherd who recognizes the worth of each person who participates in ministry with us, it is important that we communicate to them how valuable they are. We can go out of our way to speak words of appreciation to them. We can compliment them for something they have done well. We can send them thank-you notes. We can include them in our prayer time with the worship team before the service.

Men and women working together

As a woman worship leader, there is one other group that I have found it very important to learn how to work alongside in an encouraging way: *the men* who serve with me. If you are a male worship leader, it is important for you to learn how to work alongside and encourage the women who serve with you.

Men and women do not always speak the same language. We do not always resonate with the same modes of communication. Some women may have a history that makes them feel especially intimidated by a man who comes across with bold confidence. Some men may have a history that makes them bristle when a woman shows strong leadership skills. When a man approaches something in ministry a different way than a woman does, it might be tempting for the woman to pridefully dismiss him as insensitive or unintuitive. When a woman approaches something in a different way than one of her male co-laborers, it might be tempting for the man to condescendingly label her as irrational or majoring in the minors.

Fellow worship undershepherds, we must guard against such uncharitable attitudes toward one another, both within our own hearts and within our teams. It divides the church, and it destroys our brothers and sisters. It hampers ministry, and it steals joy. Men and women are of equal value in the eyes of Christ; we are to treat each other with the honor a fellow heir of Christ deserves. (See 1 Peter 3:7; Galatians 3:28)

It will not always be easy, but we men and women must ask the Lord to help us understand one another. We must try to discern how we are coming across and do our best to make sure we are not being misread. We must not jump to conclusions about one another; rather, we must give each other the benefit of the doubt. We must never be disrespectful of each other, either through sarcasm or ridicule or careless offhand comments.

In addition, it is important that we take special care to make sure we are not excluding each other. Men, are you in a band comprised mostly of guys? Make sure you do not ignore the women vocalists or marginalize the woman guitarist. Women, are you particularly good friends with the women on the team? Be sure to be wise in your conversations with them so that the men in the room are not made to feel uncomfortable.

Finally, it is imperative that men and women who work together remain pure in their relationships with one another. Furthermore, we must be careful never to give even the *appearance* of impropriety. (One thing I try to avoid is going anywhere alone with a man, and if I am talking with a man in the music room, I make sure the door is always open.) Women, dress in a way that will not cause your brothers to stumble. Men, do not speak in an inappropriate manner to your sisters.

The Treasure Of Community

In all of these relationships—musicians, audiovisual techs, creative arts teams, our congregation—we have been given a treasure of incalculable worth. The huddled front-row youth, the vociferous back-row saints, the preschooler rolling down the aisle—this is our local community, and we get to call them family. Do we realize how crazy rich we are? Do we need to be reminded?

Perhaps we would do well to follow Paul's example. In his letter to the Romans, he concludes by asking them to greet his brothers and sisters in the Lord, 27 of whom he refers to by name and many others whose names he does not list. Then he names eight more people who, in turn, send their greetings (Romans 16).

Paul, I am pretty sure, knew how crazy rich these relationships made him.

How about us? If we were writing a letter listing all the precious people God has placed in our lives to worship with and serve alongside, whose names would we write down? Maybe we should start that list now; it might take a while.

A Conversation With My Shepherd

My life

Will You show me some of the ways that my worship ministry co-laborers are a gift to me and to our church?

What is one practical way I can show my co-laborers I care about them?

Will You show me if there is any way I am not honoring members of the opposite gender as fellow heirs of Christ?

Will You please remind me why being part of Your family makes me "crazy rich"?

Your Word

According to Philippians 2:19, 25 and 4:2, what are some types of affirmations I might give to my co-laborers in ministry?

As I read Romans 16:1-15, 21-23, what are some additional ways I might affirm my co-laborers?

Your thought for me

What is one thing You want me to remember from today's lesson?

My heart before You

(Talk to your Shepherd about all or part of the following.) Here's what I need to confess to You; how I want to praise You; what I hope to do with what You've shown me; what I need You to help me with:

A PRAYER TO PRAY

Relational Shepherd, how intimately acquainted You are with me, and how attentive to my needs! You know that I do not do well on my own, so You have placed me in a family with You as our Head. A family so vast I cannot number it, Your children from all ages past and all ages to come, fellow believers with whom I will someday be seated around Your table.

In the meantime, I am so thankful that You do not make me wait until then to experience sweet fellowship with my brothers and sisters! Because You care for me, You have placed me in a community where I can love and be loved as an extension of Your deep love.

May I never take my brothers and sisters for granted! Let me pour forth praise and gratitude continually for the gift that they are to me. Let me never squander this gift by forgetting that You have given them to me for my growth and encouragement and joy. Let me never be a poor steward of this gift by neglecting to care for them in the same way You have cared for me.

By Your grace I will view them as a sacred trust, loving them fervently and receiving from them gratefully.

How precious and irreplaceable is Your church. Oh, let me treasure this community of believers with my whole heart!

CHAPTER 11

OUR SHEPHERD SPEAKS HELP

DAY 1: WE CANNOT DO IT ALONE

It loomed over me like a specter, intermittent in its appearance, sure in its return. This decision I could no longer avoid hovered with ominous gleam, haunting my dreams. It sabotaged my security and conjured up second guesses, beckoning me to the edge of the cliff and teasing me to follow it over the edge.

I had come too far to turn back. Terrifying though the prospect was, I knew that at some point I must step over: my aversion to remaining there in a limbo of indecision outweighed my fear of free-fall. Cushioned or crushed by the landing, follow the specter I must.

It appeared under many guises. Some of them were quite noble and innocuous: pursuit of excellence; maximizing people's gifts; moving forward in worship. Others were less idealized: cutting the teams to manageable size; making rehearsals less frustrating; avoiding embarrassment.

One manifestation loomed larger than all the others, causing me to sweat and tremble: hurting a whole lot of people's feelings and appearing ungracious in the process.

Let me back up. Fifteen years after coming to our church, I became the director of worship ministry. I inherited a willing group of volunteers who were neither polished nor perfected, but they had a good spirit. I loved them and was grateful for them.

As we served together, the worship ministry grew in heart and skill. Yet, over time, some unsettling issues began to arise:

- The sheer number of volunteers became unwieldy.
- Some of the volunteers did not embrace the level of commitment expected of them.
- Not all of them possessed the musical skills necessary for the type of music we sang.
- Not all of them had been given the spiritual gifts needed to help bring the congregation along with them in worship.
- Some of them did not gel socially with others on the teams.
- A handful of them did not seem to grasp the heart of worship.

It became increasingly obvious that if we were to keep moving in the direction God was leading us, the teams needed to be pared down. But these were my dear friends and co-laborers; I was unwilling to take any step that might lead to their feeling disvalued. I was scared to death that I might make a wrong decision at their expense.

Thus the specter, bringing with it a litany of doubts:

- What if this decision causes bitterness or harms someone's relationship with Christ?
- Will cutting back the teams be perceived as elitism?
- I myself have far to go musically and spiritually; will others think I am self-deceived or prideful?
- With just a little more time, would some of the team members get to where they need to be?
- Will it look like we're aiming for something higher than we are cut out to be?
- If people get angry at me for decisions made, will this affect their view of my husband—their pastor—as well?

Another thing I inherited with my new position was a worship leadership team. There were four others with me on the team, and together we sought the Lord about issues to be addressed and decisions to be made in the worship ministry. The team and I recognized the need to do something about the worship teams, but we could collectively summon neither the strength nor the wisdom to deal with it. We went round and round, evading and avoiding and coming up with nothing.

After three and a half years of this, the Lord showed me that it was time to gather some courage and meet the dilemma head-on. I journaled: "Lord, I'm going to seek You, face down, until You answer me about the direction You want our music ministry to go. And then I'll seek You face down some more until I hear from You the 'how' and the 'who.' I'm desperately dependent on You. I'll seek You, and I will obey, by Your grace."

But I knew I must not seek Him alone.

Why Do Worship Undershepherds Need Help?

It could be tempting to try to do this ministry by ourselves. Fueled by our eagerness to forge ahead with the good work, we might be reticent to slow down long enough to find the right helpers and bring them along with us. Armed with truth and clear-eyed vision, we might be unwilling to make the concessions that sharing the responsibility might require. Fortified by the confidence necessary to do the really hard things, we might think that acknowledging our need for help could somehow discredit our leadership.

Admitting we cannot carry out the call on our own is not a sign of weakness: It is a sign of wisdom. Our Shepherd Himself was surrounded by men and women who stood with Him as He fulfilled His mission: the twelve disciples; His close friends Martha, Mary, and Lazarus; Simon, who carried His cross; His beloved disciple John; His mother Mary, and the other women who stood with Him at the cross.

As His undershepherds, Jesus does hold us ultimately responsible for our ministries, but He does not expect us to do them alone. I once heard worship leader and songwriter Kathryn Scott give this analogy: A worship leader is like the driver of a vehicle. The passengers expect the driver to work the pedals and turn the wheel, but they may be called on to help sometimes. For example, the map-reader may be asked for directions when the driver gets lost. The mechanic may be asked to repair the vehicle when it breaks down.

Her analogy was of great help to me as I pondered what role I should play in the decision to pare down our teams. It helped me see that, though it was important to lead from a place of security, I didn't have to know everything, and I certainly didn't have to do it all on my own. To think otherwise would have been devastating to my ministry and to myself.

We worship leaders must seek help as we lead. Our Shepherd gives us three very good reasons why.

Our Shepherd's Voice: "You are not wise enough in yourself."

As we drive the vehicle of our worship ministry, there will be stretches of the road that confound us. Do we trust ourselves to always make the right decisions? Can we discern every nuance and ramification as we contemplate a course of action? If we are honest with ourselves, we must answer "No" to each of these questions.

The responsibility of directing our ministry with skill and grace is too important to approach in our own limited wisdom. The Bible makes this clear over and over again:

He who trusts in his own heart is a fool,
  But he who walks wisely will be delivered. (Proverbs 28:26)

The heart is more deceitful than all else and is desperately sick; who can understand it? (Jeremiah 17:9)

The way of a fool is right in his own eyes,
  But a wise man is he who listens to counsel. (Proverbs 12:15)

Where there is no guidance the people fall,
  But in abundance of counselors there is victory. (Proverbs 11:14)

Our Shepherd's Voice: "The job is too big to tackle by yourself."

One Easter season, it seemed that I was tottering under an excessive load of responsibility. On the Saturday morning before Palm Sunday, the sheer volume of details threatened to crush me. As I practiced with the vocal ensemble, prepared music for a keyboard duet, helped set up the cross outside, communicated with the sound technicians, made sure everything was in place for our 24-hour prayer vigil, and led the discussion in our worship leadership team meeting, I sensed my knees buckling. Questions were tossed at me from all directions: Did you find someone to put the banner on the cross? What color lights do we need? Who will blow up balloons for the Easter post-service praise party? When can the two men in the pantomime rehearse at church? Each new question had the potential to be the final straw to break my back. Had there not been faithful co-workers alongside me to help pick up the slack that Easter, I might well have crumbled under the weight.

Stressful seasons like this are part-and-parcel of worship ministry. Still, it is vital for our personal well-being and the success of the ministry that we enlist the help we need. As Ecclesiastes 4:9-10 reminds us:

Two are better than one because they have a good return for their labor. For if either of them falls, the one will lift up his companion. But woe to the one who falls when there is not another to lift him up.

Our Shepherd's Voice: "The burden on your heart is too great to bear alone."

As our Shepherd fashions our heart into a heart like His, we will find ourselves caring more and more deeply about the welfare of His sheep. This is good and right. After all, the apostle Paul instructs us, "Bear one another's burdens, and thereby fulfill the law of Christ" (Galatians 6:2).

But this load on our hearts can become very heavy; when it does, we will not have the strength to carry it by ourselves. Paul knew he needed others to help him bear the weight. In his letter to the Philippians, he wrote:

But I hope in the Lord to send Timothy to you shortly, so that I also may be encouraged when I learn of your condition. For I have no one else of kindred spirit who will genuinely be concerned for your welfare. (Philippians 2:19-20)

Even our Lord Jesus, as He faced the cross where He would bear the crushing load of our sins, asked His inner circle of disciples to join Him in bringing this burden before the Father (Matthew 26:36-38). If our Savior Himself needed others to come alongside Him, how much more do we?

A Conversation With My Shepherd

My life

Shepherd, here is an area of worship ministry for which I need more wisdom right now:

Will You show me if I am taking more responsibilities on myself in this ministry than I should be?

For which of Your sheep are You giving me a particular burden this week?

Your Word

In what ways do the following verses show me I must not rely on my own wisdom?

Proverbs 28:26

Jeremiah 17:9

Proverbs 12:15

Proverbs 11:14

As I read Ecclesiastes 4:9-12, what do You want to teach me about the importance of letting others help me carry out ministry responsibilities?

As I compare Galatians 6:2 with Matthew 22:35-40, will You show me how both bearing the burdens of others *and* allowing others to carry the burden with me are ways of making sure the "law of Christ" is being fulfilled?

Your thought for me

What is one thing You want me to remember from today's lesson?

My heart before You

(Talk to your Shepherd about all or part of the following.) Here's what I need to confess to You; how I want to praise You; what I hope to do with what You've shown me; what I need You to help me with:

DAY 2: SHARING THE BURDEN OF LEADERSHIP

When our Shepherd has made it so clear that we cannot shepherd His sheep all by ourselves, how is it that we ever consider stepping out on our own? Yet, that's pretty much what I did when I first took the helm of our worship ministry.

Two circumstances early on showed me that I had a fair distance to go in making good use of the godly men and women God had placed around me. In the first situation, I took it upon myself to talk with one of our worship leaders about how he could improve his leadership presence up front and contemporize his guitar skills. In the second situation, I explained to a woman who aspired to be a vocalist on our worship teams that she would first need vocal training to help her learn how to stay on pitch.

The words I used in each case were gentle and true; the help I offered was genuine. But both of these fellow believers were hurt, and they and their families left the church soon after.

How would bringing in the leadership team have helped? Though I will never know whether either of these friends would have stayed had I done things differently, I do know that I could have avoided several things by including others in the process:

- Making a decision that would affect others without counsel or input from those in ministry with me
- Acting on the decision without the prayer support of those in ministry with me
- The perception that I had a personal bias against these two people
- Second-guessing my own wisdom and motives after the fact

Having learned this indispensable (and painful) lesson early on, I wasn't about to make the same mistake four years later when a decision as monumental as paring down the teams was in the balance. If I was to jump off the cliff into a decision of uncertain outcome, I knew better than to do it without the parachute of my leadership team.

So, I brought the leadership team together and, with clammy hands and fast-beating heart, told them I believed it was time to act. I asked them to join me in listening to the voice of our Shepherd so that we would be able to collectively follow His lead.

As I glanced around the table, their faces mirrored what was in my own heart: hope that our Shepherd would guide us unmistakably down a path He had already cleared; fear that we might lose sight of Him and veer from the path. The enormity of the impact this might have on our brothers and sisters pressed down on us, and we were desperate to hear our Shepherd well.

After a month of prayer and discussions, we knew what we were to do: decrease the number of worship team members by half.

That paragraph sounds simple, like a cut-and-dried formula easily applied to a mathematical problem. It cannot begin to account for the hearts and emotions of each person involved, both on the giving end and on the receiving end of this decision.

So it was that, with quivering stomachs, yet secure intent, we called a gathering of the worship team volunteers and shared our plan with them (though not specifically who would remain in the worship ministry).

I give much credit to the worship ministry volunteers in that room for having submissive hearts before the Lord. They were gracious, affirming, and accepting; they were tearful and thoughtful. Many of them prayed for unity and humility; many spoke words of encouragement to the leadership team and to me.

I came away from the meeting overwhelmed with gratitude for how our Shepherd had prepared hearts ahead of time. I also came away more convinced than ever that, for both the sake of those around me and myself, this ministry cannot and must not be done alone.

Sharing The Burden Of Leadership For The Sake Of *Others*

How many meetings like this has the church experienced since its inception? How many times have church leaders over the centuries been required to make hard decisions that would affect their people?

How many times have congregations been asked to accept decisions made by those over them?

The believers in the early church at Antioch had a decision handed down to them, just as our worship teams did. A decision that could have been potentially divisive. The apostles and elders had gathered in Jerusalem to address a tricky question that had troubled the early church. After much prayer and deliberation, they had concluded that Gentile Christians should not be required to be circumcised like their Jewish brethren. They had written a letter to the Antioch church explaining their decision.

The council at Jerusalem knew the letter was too important to simply deliver by mail carrier, so Paul and Barnabas were sent to present it in person. The council also chose to send two additional men (Judas and Silas) to help the church understand and accept the decision (Acts 15:24-27). Scripture goes on to tell us that the men who brought the decision to the Antioch church "encouraged and strengthened the brethren."

I wonder what decision would have been made had it been left to only one apostle? I wonder how the church at Antioch would have received the decision if it had been made by only one leader? I wonder how encouraged and strengthened people would have felt if the message had been sent by mail carrier or read to them by a solitary messenger?

We worship leaders need to understand that perception is important. It is incumbent on us to do the best we can, not only to make wise decisions but also to communicate to others that we are not acting on our own initiative. Our fellow believers need to know that we respect them enough to include others in the process of making decisions that will impact them.

Sharing The Burden Of Leadership For The Sake Of *Ourselves*

You may be the most energetic worship leader in your city. Creativity may ooze out of your pores. Organization may be one of your most impressive skills. Leadership may be one of your top spiritual gifts. You may be blessed with an inordinate amount of innate wisdom. People may be drawn to your irrepressible personality. You may be a spiritual giant.

Not that I can say any of these things about myself. Even if I could, and even if you can there is not one of us who is adequate in ourselves to carry out our worship ministries in a way that will glorify God and build up our congregations. Furthermore, if we attempt to do so, we will be in danger of burning out or, worse yet, giving up altogether.

Moses was a man of uncommon qualities, possessing reserves of strength, spirituality, and shepherd-heartedness. Perhaps this is why he was unable to clearly see his own limitations. Sometimes it takes others to point out what we cannot see. In Moses' case, it was his father-in-law, Jethro:

> Now when Moses' father-in-law saw all that he was doing for the people, he said, "What is this thing that you are doing for the people? Why do you alone sit as judge and all the people stand about you from morning until evening?" (Exodus 18:14)

Moses's answer to this was one that most undershepherds can relate to: "Because the people come to me" (verse 15). Jethro, with words spoken as from the truest of friends, did not sugar-coat his reply to Moses' faulty reasoning: "The thing that you are doing is not good" (verse 17). He then proceeded to counsel Moses to bring others alongside to help share the load (verses 18-23).

Moses's response reflected the humility he was known for: "So Moses listened to his father-in-law and did all that he had said" (verse 24).

We worship leaders will do well to take note of Moses' response. For our own sake, as well as for the sake of the people we love and serve, we must surround ourselves with good and godly people who will help us.

A Conversation With My Shepherd

My life

Will You remind me of a time in my ministry when I've stepped out on my own rather than seeking the help I needed?

Am I leading with a heart of humility to receive the help You want to give me through others now?

Your Word

What can You show me from Acts 15:1-31 about the wisdom of letting others help make ministry decisions and carry them out?

How does the counsel of Jethro and Moses' response in Exodus 18:13-26 show me the importance of enlisting help as I carry out the calling You've given me?

Your thought for me

What is one thing You want me to remember from today's lesson?

My heart before You

(Talk to your Shepherd about all or part of the following.) Here's what I need to confess to You; how I want to praise You; what I hope to do with what You've shown me; what I need You to help me with:

DAY 3: FINDING THE RIGHT PEOPLE TO SHARE THE BURDEN

On Day 2, we talked about why it is important, both for ourselves and for others, that we share the burden of leadership. Today, we will discuss what qualities to look for in choosing people to help us.

When Jethro counseled Moses to enlist help, he told him to find "able men who fear God, men of truth, those who hate dishonest gain." We, too, must find people with the right heart and the right capabilities to help us. People who will help make up for our deficiencies and come alongside us in the three areas mentioned on Day 1: wisdom, practical help, and moral support.

People Of Wisdom

Much as I would like to think that I have impeccable hearing when it comes to listening to the Holy Spirit, experience has shown me otherwise. This is why the insights of my worship leadership team have been invaluable to me. Having people alongside me who care for the congregation as I do and are committed to seeking the Lord as we wrestle together with the hard things has been a gift of incalculable worth.

My leadership team and I have talked about personality conflicts on the teams and how to approach them in a godly and gentle manner. We have talked freely (yet kindly) about people's skills and gifts and how they fit in (or don't) with our worship ministry goals. We have talked about how to run rehearsals more efficiently. We have discussed how the congregation is responding to the worship ministry, taking into consideration their views while at the same time not losing sight of the vision God has given us. When the pastor and elders have asked us to do things a certain way, we have followed their lead; if we have not agreed with their decisions, we have encouraged one another to submit with the right heart. And we have prayed. A lot.

This is not a team of yes-persons. This is a team of individuals seeking the wisdom of the Holy Spirit and trusting Him to lead us corporately to the right decisions. Our goal has been to be able to say, along with the apostles and elders who brought their decision back to the Antioch church, "It seemed good to the Holy Spirit and to us" (Acts 15:28).

The Old Testament tells the story of a leadership team gone very wrong. Israel was ruled by a young king named Rehoboam. Wise counselors had been put in place around him, men who had served under his father Solomon. Early in Rehoboam's reign, when faced with a decision about whether to respond favorably to a request the people had made, these counselors urged him to listen to the people and thus earn the people's respect.

Rehoboam did not like the advice of this seasoned team, so he found another group of advisors, people who would be a little more agreeable to his point of view: he consulted the friends he had grown up with. Predictably, their response fed the young king's ego. In essence, they counseled him: "Don't listen to the people; show them who's boss" (1 Kings 12:10-11).

Rehoboam impulsively followed the counsel of his groupies, and as a result, the kingdom was tragically split in two from that point forward.

For the sake of the precious sheep under our care, as well as our own sake, it is critical that we surround ourselves with godly people of discernment and integrity. And that we listen to them well. The success of our worship ministry depends on it.

People Who Can Offer Practical Help

From the outset of my ministry, I realized that if I was to survive the cavalcade of details that threatened to trample me underfoot, I would need to rely heavily on my leadership team for help. Each leadership team and each worship leader is different; how the responsibilities are divided depends on everyone's availability and skills. In our case, some of the tasks the team has helped me with are:

- Planning and leading worship ministry workshops and gatherings
- Finding new songs that work well with our congregation

- Auditioning potential worship team members
- Hosting concerts and speakers
- Running the summer-long Worship 101 programs for our youth
- Publicity and announcements
- Emails and phone calls
- Brainstorming ideas for special services and seasons
- Out-of-town conference details (travel arrangements, registrations, etc.)
- Setting long-term goals and helping implement them
- Communicating these goals to the worship teams
- Recruiting other worship ministry volunteers to help
- Researching sound and lighting improvements

Having such a willing team by my side has enabled me to focus on the things that are priorities for me (such as planning worship services, team encouragement, personal development, and vision-casting) as well as tasks that fall exclusively in my realm of responsibility (such as staff meetings, budgeting, and scheduling).

Once again, we find good precedent in Scripture. In Acts, we read that it was brought to the attention of the apostles that some of the widows in the church were not being taken care of as they should be. The apostles recognized this as an issue that required their attention, but they were wise enough to assign it to others so that the apostles could devote themselves "to prayer and to the ministry of the word" (Acts 6:2-4).

Our role as worship leader will often require us to carry out a mountain of tasks, many of them mundane and time-consuming. Knowing what our priorities are, and enlisting our leadership team to come to our aid, will help ensure that we don't get buried under it.

People Who Will Give Moral Support

My friend and I often talk of how we "bear armor" for each other. If one of us is having a particularly daunting day, the other enters into fervent prayer, speaking words of encouragement and truth along the way, for as long as it is needed.

We borrow this image from 1 Samuel 14, where we read of one of the boldest acts of courage recorded in Scripture. For days, the Israelites had found themselves surrounded on all sides by enemy forces. Swords and spears were in short supply. In fact, only two men possessed such weapons: King Saul's son Jonathan and Jonathan's armor bearer.

One day Jonathan and his armor bearer snuck out of camp with the intent of crossing over to the garrison of their enemy, the Philistines. The odds were stacked impossibly against them. It would have been a very human response for the armor bearer to try to argue Jonathan out of it. Or to try to ease away by saying, "You go right on ahead, Jonathan. I'll just stay here and mull it over for a while."

But Scripture implies no such timidity. Rather, the immediate response of the armor bearer was, "Here I am with you according to your desire" (verse 7).

Possessing fierce determination and backed by a man of unimpeachable loyalty, Jonathan proceeded to scale the cliff that lay between him and the enemy. His armor bearer followed close behind, and upon reaching the top, the two of them, by a miracle of God, routed the enemy.

Do you have such men and women bearing armor on your behalf? When I sat in that circle of worship ministry volunteers on the day we shared with them that we would be cutting down the teams, I was literally shaking inside. If my leadership team had not been with me every step of the way as we'd sought the Lord; if they had been unable to reassure me that in doing this hard thing the Lord would be faithful to accomplish His purposes and preserve our unity; or if they had backed out at the last minute, leaving me to face our co-laborers alone—I do not believe I could have followed through with it.

A Conversation With My Shepherd

My life

Am I listening to any unwise counselors as I serve You in this ministry?

Will You bring to mind any names of people that might be able to come alongside me with practical help in this ministry?

Who are the "armor bearers" You have brought into my life?

Your Word

What lesson can I learn from 1 Kings 12:1-20 about listening to wise counsel as I serve Your sheep?

As I read Acts 6:1-6, will You show me why I must not personally carry out every aspect of my ministry?

Your Word (continued)

How does 1 Samuel 14:1–13 illustrate the spiritual principle of the value of "armor bearers" supporting me in prayer as I carry out Your calling?

Your thought for me

What is one thing You want me to remember from today's lesson?

My heart before You

(Talk to your Shepherd about all or part of the following.) Here's what I need to confess to You; how I want to praise You; what I hope to do with what You've shown me; what I need You to help me with:

DAY 4: OUR SHEPHERD, THE ULTIMATE BURDEN-SHARER

That meeting where my leadership team and I shared our difficult decision with the worship teams is not the end of the story. One more action was required: We needed to talk with each worship team member about his or her future in the ministry. My leadership team co-laborers were given the happy task of contacting the people who would remain on the teams. As director of worship ministry, I was given the difficult and distasteful task of contacting those who would not be asked to stay.

The Loneliness Of Leadership

How I longed to be the one to contact those who *would* be asked to stay. How I would have loved to call them to give the joyful news, affirming their giftedness for this ministry and expressing how glad I was about the prospect of continuing to work with them.

However, as the head undershepherd of worship, I could not pick and choose assignments according to my comfort level. This task was mine to carry out, and that was how it should be.

During the days that followed the meeting with our worship teams, I called some people, I met with others, and overall I endured one of the most emotionally grueling weeks I'd ever experienced in ministry.

My leadership team was praying hard for me and for those I would be contacting. I was praying hard too, listening intently for the words my Shepherd would give me in each conversation. Even so, the process was far from smooth. Significant ministry changes rarely are. As Kathryn Scott noted at a workshop I attended, changes like these are akin to giving birth: you know the baby needs to be born, but it's going to be messy and difficult.

I would also add: though a mother in labor is grateful for the support around her—doctor, nurse, coach—bottom line, she is the one who does not have the option of walking away. No one in the delivery room feels the responsibility quite like she does.

As I did the hard labor of telling my brothers and sisters news they did not want to hear, there was more messiness than I had hoped. I bungled one conversation and deeply hurt a dear brother and long-time leader on the worship team. I believed myself to be gloriously successful in another conversation as my friend responded with grace and near-joy, only to find out much later that she had secretly been devastated.

Even those who received the invitation to remain on the teams did not all respond as we had hoped. One young musician pulled himself off the team because he disagreed philosophically with the decision to pare down the teams. It was left to me to talk with him and hear him out, trying to explain how we had come to our conclusion. Though the conversation was congenial, it did not change his mind.

My leadership team carried all this with me. I never once felt apathy or detachment from them. They were all in, and they cared intensely for our brothers and sisters in the worship ministry and for me. It was not easy for them either.

But as the one ultimately responsible for the ministry and, in this case, for all the difficult conversations, I felt, on some level, very alone. Akin to the prophet Elijah who, as one of 7,000 people remaining who had not bowed to the false god Baal, declared with absolute straight face: "I alone am left" (1 Kings 19:10, 14).

Being a leader is uniquely lonely. Most of the time, the people around us do not have any idea that we ever feel lonely.

I remember one Easter season when everything went beautifully, or so I believed. After the season ended, our creative arts team met at my home to evaluate all that had happened.

I'd come to appreciate these friends and the unique qualities each one brought to the table. One churned out a continuous stream of delightful creativity. Another was driven by a passion for community outreach. A third peppered our meetings with one-line zingers, and a fourth kept us on track with energetic organization. One used his theological sensitivities to help us stay true to the Word. Then there were the two culturally-savvy college students who infused our discussions with youthful optimism.

That meeting, we engaged in a rousing discussion. Comment after comment was offered critiquing various aspects of what we had done, none of them rude or meant to hurt. At the close of the meeting, everyone felt lighthearted and good about having had a profitable conversation. Everyone except me. I closed the door after the last person left and sank down in my chair, defeated.

Was it wrong for them to evaluate with honesty? Not at all. Was I the only one who had contributed to the Easter season? Hardly. Was I warranted in feeling discouraged and alone? No. Yet that is how I felt.

It comes with the territory. Even with the best support teams around us, we worship leaders will be the ones initiating the difficult conversations. We will be the ones quieting down the worship team at rehearsal when really all we want to do is join in the banter. We will be the lightning rods for the sharp thunder-claps of criticism. We will bear the ultimate responsibility for a disappointing evaluation after a special service. No other person can feel our loneliness like we feel it.

Except One.

Our Shepherd Enters Into Our Loneliness

We children of our Father belong to someone who enters into our skin, saturates our spirit and searches out the deep things. He feels them with us, from the inside out. With the raw material of our elusive emotions, He could pen an elegant and epic poem.

He gets us.

Scripture tells us that we have a high priest who sympathizes with all of our weaknesses (Hebrews 4:15). Jesus enters into our loneliness in a way that no mere human ever could.

When Luke records the simple words...

And she gave birth to her firstborn son; and she wrapped Him in cloths, and laid Him in a manger, because there was no room for them in the inn. (Luke 2:7)

there is something impossibly profound going on here. Jesus, very God of very God, eternal King and Ancient of Days, entered into our loneliness. He was left out too. Of heaven. Of earth. He was left out for the purpose of bringing us *into* His fellowship with the Father.

His nearness—all the good we need

What does it mean to us that our Shepherd enters into our lives, coming near to us in our time of need? It means everything. As the psalmist Asaph confidently declared: "As for me, the nearness of God is my good" (Psalm 73:28). God's nearness was enough for Asaph, and it is enough for us. Our Shepherd's entering in is *all* the good we need.

My daughter called me one night a few years ago. She was on a train and informed me that she would be riding the Chicago transit system all night as part of a college project to help students understand the situation of homeless people.

These are words to make a Boise, Idaho mother's thoughts jump to unwelcome places. In that moment, I knew I could either surrender to fear or console myself with the one truth I needed to believe more than any other: God was *with* my daughter. This truth was all I had, but it was all the good I needed.

Time and time again, when God's people needed reassurance or encouragement, His presence was the one anchor-truth given them:

To Joshua: Have I not commanded you? Be strong and courageous! Do not tremble or be dismayed, for *the Lord your God is with you wherever you go* (Joshua 1:9).

To Joseph: Then Israel said to Joseph, "Behold I am about to die, but God *will be with you*, and bring you back to the land of your fathers" (Genesis 48:21).

To Gideon: But the Lord said to him, "Surely I *will be with you*, and you shall defeat Midian as one man" (Judges 6:16).

To the Israelites: When you pass through the waters, I *will be with you* … (Isaiah 43:2).

To the disciples: Go therefore and make disciples of all the nations … and lo, *I am with you always*, even to the end of the age (Matthew 28:19-20).

To the Corinthian church: Finally, brethren, rejoice, be made complete, be comforted, be like-minded, live in peace; and the God of love and peace *will be with you* (2 Corinthians 13:11).

The nearness of God always has been and always will be enough for God's people.

His nearness—how it helps us

Recently my husband met with a woman who came to him for help in her grief. Her teenage son took his life four months ago, and since then she has lived in a fog of sorrow, shadowy and unshakable.

She does not yet know Christ, so Greg listened to her heart and held out to her comforting truths that he prays she will someday embrace. Over dinner, he and I talked about what this woman must be going through and wondered aloud how the truth of God's nearness would help her, if she were able to receive it.

Indeed, what help is it to *any* of us that our God is near? It would take a much larger book than this one to catalogue all the ways His nearness helps us, but here are a few recurring themes we find in Scripture:

- His nearness gives guidance (Psalm 139:7-10)
- His nearness gives reassurance in the dark (Psalm 139:11-12)
- His nearness gives rest (Exodus 33:14)
- His nearness brings favor (Exodus 33:15-16a)
- His nearness teaches us (John 14:26)
- His nearness brings peace (John 14:27)
- His nearness means He listens to us and answers us (Psalm 116:1, 2)

In the lonely moments of leadership, we are *not* alone; our Shepherd is with us. And His is no powerless presence standing idly by and calling out, "You've got this!" When we look around us and it seems we alone are left to shoulder the heaviest burdens, our Savior says, "Look again. I'm still here, and *I've* got this."

A Conversation With My Shepherd

My life

> Do I feel lonely now as a leader of Your flock? If so, how are You speaking Your presence to me?

> Will You remind me of a time when You have made Your presence especially known to me as I've carried out this ministry?

> In which of the following ways do I need to know that You are near right now: guidance, reassurance, rest, favor, instruction, peace, or answers to prayer?

> Can I say and know with confidence that Your nearness is my good?

Your Word

> In 1 Kings 19:9-18, what will You show me about the ways You meet Your undershepherds when they feel lonely?

Your Word (continued)

How do Luke 2:7 and Hebrews 4:15 prove that You want to enter our world and be near us?

What does Psalm 73:25-26, 28 teach me about Your nearness?

Your thought for me

What is one thing You want me to remember from today's lesson?

My heart before You

(Talk to your Shepherd about all or part of the following.) Here's what I need to confess to You; how I want to praise You; what I hope to do with what You've shown me; what I need You to help me with:

DAY 5: TAKING HIS HELP TO HEART

Worship undershepherds are expected to live in constant awareness of their Shepherd's presence, right? After all, don't we lead our congregations with songs declaring that our God is near? Don't we draw attention to Scriptures that hammer home what we sing? Scriptures like:

> God is our refuge and strength,
> A *very present help* in trouble. (Psalm 46:1, emphasis added).

Yet, in our lonely seasons, we undershepherds may find ourselves sighing, Eeyore-like, "Makes no difference." Makes no difference that we have a whole congregation of brothers and sisters singing these truths right along with us. Makes no difference that we have a leadership team committed to helping us bear the burden of leadership. We still feel alone.

Though we are not.

How Do We *Know* He Is Near?

How do we know God's very-present help as a reality in our lives? What makes this a tangible truth rather than a theory? We do not *see* Him (not yet). Most of us never hear Him speak in audible tones. We do not literally feel the warmth of His wings sheltering us. So how do we *know* He is near?

The Apostle John must have anticipated such a question from God's children:

> We know by this *that He abides in us*, *by the Spirit* whom He has given us. (1 John 3:24b)

God's Spirit abiding in us? This is amazing. Outrageously generous. Mind-boggling. The Spirit of our infinite God Himself draws nearer than near, inhabiting our heart and whispering to our soul that we are His (Romans 8:16)!

What profound comfort the disciples must have felt when they heard these words of Jesus even as His departure was imminent:

I will ask the Father, and He will give you another Helper, that He may be with you forever; that is the Spirit of truth, whom the world cannot receive, because it does not see Him or know Him, but you know Him because He abides with you and will be in you. (John 14:16-17)

The Holy Spirit is called our Helper for good reason. He does not manifest Himself in our lives as some polite houseguest quietly warming Himself in a corner by the fireplace, unwilling to interrupt our routine. If this is what His presence meant, what would be the good in that? Happily, this is *not* the God we belong to. *Our* God strides into our lives with power and promise, taking over the household and making His presence known.

Yes, our God is a very present help. And He wants us to know it to our deepest parts.

We Need Him; We Have Him

What would have happened in my spirit if I had wallowed in my aloneness during our worship team cutbacks, allowing it to overshadow me? Would I have been able to carry out the difficult conversations with grace? Would I have been able to initiate them at all? As an undershepherd desiring to please my Shepherd even in my aloneness, I knew I had no choice but to trust Him to stamp the reality of His presence on my spirit. As I tremblingly undertook what I knew to be right, this was the truth that sustained me:

As for me, You uphold me in my integrity,
And You set me in Your presence forever. (Psalm 41:12)

What kind of extravagant kindness is this that sets us eternally in the presence of the God who dwells in unapproachable light? It's the kindness of a Savior who has entered into our loneliness and will not leave us to bear it alone. It's the love of a Friend who promises never to abandon us as orphans (John 14:18).

When our children were young, we took a trip across several states to visit Greg's sister. One of the states we passed through was Nebraska, and on this particular day in this particular year the Nebraska skies turned green. An eerie green, menacing and still. Exactly like the sky we'd seen in the movie *Twister* the week before. But this was no big screen, and we were not seated in a sheltered theater.

With the startling effect of a jump scene, baseball-sized hail began pommelling our car. Above the deafening roar we strained to hear the radio announcer who was informing us that between two certain towns there was a severe tornado warning. (We were squarely between the two towns.) He continued to intone with deliberate gravity: "If you are in a vehicle, find safety under an overpass." (Unfortunately, all the semi-trucks had received the memo before we did.) "If you can't find an overpass, pull over to the side and get out of your car and into a ditch." (Did I mention the hail was of biblical proportions?)

Blanched with fright and unsure what to do, Greg and I tried to remain calm for the kids. Then we heard the timid voice of one of our children from the back seat: "Shouldn't we pray or something?"

In that moment I remembered: Before we had headed out that morning, I had grabbed a quick few minutes to read the Bible and pray. "Kids!" I said. "God knew this was going to happen to us today, and He wanted us to know that He is with us right now. Listen to what He showed me this morning!" I opened my Bible to Psalm 148:4, 8 and read:

Praise Him, highest heavens,
And the waters that are above the heavens! ...
Fire and hail, snow and clouds;
Stormy wind, fulfilling His word.

It was one of those light-bulb moments described by author Ruth Myers:

Humility says, like the cherished hymn, "I need you. Oh, I need You!"
Then it lets faith take over with the glad affirmation: "I have You! Oh, I have You!" [44]

⌈In that instant, we went from acknowledging our *need* for His presence to gratefully affirming the *fact* of His presence.⌉

The tornado never materialized. Dorothy and Toto did not fall from the sky. We were none the worse for wear, though our pock-marked car had taken a good beating.

Since that incident there has not been another occasion for me to claim Scriptures about hail. But I will never forget that, one summer day in Nebraska, my Shepherd spoke in a voice so intentional and unmistakable that not even the most ferocious of hailstorms could drown it out:

"You are not alone. I am here, and I will help you."

Worship leaders, take heart: We are not alone. We have a Helper, and He is with us.

A Conversation With My Shepherd

My life

> Is there any way I am treating Your Spirit as a "polite houseguest" in my heart rather than inviting You to make Yourself at home, speaking truth and help to me?

> How are You showing me Your extravagant kindness today?

> Here are some things in my ministry for which I am very aware that I *need* You and that I *have* You:

Your Word

What does Psalm 46:1-3 teach me about Your presence?

According to the following Scriptures, how do You reassure me of Your presence in my life?

1 John 3:24b

Romans 8:14-17

John 14:16-17

How can You reassure me from Psalm 41:12 and John 14:18 that, though I may feel alone as I carry out Your call, I am not alone and never will be?

Your thought for me

What is one thing You want me to remember from today's lesson?

My heart before You

(Talk to your Shepherd about all or part of the following.) Here's what I need to confess to You; how I want to praise You; what I hope to do with what You've shown me; what I need You to help me with:

A PRAYER TO PRAY

Very-Present Shepherd, Your Word assures me that You never intended for me to lead this ministry on my own. When I try, will You please remind me that this is not Your way?

Thank You for the brothers and sisters You've given me to help carry the load. Thank You for those who give of their time freely, looking for no compensation other than to see Your church built up for Your glory. I am honored to have them by my side. Let me glean from their wisdom, accept their help, and take encouragement from the moral support they give me.

Are there others You might be bringing to help me? Please open my eyes to recognize them when I see them.

I know that helpers may come and go, and there will inevitably be seasons when I feel alone. While I desire never to take my co-laborers for granted, I joyfully acknowledge that the best help is You, Yourself.

Your nearness is my good, and it is all the good I need. So will You please meet me in my lonely moments? Will You teach me how to grasp Your hand and live fully in Your presence, taking joy in Your company and looking to You as my ultimate resource?

CHAPTER 12

OUR SHEPHERD SPEAKS THANKFULNESS

DAY 1: THANKFULNESS—AN OFFERING OF WORSHIP

I stood up, rolled my chair under the desk, and took one long last look around my office: boxes stacked by the door, full-brimmed with photos and coffee cups; binders jammed with copies of music; framed "He Will Rejoice Over You With Singing," encouragement from a friend; scuffs on the wall behind the congas; fabric painting of African musicians; little elephant candle, gift from our church's Bosnian custodian, now my friend, for whose salvation I continually plead; file drawers whittled down to the essence of nine years' work…and the clock on the wall. How often in the course of this ministry had I glanced repeatedly at its hands, frequently dismayed by the cyclonic speed at which they rotated? Nine years; 78,840 rotations of the big hand.

No, Greg and I weren't leaving the church. We are still deeply rooted there in the congregation that we both dearly love. I am still actively serving in the worship ministry. I was simply making way for the person who would take my place as the next director of worship ministry. God had made it clear to me that my time in that role was completed.

I walked to the door, switched off the lights, and turned my head back toward the window. The field outside was awash in golden glow, the sky suffused with brilliant oranges and violets. I was drawn irresistibly, lured by the beauty and won over by the pronouncement: "I will give My glory to no other."

I moved toward the window, eyes transfixed by the dazzling majesty—or was it by God Himself? Heart overflowing, tears spilling, I began to sing a familiar worship song. Quietly and reflectively at first, gradually crescendoing to boisterous joy. The lyrics tumbled out, phrase upon phrase describing God's presence in high places and low places, His faithfulness in triumphs and battle scars. In that moment, there was room for nothing in my heart besides thankfulness. No pride, no regrets, no misgivings, no nostalgia, no fear. Only gratitude, pure and profound.

Why It's Important For A Worship Undershepherd To Be Thankful

Thankfulness is an art. It's a discipline. It does not always come naturally. Much more ready on our lips are words of disappointment and complaint. These are the words that do not have to be summoned; they appear without warning and fly from our tongue without effort.

But gratitude? Now here is something that doesn't spring up from our heart ground like some prolific indigenous plant. A crop of thankfulness requires careful and intentional care. What words does our Shepherd have for us as we cultivate this garden of gratitude?

Our Shepherd's Voice: "Thankfulness informs true worship."

Is this deliberate cultivating something we worship undershepherds are willing to do? Do we believe deep-down that it is worth the effort? Perhaps if we see thankfulness as a catalyst to worship, we will be more ready to nurture it into a full-fledged way of life.

Listen to these familiar words:

Enter His gates with thanksgiving
And His courts with praise.
Give thanks to Him, bless His name. (Psalm 100:4)

These words are painted above the entrance to our church sanctuary, and I've often considered them a good reminder. But I am not sure I've always viewed them as the mandate they are. I have not always seen thankfulness as a prerequisite to worship.

This verse tells us that worship flows from a heart that is thankful. Reading it now, I ask myself: Is it even possible to worship without a thankful heart? Isn't worship a glad capitulation of my will to the will of God (Romans 12:1-2)? If so, is it even conceivable that I could worship while holding discontentment in my heart?

Furthermore, if my heart is callous to the good gifts He showers on me, doesn't this mean that some part of me is not submitted to Him, not willing to give Him all the praise He is due? Is it thinkable that I could glorify the Lord of all creation while at the same time failing to acknowledge the good and perfect gifts that come from His gracious hand (James 1:17)?

True worship finds its source in a heart that is thankful. Thankfulness is the ingredient of worship that turns it from token into treasure.

God does not *need* anything from us. He owns everything, including us. All our gifts and sacrifices—yes, even our talent and our time—mean *nothing* to Him if not offered from a heart of gratitude. Hear from the lips of the Father Himself what comprises acceptable worship:

If I were hungry I would not tell you,
For the world is Mine, and all it contains.
Offer to God a sacrifice of **thanksgiving**
And pay your vows to the Most High …
He who offers a sacrifice of **thanksgiving** *honors Me.*
(Psalm 50:12, 14, 23a, emphasis added)

Our Shepherd's Voice: "Thankfulness turns your eyes from yourself to Me."

Besides being the essential element that informs true worship, thankfulness also twists our head back around from ourselves (am I happy? do I feel satisfied? do I have enough?) and toward our Shepherd in whom the answer to all these questions is a resounding "Yes!":

- Thank You, Lord, that in Your presence is fullness of joy
- Thank You, Jesus, that You are the Bread of Life, the water that quenches all thirst
- Thank You, Father, that You provide more than we could ever ask or think

Self-seeking is antithetical to worship; thanksgiving is the perfect antidote because it makes all self-seeking redundant and irrelevant. If we gratefully acknowledge that, in Christ, we possess everything good, there will be no point in trying to reach for anything besides Him.

Our Shepherd's Voice: "Thankfulness inspires others to worship."

God is pleased by worship that stems from a thankful heart. *We* are blessed when we worship from a heart unshackled from self and governed by gratitude. But there is a third party to consider, and that is our *congregation.* When our own worship is freed to be all that God intends it to be, we can inspire *others* to flourish as worshipers of the one true God.

As faithful tenders of our Shepherd's flock, we have a responsibility to live out the beauty of a heart thoroughly saturated with thankfulness so that others will want such a heart for themselves. Furthermore, we worship leaders have the unique opportunity of helping our congregation see that there is very good reason to be thankful.

It is not a responsibility to be taken lightly. There may be newer Christians among us who have not walked with their Shepherd long enough to see the arc of His faithfulness over time. If we've traveled with Him a distance, we have the joyful privilege of recounting for them His grace over the long-haul. There may be more seasoned Christians in our midst who are weary because of the length of the journey or distracted by its demands; we are given the sacred trust of reminding them to look up again and see that God is generous and gracious, always.

If we love these sheep in our care, won't we want to say, along with the Psalmist:

> *I will sing of the lovingkindness of the Lord forever;*
> *To all generations I will make known Your faithfulness with my mouth.*
> (Psalm 89:1)

A Conversation With My Shepherd

My life

How are You cultivating a heart of thankfulness in me?

Has my heart been callous to any of the good gifts You've showered on me recently?

Will You show me how I can help my congregation see that there is very good reason to be thankful?

Your Word

What can You teach me from Psalm 100:4 about the relationship between thanksgiving and worship?

What can I learn from Psalm 50:10-14, 23a about worship that is acceptable to You?

What can Psalm 89:1-2, 15-16 teach me about leading Your people in grateful worship?

Your thought for me

What is one thing You want me to remember from today's lesson?

My heart before You

(Talk to your Shepherd about all or part of the following.) Here's what I need to confess to You; how I want to praise You; what I hope to do with what You've shown me; what I need You to help me with:

DAY 2: THE FLOW OF THANKFULNESS—THANKFULNESS IN *RETROSPECT*

A Continuous Stream—Past, Present, And Future

A thankful heart can't choose its moments any more than a drifting twig can choose its current. Each of us floats along the stream of life, carried along a course of the Creator's design. We can either sail through, buoyed by gladness along the way, or we can struggle and gasp, drenched in discontent.

Can we rightly be called grateful people if we allow amnesia to set in and fail to remember the grace God has poured into our days and years up until now? Can we be labeled thankful if we enthuse about the big occasions of obvious blessing while letting all the little ones slip by unnoticed? Are we truly thankful children of our Father if we think that at some point He might stop pouring out His blessing, as if there was a cap on His generous heart?

Life is a continuous current of moments that flow one into the other. A thankful heart will settle into the flow of life's stream, carrying with it a song of praise as it rides the waves and bobs in the eddies. A heart of gratitude will glance back from time to time to remember what has transpired; it will peer ahead from time to time to catch glimpses of what might be around the bend. It will choose to rejoice with thanksgiving in all moments past, present, and future, eyes open to absorb the gifts to be found there.

In Chapter 4, we looked at how choosing to recount God's faithfulness will be the ballast that keeps us steady when even our strongest resolve to worship has been thrown off-kilter by life's storms. The purpose of this present chapter is a little less weighty. Here, we are talking about thankfulness as a means of injecting a celebratory spirit into our days. Sometimes we need to allow ourselves the luxury of sitting back and being merry. Think of this chapter as blowing a horn at the culmination of a birthday party when the cake is brought out. It's time to soak in the joy and let it bring a smile to our face.

You have your reasons to celebrate; I have mine. Perhaps as I share some of my own reasons to be thankful over my nine years of worship ministry, your heart will be inspired to come up with reasons of its own. That is my prayer for you.

Rejoicing In The Past

The morning following my last time at the helm of worship team rehearsal, I spent a few minutes with my Shepherd letting it all sink in. Nine years: Insecurity and euphoria, failure and faith, puzzlement and perseverance, labor and rest, discouragement and amazement, exhaustion and energy, solemnity and laughter, timidity and courage, camaraderie and isolation. I'd experienced all of these things.

I had stood shoulder to shoulder with co-laborers who had worshiped and served with me, brothers and sisters who had cheered me on and shown me grace. I had learned right along with my congregation—sometimes haltingly, sometimes with bursts of brilliant awakening—what it meant to be a family worshiping together.

As I reminisced that morning, I began to see how at every juncture my Shepherd's hand had left its unmistakable imprint. He had been writing His story in my life and in my church all along. The more memories my mind gathered, the greater my gratitude grew.

His Word tells us it is good and right to remember all He has done for us:

He has made His wonders to be remembered;
The Lord is gracious and compassionate (Psalm 111:4).

Bless the Lord, O my soul,
And forget none of His benefits (Psalm 103:2).

I shall remember the deeds of the Lord;
Surely I will remember Your wonders of old.
I will meditate on all Your work
And muse on Your deeds (Psalm 77:11-12).

As I "mused" on all that my Shepherd had done, I couldn't help but rejoice:

Rejoicing in the Shepherd's leading

First, there had been the leading of the Holy Spirit as He had opened doors and cleared paths, prompting and confirming along the way: the sudden and unexpected vacancy of the worship leader position; my heart warmed ahead of time to the idea of taking up this mantle; Greg, the elders, and the worship leadership team in agreement about asking me.

Rejoicing in the Shepherd's encouragement

Then, there had been the gifts of encouragement from the Spirit, given at just the right moments: Matt Redman's "Heart of Worship" story[45] and its reassurance that, though we may not always get the music right, it is always about Jesus; knowing from the outset what my ministry theme verse was so that I had the trembling courage to accept this call:

> *Not that we are adequate in ourselves to consider anything as coming from ourselves, but our adequacy is from God.* (2 Corinthians 3:5)

Rejoicing in the Shepherd's people

Add to these gifts of encouragement the people God had brought to our church and incorporated into the worship ministry at exactly the right moment: co-laborers without whose skill, heart, and friendship I might not have had the strength to see my call to its completion.

Rejoicing in the Shepherd's power

Woven through all of these things had been the power of the Spirit to accomplish His purposes in every worship service, every season, and every circumstance. *He* was the one who had led us to the songs He wanted us to sing, astounding us with their timeliness and humbling us with their effectiveness. *He* was the one who had directed the service flow and organized the individual elements into a seamless whole. *He* was the one who had raised up the musicians and artists, equipped the technicians, and inspired the message. *He* was the one who had enlivened all our hearts to respond to His voice. In all of this, *He* was the one who had taken our imperfect efforts and transformed them into works of value, for His glory.

Rejoicing in the Shepherd's lessons

Furthermore, with each step of the journey, the Shepherd had taken this wet-behind-the-ears little undershepherd and gently taught her the invaluable skills, values, and principles necessary to lead His sheep in worship. As the time neared for me to transition out of leading this ministry, I shared with our congregation in a newsletter article some of the things He had taught me:

- Christ is the head of the church, and He will move us forward in His own way and in His own time.
- The Lord's plans are much better and bigger than our own.
- The Lord goes before and prepares hearts for worship.
- God puts together the parts of the body as He sees fit.
- I cannot (and should not) do this ministry on my own.
- It is possible (and imperative) to sincerely worship the Lord while at the same time serve the congregation by playing skillfully and engagingly.
- As an instrumentalist on the worship team, often less is more.
- There will always be someone who is better at what I do than I am, but God only expects me to give Him my best (with no apologies).
- We must practice and prepare diligently but hold all things loosely.
- When I am least secure is often when His power is most visible.
- Ministry is much more about people than about music.

- I can trust God to help my brothers and sisters respond with grace, even when it is necessary to have difficult conversations and make difficult decisions affecting them.
- Diligent and fervent prayer must precede everything.
- None of this ministry is about me, so there is never a need to be defensive or fearful or discouraged by someone else's responses.
- Though I take great joy in worshiping with my brothers and sisters on a Sunday morning, worship should infuse every other waking moment as well.
- I am not indispensable, and when it's time to move on to a new calling, God will raise up the right person to take my place.

Rejoicing in the Shepherd's refinement

Finally, in addition to these lessons, my Shepherd had taught me deeper, more personal things: imperfections hammered out on the anvil of adversity, impurities refined in the cauldron of criticism, pride lopped off by the shears of shame. The work was sometimes jarring in its suddenness, other times imperceptible in its subtlety, but the result was always and only wrought by His sure and loving hand.

Continuing Down The Stream

As we float along life's stream, glad reminiscence is not the only thing that will keep us whistling a song of thankfulness. Such music will also require eyes and heart open to the gifts along the way. This is where we will turn our focus tomorrow.

A Conversation With My Shepherd

My life

When is it easiest for me to have a thankful heart: when I remember what You've done in the past, when I notice what You're doing in the moment, or when I think about what You will do in the future?

Is there some way You can help me inject a more celebratory spirit into my days?

If You were to ask me to leave this ministry today, what are some of the things You would want me to be thankful for as I looked back?

Is there anything I would have difficulty thanking You for? If so, will You help me lay this at Your feet now?

Your Word

Taking the following verses all together, what can I learn about being thankful for the things You've done in the past (Psalm 111:4; Psalm 103:2; Psalm 77:11-12)?

In Psalm 111, what are some of the things that Your people have praised You for in retrospect ("He has …")?

Your thought for me

What is one thing You want me to remember from today's lesson?

My heart before You

(Talk to your Shepherd about all or part of the following.) Here's what I need to confess to You; how I want to praise You; what I hope to do with what You've shown me; what I need You to help me with:

DAY 3: THE FLOW OF THANKFULNESS—THANKFULNESS IN *THE MOMENTS*

Appreciating The Present

As I journeyed down the current of life and ministry during those nine years, did I see all of the good things God was doing in the moments they were happening? No. It is often easier to view them in hindsight, which is why we do well to look for them from that vantage point. I do, however, wish I had searched more diligently for them as they occurred.

Gladness in the moments

There is a prayer in Scripture that reveals much about what it means to be thankful in all the moments that make up the span of our lives:

> *Lord, You have been our dwelling place in all generations.*
> *Before the mountains were born*
> *Or You gave birth to the earth and the world,*
> *Even from everlasting to everlasting, You are God… .*
> *For a thousand years in Your sight*
> *Are like yesterday when it passes by,*
> *Or as a watch in the night… .*
> *So teach us to number our days,*
> *That we may present to You a heart of wisdom… .*
> *O satisfy us in the morning with Your lovingkindness,*
> *That we may sing for joy and be glad all our days.*
> (Psalm 90:1–2, 4, 12, 14)

What sorts of life experiences would prompt the psalmist to pray such a prayer? What life streams had carried him to this place where he was able to embrace both the birth-to-death eternal view and the moment-by-moment temporal view?

We know that it was a journey of tragedies and detours, failures and cataclysmic consequences. Moses, the author of this psalm, understood the value of singing for joy and being glad all his days, no matter what they held. He grasped the importance of seeing each day from God's eternal perspective, knowing that this would train his heart to be glad in God all his life. As he grasped the life-giving truth that his Shepherd lived to satisfy him with lovingkindness each and every day, he passed it along to others. His psalm is one big invitation to pray with him: "Let's thank the Lord together for His lovingkindness. *This* is what it means to worship."

Spiritual awareness in the moments

Our family once took a journey that surprised us with events not included on our itinerary. This experience wasn't as life-changing as the one endured by Moses and the Israelites in the wilderness, but it was memorable enough to forever earn the moniker, "The Reider Adventure."

That summer, we decided to take our three young children on a drive to see their cousins. A 3,000-mile drive from Boise to Iowa and back, our main resources being a bundle of books and a crumpled-up map of the United States that I could never figure out how to refold properly.

The night before we left, Greg carefully tied our suitcases to the top of the minivan, secured the tarp, and stepped back to look at his masterpiece.

"Good job, Honey," I said encouragingly. "It looks so neat, and pretty too."

Early the next morning we all piled into the car, sleepy-eyed and high-hoped, and headed down the road. An hour later, I happened to glance at the side mirror, and my groggy brain registered that two suitcases were hanging precariously over the edge of the roof.

"Um. I think you'd better pull over, Greg."

We pulled over at the next off-ramp to re-secure the pile, only to discover that three other suitcases had previously made their escape. This was not welcome news.

After quickly re-tying our diminishing possessions, we were on the freeway again, this time heading back toward home, eyes peeled for any signs of our luggage. As we neared our exit, we noticed tiny clothes scattered all over the freeway on the opposite side of the median. After discussing the slim odds of *another* family losing their luggage on this same morning, we astutely concluded that these must indeed be our runaway belongings.

By now it was morning rush hour, but my husband valiantly (if not sensibly) dodged in and out of the four lanes of traffic, recovering every single item except our son's toothbrush.

The suitcases, however, had exploded. So we drove back to town, ate breakfast out of our ice chest, shook debris off of grease-stained clothes, bought two new suitcases, and headed out again, several dollars poorer and six hours behind schedule.

Sometimes things just go so wrong that the absurdity makes you laugh. Greg and I decided at this point that we could either let this turn of events ruin the rest of our trip, or we could see it as an opportunity to teach our children how to choose good humor and worship God in all moments.

To avoid giving the mistaken impression that we are a super-spiritual family whose vacations are characterized by an atmosphere of love and laughter from beginning to end, I want to stop and acknowledge something right here: we have had more than our fair share of arguments and bad attitudes when it was all we could do to stay in the same car with each other. *This* just happened to be one of those moments when our Shepherd slammed us on the shoulder with His rod and said, "Listen up! This is important, and you need to get this."

It was a good thing we listened. Our plan for the day had been to drive through Yellowstone, catch a glimpse of Old Faithful, and spend the night at a hotel outside the park. However, that afternoon our car broke down. Twice. When we did eventually arrive at Old Faithful, we had missed its performance by ten minutes.

Grabbing a quick dinner, we continued on, anxious to get a good night's sleep. We began cheering loudly when we finally found the park exit late that night, but the hurrahs soon died down as we pondered, "Why does the east exit have a sign that says 'South Exit'?" So we turned back around and drove slowly through the park again, trying to avoid the ubiquitous bison that kept startling us. Finally, we landed at our hotel for a brief night's sleep.

Two days and several car breakdowns later, we were greeted by our dear family in Iowa who spent the whole first day helping us dry out the entire contents of our suitcases (including shoes and ties) because our tarp had provided—how shall I put this—inadequate coverage as we had driven through a 12-hour deluge.

A few days later, we courageously piled in the car again to begin our trip home. The high point of this leg of our journey was when our engine caught fire in the middle of the Idaho wilderness. While Greg hitchhiked to the nearest town for help, the kids and I wrote a song called "Oh, What an Adventure" (to the tune of "Oh, How I Love Jesus"). The poetic artistry of this song would move you to tears (who would *not* be touched by the beauty of such lyrics as, "After missing Old Faithful they left with cold despair"?). Rather than awe you with more examples, I will conclude with the lesson that was driven home to us on that hot July day:

Something extraordinary was happening here; these weren't random mishaps. From those first wayward suitcases, our Shepherd had graciously heightened our spiritual awareness so that we would catch the joy in the moments. This was the stuff out of which young minds and hearts were being formed. This was fuel for the fires of thanksgiving He wanted to ignite in our little family.

When we think back to this vacation, it's not the sweet time on the Iowa farm that we remember most (wonderful though it was). It's the delays and disappointments, the U-turns and breakdowns. It was in *these* moments that God made His presence especially known, teaching us the joy of choosing thankfulness *every* moment.

I love this prayer from *The Valley of Vision*:

My cup runs over.
Suffer me not to be insensible to these
    daily mercies. [46]

Isn't a thankful person one who is not oblivious to the Shepherd's daily mercies?

Thankfulness in the moments has its learning curve

Becoming a thankful person does not happen haphazardly; it happens over time, moment by moment, day by day. Just as Moses prayed, "Lord *teach* us to number our days," we, too, need to pray, "Lord, *teach* us how to value each day, handing it right back to You as an offering of thanksgiving." It didn't come naturally to this undershepherd any more than it comes naturally to us.

Last year I made it my goal to try to cultivate a more thankful heart. One tool I used (at the inspiration of Ann Voskamp's book *One Thousand Gifts*) [47] was to keep a journal of thanksgiving, jotting down things that evidenced my Shepherd's loving hand in the course of a day. A year later, I still have far to go in acquiring a heart of thanksgiving, but I do see myself becoming more attendant to the little joys that are to be found in the moments.

As a worship leader, I often found it difficult to notice those gifts my Shepherd handed to me during each day. I would become consumed with working out a musical transition as I prepared for rehearsal. I would fume about an unkind email in my In-Box. I would let the bored-looking faces in the pews blind my eyes to the engaged ones. I would obsess about preparing details for the next big event rather than taking in the everyday beauty of the task right in front of me.

I wish I had done better.

Yet I do believe that at the end of my nine years of ministry I was a more thankful person than at the beginning. Little by little, my Shepherd had been teaching me that, in *every* moment, there is something to be thankful for.

How blessed are the people who know the joyful sound!
O Lord, they walk in the light of Your countenance.
In Your name they rejoice all the day. (Psalm 89:15–16a)

A Conversation With My Shepherd

My life

What joys are You wanting me to catch in this moment?

Are my eyes open to see You in the moments of this day?

How can I learn from You to be more aware of Your daily mercies? Is there something specifically that I can do to become more aware?

Your Word

What can I learn from Your servant Moses about cultivating a thankful heart through all the moments of life, even the difficult ones (Psalm 90)?

Your thought for me

What is one thing You want me to remember from today's lesson?

My heart before You

(Talk to your Shepherd about all or part of the following.) Here's what I need to confess to You; how I want to praise You; what I hope to do with what You've shown me; what I need You to help me with:

DAY 4: THE FLOW OF THANKFULNESS—THANKFULNESS IN *PROSPECT*

As we continue along the current of life and ministry buoyed by thankfulness, it is good to both glance backwards in gratitude and appreciate the scenery along the way. But these things are not enough to keep a song of gladness on our lips: we must also keep looking farther down the stream with expectant hope.

As I prepared to write this concluding chapter, I had trouble deciding what to emphasize: Thanksgiving or Hope? The two ideas are interdependent; it is difficult to separate them. Thankfulness gives hope credence: When our eyes are open to all that God has done and is doing, our hearts are more ready to believe that He will continue to do it. We will be better able to thank Him in advance for what we cannot yet see.

Hoping For The Future

A few weeks ago, I sat down on the first day of the new year and listed some of the things I am looking forward to in this year. As I contemplated the items on my list, I realized that for each hope there was an accompanying fear. This year, Greg and I will become grandparents for the first time: what if we have forgotten how to care for young children in the time since our own children were young? Soon the long process of writing this book will be completed: what if no one outside my immediate sphere of friends and family ever reads it or is encouraged by it?

It is one thing to thank God for the tangible gifts He has *already* given us; it takes a whole new level of determined gratitude to thank Him for things *before* we receive them. We know His general promises (He will always do what's best; He will never leave us; He will come to our aid), but we do not know the specifics of how He will carry out His promises: What energy, wisdom, and time will He enable me to give each grandchild? How many people will He prompt to read this book?

Thankfulness, by faith

Thankfulness in *retrospect* and *in the moments* requires open eyes and receptive heart; thankfulness in *prospect* requires faith, the kind described in Hebrews 11:1:

> *Now faith is the assurance of things hoped for, the conviction of things not seen.*

What will be the difference between a worship leader who is able to help his fellow sheep worship with joyful faith and one who is not? It will be his ability to recognize and appreciate the Shepherd's generosity through the years and give thanks for His generosity yet to be seen.

What kind of a leader does your congregation see standing before them? Is it one who forgets that we worship a faithful God who is the same yesterday, today, and forever (Hebrews 13:8)? Or is it one who boldly and assuredly proclaims:

> *This I recall to my mind,*
> *Therefore I have hope.*
> *The Lord's lovingkindnesses indeed never cease,*
> *For His compassions never fail.*
> *They are new every morning;*
> **Great is Your faithfulness.**
> (Lamentations 3:21-23, emphasis added)

Last week my writing stalled, and I became discouraged. As I shared my disappointment with my husband, he looked at me with compassion and said, "Honey, I think you're feeling like this because you've been climbing this mountain for so long. God has brought you this far, and the summit is within reach. But a storm has settled in, and you're being forced to pitch your tent and spend the night a few yards short of your goal."

The next evening he brought home a little flag for me to keep in view as I write the last few pages of this book. "So you can plant it on the summit when you reach it."

A couple of days later, a friend with whom I had shared about the flag mailed me a card. On the front was a picture of a person standing on a mountaintop, flag in hand. Inside was the Scripture, "Our steps are made firm by the Lord..." (Psalm 37:23, NRSV[48]), and my friend's words: "To the summit!!"

Do you know that these cheerful assumptions of God's continuing faithfulness were just what I needed to put strength in my stride and gladness in my heart? This is what hopeful thanksgiving does: it allows gladness to make an early arrival.

Helping the congregation thank Him, by faith

As I take up my pen again today, I am holding a card another friend placed in my mailbox early this morning. These are some of the words she wrote: "Today is the day you *will* finish this book and rejoice at how He has carried you so faithfully, all by His grace! I know He *will* use it to bless His church and cause them to delight in Him!"

My goal in writing this book is the same goal I had those nine years I led our worship ministry: to bless and build up God's church for His glory. My friend's mailbox card helped me thank God by faith that He will accomplish this, however He chooses to use this book.

Can we stand in front of our congregations and encourage them in the same way? Psalm 48:9 says:

We have thought on Your lovingkindness, O God
In the midst of Your temple.

Can we come before our fellow sheep and help them meditate on their Shepherd's lovingkindness? Even when it may take faith for them to do so? Have we been cultivating our own heart of thankfulness for things past, present, *and* future so that we can with complete conviction say to them:

*"Church, our Savior has gathered us to this place in His name; let's thank Him **in advance** for the good things He will place in our hearts as we worship."*

*"Beloved family, we are all grieving the loss of one of our own; let's come with gratitude before our High Priest, knowing our loved one is with Him and believing that Jesus **will** comfort us in this time of loss."*

*"Little sheep, we seem to have lost our way a bit lately. Let's humbly bow before our Good Shepherd and thank Him for His **promise** to show us the way back again."*

What a gift we will give our Shepherd's precious sheep when, out of a heart brimming with thankfulness, we invite them to join us in coming before Him with gladness! Friends, let us not speak one word in front of them academically or hypothetically. Let's ask our Shepherd to cause every word we speak, every phrase we utter, and every thought we communicate to bubble up from the innermost parts of our being where His Spirit causes true joy to reside. Then, by God's grace, we will be able to lead them with sincerity as we lift our voices together and say:

> *The Lord is my shepherd,*
> *I shall not want…*
> *Surely goodness and lovingkindness **will** follow me*
>   *all the days of my life,*
> *And I **will** dwell in the house of the Lord forever.*
> (Psalm 23:1, 6, emphasis added)

The God we worship always has been and always will be a loving and faithful Shepherd. So, worship undershepherds, be glad! Put on your party hats and blow your birthday horns. Give thanks with all your heart, because He is not finished giving us good things.

A Conversation With My Shepherd

My life

Will You remind me of some things I am hoping for?

What are You showing me of Yourself that will carry me as I continue to hope?

Is there something that people in my congregation are needing to trust You for right now?

How can I help them meditate on Your lovingkindness even as they wait to see what You will do?

Your Word

What does Lamentations 3:21–26 show me about the reasons I can hope with thankfulness even while I wait for You?

Your Word (continued)

What can I learn from Psalm 48:9-14 about leading Your people in thankful worship?

No matter what lies before me, what are some things for which I can thank You ahead of time, knowing You will do them (Psalm 23)?

Your thought for me

What is one thing You want me to remember from today's lesson?

My heart before You

(Talk to your Shepherd about all or part of the following.) Here's what I need to confess to You; how I want to praise You; what I hope to do with what You've shown me; what I need You to help me with:

DAY 5: THANKFULNESS OVERFLOWING

As I stood at the window that last evening in my office, captured by the beauty of the setting sun and singing the words, "You are faithful, God, You are faithful," my only thought was, "It's all *You*, Lord." My heart held neither false modesty nor forced humility. It was simply filled with consummate thankfulness to my Shepherd who had taken a woefully weak and inadequate undershepherd and made something beautiful out of her small but trusting offering. I was overcome.

I think Paul had a moment like this when he took up his pen to write a letter to his brothers and sisters at Ephesus:

Blessed be the God and Father of our Lord Jesus Christ, who has blessed us with every spiritual blessing in the heavenly places in Christ (Ephesians 1:3)

and then, as if completely incapable of stopping himself, poured out praise upon praise for all the blessings God had lavished on them because of Jesus: "He chose us... He predestined us to adoption... He made known to us the mystery..."

I think the writer of this hymn had a moment like this too:

Soul, then know thy full salvation
Rise o'er sin and fear and care
Joy to find in every station,
Something still to do or bear.
Think *what Spirit dwells within thee,*
Think *what Father's smiles are thine,*
Think *that Jesus died to win thee,*
Child of heaven, canst thou repine. [49]

And I'm quite sure the author of this psalm had a moment of uncontainable gratitude when he wrote the following words to his Shepherd:

My mouth is filled with Your praise
And with Your glory all day long.
But as for me, I will hope continually,

And will praise You yet more and more.
O God, You have taught me from my youth,
And I still declare Your wondrous deeds.
And even when I am old and gray, O God, do not forsake me,
Until I declare Your strength to this generation,
Your power to all who are to come.
For Your righteousness, O God, reaches to the heavens,
You who have done great things;
O God, who is like You? (Psalm 71:8, 14, 17–19)

Can you envision the psalmist adorned in this garment of gratitude as he leads God's people in worship? Can you see the exquisite cloth of praise he wears, woven together with threads of thankfulness, past, present, and future?

Fellow worship undershepherds, our Shepherd stands ready, cloak in hand, waiting to clothe us with these same garments. His vial of blessing is poised over us, ready to saturate our bowed heads and fill our out-held cups until we overflow with thanksgiving.

As we receive this grace of His, allowing it to flow down and spill over, working its way deep into our souls, let us be worship leaders who lead His flock with joy until, one day, we will all be gathered together in those promised fields of which now we can only dream.

Soon shall close thy earthly mission,
Soon shall pass thy pilgrim days,
Hope shall change to glad fruition,
Faith to sight, and prayer to praise. [50]

A Conversation With My Shepherd

My life

Will You please adorn me with a garment of gratitude now as I fill up this space with some of the great things You *have* done, *are* doing, and *promise* to do for me and for my congregation?

Your Word

What are some of the riches You've lavished on me, because of Christ, according to Ephesians 1:3-14?

In Psalm 71, what are some phrases that show thankfulness about the past, the present, and the future?

The past (phrases like "I have," "You have")

The present (phrases like "You are," "I will" present implied)

The future (phrases and words like "You will," "hope," "until," "more," "I will" future implied)

Your thought for me

What is one thing You want me to remember from today's lesson?

My heart before You

(Talk to your Shepherd about all or part of the following.) Here's what I need to confess to You; how I want to praise You; what I hope to do with what You've shown me; what I need You to help me with:

A PRAYER TO PRAY

Shepherd of my joy, the thankfulness I hold in my heart far exceeds the ability of my mouth to express it. How can mere words convey the magnitude of the gifts You have given me?

Let me never forget how blessed I am. Every day, let me see Your loving face before me drawing out my heart in thankfulness.

You have always spoken the right words of encouragement to my heart, at the exact moments I needed them:

*In my dry seasons, You have spoken **refreshment.***

*In my weariness, You have spoken **perseverance.***

*In my weakness, You have spoken **strength.***

*In my pride, You have spoken **humility.***

*In my inadequacy, You have spoken **reassurance.***

*In my confusion, You have spoken **identity.***

*In my striving, You have spoken **patience.***

*In my willfulness, You have spoken **submission.***

*In my self-absorption, You have spoken **community.***

*In my helplessness, You have spoken **help.***

*In my ingratitude, You have spoken **thankfulness.***

I have received untold riches, yet I acknowledge that all of them added together are but a mere taste of those that are to come. I know that You have prepared, for those who love You, things which eye has not seen and ear has not heard, things which have not yet entered any heart.

Oh, I do love You, Good Shepherd. And I live to worship You.

APPENDIX A

IDEAS FOR SEEKING REFRESHMENT FROM THE SHEPHERD

Be present to the Lord.

Our Shepherd is always present to us. Make it a point to be aware of His presence in every moment of the day.

Ask God questions in the morning about the day to come.

Begin each day by talking with Him, asking for His direction and inviting Him to make your heart ready for whatever He has planned. Pray as Thomas à Kempis did: "Make me a pious and humble follower... that I may walk according to Your every nod."[51]

Remember one thought from the morning's quiet time.

It might be the thought to give thanks in all things. Or the thought that He is the sun and you are the moon reflecting Him. Or the thought to think of others first. One thought can put the whole day into a trajectory of worship.

Take a day to write down how to worship in each next thing.

Keep a notepad handy, and throughout the day write down how to worship God in each next thing: Before making a phone call, write "Love this person as God does." Before putting together a worship set, write "Lay aside my own agenda." Keep in mind the verse "I will bless the Lord at all times, His praise shall continually be in my mouth" (Psalm 34:1).

Record thoughts.

Smart phones can be a wonderful tool to help us remember what the Spirit is impressing on us in the moment. Take a moment to record ideas, encouragements, journal entries, observations, or little ways He is making His presence known.

Pray. At all times.

It's a specific discipline and it's also an attitude. Charles Spurgeon said, "We should pray when we are in a praying mood, for it would be sinful to neglect so fair an opportunity. We should pray when we are not in a praying mood because it would be dangerous to remain in so unhealthy a condition."[52]

Memorize Scripture.

An acquaintance recently commented to me, "I don't see why people say it's important to memorize Scripture. I have a moment-by-moment conversation with God all the time, and I know what the Bible says. So why do I need to memorize it?" Why? Besides the fact that we are instructed to hide it in our heart, which is reason enough (Psalm 119:11), it keeps us in the truth. It gives us good meat to chew on during the busy hours of the day and the solitary hours of the night. If the Word of God is the sword of the Spirit, we need to keep it sharpened so we can use it at a moment's notice.

Meditate on the Word.

This is just another dimension of getting the Word in us. It's taking a passage of Scripture and asking the Holy Spirit to speak to us through it. It's waiting until we hear from Him. It's reflecting on it and applying it throughout the day. This is what it means to "let the Word of Christ dwell in you richly" (Colossians 3:16).

Keep a journal.

There is something about writing down the things our Shepherd impresses on us that helps us process them and remember them. It is also deeply reassuring to look back over a season and read of His faithfulness, even in the moments when we couldn't see Him.

Jot down things to be thankful for.

Ann Voskamp, in her book *One Thousand Gifts,*[53] chronicles her journey into joy, grace, and thanksgiving as she formed a habit of writing down gifts from God throughout her day. Her book inspired me to try it, and as a result I am finding myself being transformed into a more thankful and observant person.

Schedule breaks during the day.

When I am immersed in a project, or when I have a list in front of me and am checking it off systematically, it is very difficult for me to stop. I don't switch gears easily. Taking a break is something I have to intentionally discipline myself to do, but I am never sorry afterward. For just those few moments I am able to hear my Shepherd's gentle voice so that I can return to the tasks at hand with a rejuvenated spirit.

Go for a walk and pray out loud.

Sometimes long days in the office doing worship ministry can get tedious; simply taking a 15-minute walk around the grassy area behind the church, speaking with my Shepherd, clears my heart and mind so that I can approach ministry again with an ear to hear how the Spirit is leading me.

Text prayers with a friend.

Each morning my friend and I text each other the things we can pray for each other during the day. Then throughout the day we will send little reminder texts: "How are you doing with this? Are you remembering to delight in His goodness today? Are you being careful to speak words that bless?"

Let the music speak.

Do you wake up sometimes with a worship melody in your heart? Think about the lyrics to that song throughout the day; it may be that God has brought it to mind to encourage you specifically in the day ahead. In the middle of your ministry day, do you find that choosing and arranging songs for worship can become simply a chore, not a joy? It might help to walk away from your work place and sing a song to your Shepherd.

Praise the Lord right along with His creation.

When we run to our window to catch the rising sun casting its pink and orange glow; when we carefully craft musical transitions, ideas, and flow; when we walk through an art exhibit and acknowledge that God is the God of all creativity—all of these are ways of reminding our souls that God is worthy to be praised!

Read.

Anything that is edifying. Devotional books. Prayers. Articles. Lyrics. Blogs. When we hear how God has spoken to others, we can glean things He would speak to us as well.

Highlight phrases of lyrics from the songs for this Sunday's worship.

Sometimes I sit down with my friend Melissa who is on the worship team with me, and we sing through the songs and highlight phrases that have been especially meaningful to us. When we come together to sing with the team and the congregation on Sunday mornings, our hearts have been opened wide to let His Spirit drive home the lyrics even as we think of the details of notes and transitions.

Come to the sanctuary early in the morning.

Some of the sweetest times of my worship ministry have been the Saturday mornings when I come to church early and draw near to God. I pray for the people who will worship with me the next day; I pray for God to renew my heart; I walk the aisles and sing. I always leave these times more restful and refreshed.

Prepare spiritually for Sunday.

Sundays can be intense for those of us in worship ministry. It can be helpful to play and sing through the worship set before Sunday morning, not to figure out musical details, but simply to worship. On Saturday evenings, try to get to bed early, perhaps reading from a devotional book before falling asleep. Once in a while, wake up early on Sunday morning and go for a prayer walk.

Conferences.

Worship conferences have provided some pivotal moments in my worship ministry. I have often come away encouraged, inspired, and armed with new resources to carry me through the next season of ministry.

Creative pursuits.

Ironically, for worship leaders sometimes creativity gets put on the back burner, giving way to the more urgent demands of ministry. Take time to do something creative, for the sheer joy of it. Sit down and scratch out a short song; grab some drumsticks and pound out random and loud rhythms; crank up a song and sing out absolutely ridiculous background vocal improvs.

Serve "offstage."

My mom is in a nursing care facility. She speaks, but it is mostly unintelligible. However, she is a worshiper. Some of my sweetest moments of worship have been just my mom and me, sitting in the chapel, as I play and sing worship songs, stopping every few lines to say, "Isn't this true, Mom? God is so faithful! How good He has been to us!" No one else hears, and no one else sees. But I come away from these times knowing Jesus has been in our midst.

Commit to a habit of rest during the busy seasons.

It seems counterintuitive to build rest into the busy seasons, but these are the times we need it most. One December, I decided to take a few short minutes each morning and night to sit in the living room, lights low, and do one simple thing such as pray, read the Word, drink a cup of tea, listen to music, read a book, or talk with my family. It wasn't much, but it was the very thing I needed to find refreshment in the busyness of that season.

Special days alone with God.

Once in a while I am able to clear my calendar and spend a whole day alone with my Shepherd. One such day I climbed to the top of a hill at a park in town. As I sat up there on a blue-skied, sun-drenched day, overlooking the city and praying, I saw five little children walking the dirt path up the hill. It's very steep, and they slid and slipped all the way up. When they arrived at the top, the littlest girl lifted her head and saw the view, exclaiming with awestruck voice, "Oh my gosh—it's so beautiful!" With that, I was reminded that it is worth taking time to regain childlike wonder so that I can see again that life *is* beautiful in Him.

APPENDIX B

ASKING THE SHEPHERD ABOUT MYSELF, MY TEAMS, AND MY CONGREGATION

As you consider each topic on the chart, ask your Shepherd to show you specific aspects of this topic that will help you assess yourself, your teams, and your congregation. Then ask Him to help you evaluate each one as follows:

K = Keep (do not change). This is for those items that you believe should not be changed because (a) they seem to be in a healthy place right now, or (b) they are simply the way God has made you and your fellow sheep to be.

P = Pray (ask God to change). This is for those items that you believe should be changed but that you can do nothing about except pray.

W = Work to change. This is for those items that you believe can and should be changed, either now or in the future, as your Shepherd leads you to address them.

Sample Chart:

4. MUSICAL AND TECHNICAL SKILLS

Specific aspects might include vocal and instrumental ability (harmonies and blends, sight reading, rhythm and tempo, styles, technique, improv), musical comfort level of both congregation and teams, working together musically as a team, understanding of audiovisual technology, learning new songs, clapping, etc.

	SPECIFIC ASPECTS	K, P, W
Me	My ability to work well musically with the band	W
	My sense of rhythm and tempo	K
	My comfort level when playing an instrument during worship	P
	My understanding of audiovisual technology	W
My teams and co-laborers	Their ability to work musically as a team	W
	Their sense of rhythm and tempo	W
	Their comfort level when playing their instruments	K
	The vocalists' understanding of how to use microphones	K
	The audio team's understanding of sound technology	W
My congregation	Their ability to learn new songs	W
	Number of qualified volunteers who have not yet considered being involved in the worship ministry	P
	Their gentleness in expressing opinions regarding sound levels	P

1. HEART OF WORSHIP

Specific aspects might include time spent alone with the Shepherd, ability to absorb and live out His truths, teachability, passion about worshiping God, etc. *(Note: With this topic in particular, it is important to remember that we cannot truly know the heart of anyone besides ourselves. But, as worship leaders who live in community with our teams and congregations, we can ask our Shepherd to give us insight: Is this simply how He has made them? Are they doing well? Is more prayer needed? Do they need help?)*

	SPECIFIC ASPECTS	K, P, W
Me		
My teams and co-laborers		
My congregation		

2. LEADERSHIP (of the worship ministry as a whole)

Specific aspects might include strengths and weaknesses in leadership roles, priorities and vision, being on the same page with others, trust and respect, perceptions, etc.

	SPECIFIC ASPECTS	K, P, W
Me		
My teams and co-laborers		
My congregation		

3. WORSHIP CONTENT

Specific aspects might include theological discernment when choosing lyrics, service flow, preference of worship styles, understanding of the meaning of lyrics, attentiveness when someone reads Scripture or talks, appreciation for certain elements of the service, etc.

	SPECIFIC ASPECTS	K, P, W
Me		
My teams and co-laborers		
My congregation		

4. MUSICAL AND TECHNICAL SKILLS

Specific aspects might include vocal and instrumental ability (harmonies and blends, sight reading, rhythm and tempo, styles, technique, improv), musical comfort level of both congregation and teams, working together musically as a team, understanding of audiovisual technology, learning new songs, clapping, etc.

	SPECIFIC ASPECTS	K, P, W
Me		
My teams and co-laborers		
My congregation		

5. SIZE AND DEMOGRAPHICS

Specific aspects might include demographics of the congregation compared to the worship ministry, ratio of men to women, representation of different ages, church traditions represented and the perspectives that brings, how different economic brackets or education levels affect community, number of people, etc.

	SPECIFIC ASPECTS	K, P, W
Me		
My teams and co-laborers		
My congregation		

6. HISTORY

Specific aspects might include how previous experiences have affected attitudes, the fruit that has been seen, how crises and hurts have formed perspectives, significant changes in the church family, how past performance has affected present expectations, etc.

	SPECIFIC ASPECTS	K, P, W
Me		
My teams and co-laborers		
My congregation		

7. CONNECTING IN WORSHIP

Specific aspects might include the formality or informality of worship, the expressiveness with which Scripture is read, the thoughtfulness of prayers, eye contact, responsiveness and attentiveness to one another, etc.

	SPECIFIC ASPECTS	K, P, W
Me		
My teams and co-laborers		
My congregation		

8. RELATIONSHIPS

Specific aspects might include the ability to relate well to one another, relationships outside of worship times, relational strengths and weaknesses, communication between different groups (worship ministry, staff, elders, other ministries), etc.

	SPECIFIC ASPECTS	K, P, W
Me		
My teams and co-laborers		
My congregation		

9. TIME

Specific aspects might include time available for worship ministry, how time is spent outside of Sunday mornings, ability to follow through on commitments, consistency of attendance, how much time is available for worship music during services, margins (or lack of margins) and how this affects stress levels, etc.

	SPECIFIC ASPECTS	K, P, W
Me		
My teams and co-laborers		
My congregation		

Appendix C
References

[1] All Scripture references in this book, unless otherwise noted, are taken from the New American Standard Bible (NASB), Copyright © 1960, 1962, 1963, 1968, 1971, 1972, 1973, 1975, 1977, 1995 by The Lockman Foundation. Used by Permission.

[2] Basil Miller, *George Muller, The Man of Faith* (Grand Rapids: Zondervan, 1941), 50.

[3] John Bunyan, *The Pilgrim's Progress*, ed. Roger Sharrock (London, England: Penguin Group, 1985), 250. (Italics mine.)

[4] Ann Voskamp, *One Thousand Gifts* (Grand Rapids, Michigan: Zondervan, 2010), 31

[5] Scripture taken from the King James Bible (KJV), Copyright © 2002 by Evangelical Press.

[6] Matt Maher, "Apathy in Leadership," *Worship Leader Magazine*, Vol. 17, No. 3 (May 2008), 32

[7] Rory Noland, The Heart of the Artist: A Character-Building Guide for You & Your Ministry Team (Grand Rapids, Michigan: Zondervan, 1999), 328

[8] Ann Voskamp, *One Thousand Gifts* (Grand Rapids, Michigan: Zondervan, 2010), 106

[9] John Hughes, Peter Williams and William Williams, "Guide Me, O Thou Great Jehovah." Public Domain.

[10] Charles Ringma, Whispers from the Edge of Eternity: Reflections on Life and Faith in a Precarious World (Vancouver, British Columbia: Regent College Publishing, 2005), 156

[11] John Wyeth and Robert Robinson, "Come Thou Fount." Public Domain.

[12] Andy Park, *To Know You More: Cultivating the Heart of the Worship Leader* (Downers Grove, Illinois: InterVarsity Press, 2002), 13

[13] Thomas à Kempis, *The Imitation of Christ,* trans. Aloysius Croft and Harold Bolton (Peabody, Massachusetts: Hendrickson Publishers, 2004), 55

[14] Horatio G. Spafford and Philip Paul Bliss, "It Is Well With My Soul." Public Domain.

[15] Frances Ridley Havergal and Henri Abraham Cesar Malan, "Take My Life and Let It Be." Public Domain.

[16] It is not within the scope of this book to address the situations that might disqualify a worship leader from ministry. Each worship leader must examine his or her own heart before the Lord and discuss with the pastor and spiritual leaders of the church whether to step down or not.

[17] John Bunyan, *The Pilgrim's Progress*, ed. Roger Sharrock (London, England: Penguin Group, 1985), 245

[18] Madame Guyon, "Live to Love," *The One Year Book of Poetry: 365 Devotional Readings Based on Classic Christian Verse*, compiled and written by Philip Comfort and Daniel Partner (Wheaton, Illinois: Tyndale House Publishers, Inc., 1999), January 12

[19] Edward Mote and William Batchelder Bradbury, "The Solid Rock." Public Domain.

[20] Dwayne Moore, *Pure Praise: A Heart-Focused Bible Study on Worship* (Loveland, Colorado: Group, 2009), 42

[21] Christian Henry Bateman, Come, Christians, Join to Sing." Public Domain.

[22] Charles Wesley and Thomas Campbell, "And Can It Be?" Public Domain.

[23] Alison Siewert (Editor), Andy Crouch, Matt Frazier and Sundee Frazier, article by Andy Crouch, "Leading Versus Performing," *Worship Team Handbook* (Downers Grove, Illinois: InterVarsity Press, 1998), 38–40

[24] Darlene Zschech, "The Presence of God," *Worship Leader Magazine*, Vol. 19, No. 8 (November/December 2010), 28

[25] Various authors, "The Great God," *The Valley of Vision*, ed. Arthur Bennett (Carlisle, Pennsylvania: The Banner of Truth Trust, 1975), 8

[26] Glenn Packiam, *Secondhand Jesus: Trading Rumors of God for a Firsthand Faith* (Colorado Springs, Colorado: David C. Cook, 2009),

[27] Matt Redman and Friends, *Inside-Out Worship: Insights for Passionate and Purposeful Worship* (Ventura, California: Regal Books from Gospel Light, 2005), 19

[28] St. Francis of Assisi and William Henry Draper, "All Creatures of Our God and King." Public Domain.

[29] "Patience.", Encarta World English Dictionary [North American Edition] © & (P) 2009 Microsoft Corporation. Developed for Microsoft by Bloomsbury Publishing Pic. *www.bing.com.* (Accessed May 15, 2013.)

[30] Scripture taken from the New King James Version. Copyright © 1982 by Thomas Nelson, Inc. Used by permission. All rights reserved.

[31] Charles Spurgeon, *The Treasury of David,* abridged by David Otis Fuller (Grand Rapids, MI: Kregel Publications, a division of Kregel Inc., 1976), 511

[32] Tom Kraeuter, Guiding Your Church Through a Worship Transition: A Practical Handbook for Worship Renewal (Lynnwood, Washington: Emerald Books, 2003), 96

[33] Edward Taylor, "Am I Thy Gold? … Canticles II", *The One Year Book of Poetry: 365 Devotional Readings Based on Classic Christian Verse*, compiled and written by Philip Comfort and Daniel Partner (Wheaton, Illinois: Tyndale House Publishers, Inc., 1999), February 24

[34] Matt Redman, *The Unquenchable Worshipper: Coming Back to the Heart of Worship* (Ventura, California: Regal Books, from Gospel Light, 2001), 63

[35] Rory Noland, Thriving As an Artist in the Church: Hope and Help for You and Your Ministry Team (Grand Rapids, Michigan: Zondervan, 2004), 247

[36] William Cowper, "Walking With God," *The One Year Book of Poetry: 365 Devotional Readings Based on Classic Christian Verse*, compiled and written by Philip Comfort and Daniel Partner (Wheaton, Illinois: Tyndale House Publishers, Inc., 1999), February 3

[37] Tommy Walker, "The Resume," *Worship Leader Magazine*, Vol. 16, No. 5 (July/August 2007), 27

[38] "Symbiosis." Oxford Dictionaries. *oxforddictionaries.com*. (Accessed May 22, 2013.)

[39] Gordon MacDonald, "The Fold," *Worship Leader Magazine*, Vol. 20, No. 7 (October 2011), __

[40] C. S. Lewis, "Answers to Questions on Christianity," *God in the Dock: Essays on Theology and Ethics* (Grand Rapids: Eerdmans, 1970), 61-62

[41] Carolyn Arends, "Wrestling With Angels: Taste the Soup," *Christianity Today*, Vol. 56, No. 8 (September 2012), 76

[42] Dietrich Bonhoeffer, *Life Together / Prayerbook of the Bible*, transl. Daniel W. Bloesch and James H. Burtness, ed. Geffrey B. Kelly (Minneapolis, Minnesota: Fortress Press, 2005), 36

[43] Matt Redman and Friends, *Inside-Out Worship: Insights for Passionate and Purposeful Worship* (Ventura, California: Regal Books from Gospel Light, 2005), 51

[44] Warren and Ruth Myers, *31 Days of Prayer: Moving God's Mighty Hand* (Sisters, Oregon: Multnomah Publishers, Inc., 1997), 161

[45] Matt Redman, *The Unquenchable Worshipper: Coming Back to the Heart of Worship* (Ventura, California: Regal Books, from Gospel Light, 2001), 102-104

[46]Various authors, "Evening Praise," *The Valley of Vision*, ed. Arthur Bennett (Carlisle, Pennsylvania: The Banner of Truth Trust, 1975), 225

[47] Ann Voskamp, *One Thousand Gifts* (Grand Rapids, Michigan: Zondervan, 2010)

[48] New Revised Standard Version Bible, copyright 1989, Division of Christian Education of the National council of the Churches of Christ in the United States of America. Used by Permission. All rights reserved.

[49] Henry Francis Lyte and Wolfgang Amadeus Mozart, "Jesus, I My Cross Have Taken." Public Domain. Emphasis added.

[50] Henry Francis Lyte and Wolfgang Amadeus Mozart, "Jesus, I My Cross Have Taken." Public Domain.

[51] Thomas à Kempis, *The Imitation of* Christ, trans. Aloysius Croft and Harold Bolton (Peabody, Massachusetts: Hendrickson Publishers, 2004), 115

[52] quoted by Warren and Ruth Myers, *31 Days of Prayer: Moving God's Mighty Hand* (Sisters, Oregon: Multnomah Publishers, Inc., 1997), 162

[53] Ann Voskamp, *One Thousand Gifts* (Grand Rapids, Michigan: Zondervan, 2010)

Acknowledgments

Every pen scratch and keyboard clack in the writing of this book was emboldened by an army of prayer warriors, stretcher bearers, and trumpeters. I say with no trace of hesitancy, no hint of hyperbole: I could not have written it without you.

Greg, with the words "I think you need to put your passion on paper," you spoke the courage I needed to begin this endeavor. Your strong hugs, silly songs, and soft reassurances ever since have kept me going. More than anyone I know, you possess the heart of a shepherd. I am so glad my heart belongs to you.

Melissa, did I struggle over a single phrase without your in-the-moment prayers? Did I complete a single day's labor without your "Strong work!"? Did I contemplate a single chapter or devotional without your wise and discerning contribution? With every text, phone call, walk, and workout, you've believed, hoped, mused, and worshiped with me. I think you know the breadth and depth of what that has meant, and how eternally grateful I am for this treasured friendship.

My children (Daniel and Jonathan and their sweet wives Molly and Michelle, and Amanda), you've prayed for me, bounced ideas off me, and believed in me. You've taken me seriously and teased me mercilessly, fo' sho.' Daniel and Amanda, a special thanks for your insightful and wise editing suggestions. Amanda, I also thank you for the weekly pep talks on the phone, me strolling through subdivisions and you dodging street musicians. Thanks, too, for standing on a stool to take my author picture so I would look better. To all five of you, I want to say I am more blessed than you will ever know to be called your mom.

Lynne, I smile to think of your kind and intentional encouragement as we sat by the river or leaned over your counter, my manuscript spread out before us. Thank you for the phrases you let bless you, the word choices you rejoiced over. Thank you, cherished friend, for knowing me well and for daring to hope with me, always.

Gaylie, you were the one who years ago saw my dreams painfully dented and painstakingly refashioned, all the while reminding me that God was doing something very good. Your commiseration, laughter, and prayers all along have made me deeply grateful for the journey we share as perennial friends.

Jon, Judy, Scott, and Lisa—my dear friends and editors—you read my entire manuscript before I cut it by the first 24,000 words. With each smiley face and asterisk, each question mark and cross-out, you made it stronger. More importantly, with each timely affirmation and each great expectation, you made me stronger. *Judy*, I especially want to thank you for all the little celebration gifts, and for telling the entire staff at Chili's how proud you were of me.

Dad, Denise, and Frank, my whole life you've shown me what it means to receive grace and what it means to give it. You saw firsthand the stages I went through, the refinement I endured (often at your expense). Yet you always loved me, and you always cheered me on, right up through the writing of this book. I'm so privileged to be your daughter and sister.

Other friends and family members, I started to list you one by one. And then I thought, "But I'll leave someone out." Then another thought overrode *that* thought: "How can I not name some of those who have sent me emails, asked me how they can pray, read bits and pieces of my manuscript, and buoyed me with their unflagging optimism?" So, with full knowledge of the risk and a modicum of trepidation, here goes: *Jennifer, Darlene, Cecilia, Laura, Brittney, Sarah, Julie, Alison, Patsy, Donna, Gail, Angela, Susan, Luke, Bethany, Karen, Carolyn, David, Janet, Cassie, Natalie, Ruth, Stephanie, my brothers and sisters on the worship and A/V teams, my Growth Group, Greg's men's studies, our elders and wives, our church staff, Wendy, Thom, Jill, Audrey, John, Greg's brothers and sisters*—from the bottom of my heart, I thank you.

My church family, your love for your Shepherd drew us to you from the very beginning, and your love for us and our children has warmly embraced us in the 26 years since. I cannot imagine a sweeter place in which to serve and worship.

NCC Publishing, from the moment Ray said, "Let's all pray about this and see how God leads," I felt sure you were the team He was calling to take this book to publication. *Ray and Sharon, Mike and Debbie, Stephanie*—your dedication, humility, professionalism, faithfulness, and sensitivity show that you want nothing more than to please your Shepherd as you work with each author. I'm sincerely honored to be one of those authors.

Tom Kraeuter, you cannot know how much your kind phone call after you first read my manuscript encouraged me. Or the many phone calls and emails since then. Your books and workshops have powerfully impacted my worship teams, my church, and me. Beyond that, time and again you've made yourself generously available to me for counsel, advice, encouragement, and help. It has been invaluable. (Oh, and I couldn't help quoting you in my book. You will be glad to know I've spelled your name right.)

Rory Noland, since the beginning of my worship ministry, your books have helped keep my heart, and the hearts of my co-laborers, in the right place. Thank you for meeting with me to critique my first chapter. It was your honest and astute insight that informed much of what I wrote in the remaining chapters. It was your thoughtful encouragement that spurred my resolve to complete the book.

Jamie Morrison, your expressed desire to mentor authors first drew me to you at the Write-to-Publish conference. Every encounter after that proved your desire to be sincere. You assured me, "If God wants this book written, He will provide the resources." You saw the devotional potential of this book and gave me its structure. You prayed with me over the phone, a prayer so poignantly appropriate that I knew it came from God's heart to mine. May He keep prospering your ministry and your business.

Great Shepherd, where I've been distractible, despondent, disobedient, and dull, You've been my vision, my hope, my grace, and my spark. No word I know can convey the magnitude of what You've done for me. Forever I will live to thank You.

ABOUT THE AUTHOR

Jeanelle Reider is a lifetime worshiper and longtime worship director with a tender affinity for worship leaders and a first-hand knowledge of the challenges they face. As a senior pastor's wife, she has deep affection for the local church. As a distractible sheep of her Shepherd, she lives her days longing for His "Well-done" yet thankful for His "You can do better."

Jeanelle and her husband Greg live in Boise, Idaho.

You can read more about Jeanelle and her ministry on the web at:

www.TheOneVoiceThatMatters.com

www.NCCPublishing.com

Made in the USA
Lexington, KY
02 February 2015